As Orange Goes

Twelve California Families and the
Future of American Politics

Twelve California Families and the Future of American Politics

KARL A. LAMB
UNIVERSITY OF CALIFORNIA, SANTA CRUZ

As Orange
Goes

W · W · NORTON & COMPANY · INC ·
NEW YORK

For Stacy, Jan, and Julie,
and the Children of Orange County

Copyright © 1974 by W. W. Norton & Company, Inc.
FIRST EDITION
ALL RIGHTS RESERVED
Published simultaneously in Canada
by George J. McLeod Limited, Toronto
Library of Congress Cataloging in Publication Data
Lamb, Karl A
   As Orange goes.
   Includes bibliographical references.
   1. Orange Co., Calif.—Politics and government.
   2. Orange Co., Calif.—Social conditions. 3. Political
participation—Orange Co., Calif. I. Title.
JS451.C29074   320.9'794'9605   74–7228
ISBN 0–393–05520–5
This book was designed by Robert Freese.
Typefaces used are Bodoni and Electra,
set by The Haddon Craftsmen.
Printing and binding were done by Vail Ballou Press, Inc.
PRINTED IN THE UNITED STATES OF AMERICA

1 2 3 4 5 6 7 8 9 0

Contents

Preface

A Note on Method

THIS BOOK seeks to illuminate large issues by examining the experiences and attitudes of twenty-three people, representing twelve families, who live in a single neighborhood. I have known them for more than three years; I have spent more than forty hours in some of their homes; and I count them as friends. The book exists only because they were willing to discuss candidly some of their most deeply held convictions, and I am grateful to them all.

An immediate question arises. Are the twelve families described here typical of the registered voters of Orange County, of American suburbanites in general, or of the substantial population group which I have called "the affluent technocrats?" While "Ramona Heights" shares many features with other suburban developments in Orange County and throughout the nation, the answer must still be "no." In spite of an effort at random selection within the neighborhood, twenty-three is too small a number to advertise as representative of these larger groups. The microsample should not be seen as statistically representative, nor should individuals within it be regarded as speaking for others who may share their socio-economic characteristics or attitudinal patterns.

The chances of including Birch Society members in the microsample as the result of random selection were statistically nearly zero, and I felt it important to converse with some of the people whose activities have given Orange County much of its image. I knew of their membership when I first called on Frank and Mary McGee, but did not say so. This was the only misrepresentation made to any of my respondents, and I apologize for it now.

Because it is not a study in quantitative social science,

what this book says about American politics in the 1970s is suggested or implied, rather than being "proven" through statistical tables and applications of the mathematics of probability. I trust the reader can accept the material for its intrinsic interest and make judgments about its wider applicability on the basis of its resonance with his own experience. I have not been shy about pointing out agreements and contrasts between the material and the extant literature in American political science and sociology.

Some philosophers, and an increasing number of social scientists, argue that social reality is best comprehended and analyzed from the viewpoint of those persons experiencing it. This is the claim of phenomenology.[1] If the claim has validity, then one may get closer to the bone of truth by conversing with a small number of people at great length and in some depth, rather than by conducting interviews, however well designed, with a statistically significant sample. For the latter procedure reduces the responses of human beings to a numerical value, and it is hard to escape the suspicion that it violates their humanity.

Having raised this methodological issue, I prefer not to pursue it. I will put the other foot forward by reporting that in the fall of 1970, while conducting initial interviews with the voters of Ramona Heights, I participated in the design and administration of a survey of voter attitudes conducted in Los Angeles and Orange counties under the direction of Professor Joel Barkan by trained students from the Los Angeles and Irvine campuses of the University of California. The survey yielded a statistically reliable portrait of political attitudes of Southern Californians on the eve of the 1970 elections. One of its sub-samples was of suburbanites in Ramona Heights and the surrounding area, the homes of the affluent technocracy. In fact, the twenty-three voters of Ramona Heights are not unlike other affluent technocrats and other Southern Californians, when one controls for the traditional variables of income, education, occupation, age, sex, and religion. One finding of the survey was that such traditional variables are the most dependable correlates of

[1]As a philosophical school, phenomenology traces its origins to the attempt of Edmund Husserl to heal the schism between reason and tradition introduced by Descartes. Phenomenology has been elaborated by Jean-Paul Sartre and Martin Heidegger, among others, and applied to the social sciences by such thinkers as Maurice Merleau-Ponty, Alfred Schutz, and Maurice Natanson. A beginning point for further pursuit of the topic is Maurice Natanson, ed., *Phenomenology and the Social Sciences* (Evanston, Ill.: Northwestern University Press, 1973). Particularly valuable is Natanson's introduction, vol. 1, pp. 3–44.

party identification and candidate preference. This only underscores, for Southern California, the findings of other recent studies: a suburb is a geographical place, not a state of mind; suburbs do not make Republicans.[2]

The Limits of Fiction

To fictionalize the name of the community one studies is an honored tradition of social science. A main purpose of my work was to examine political attitudes in Orange County, California, and there was no reason for the county to masquerade under a false name. However, to the best of my knowledge, there is no community in Orange County called Ramona Heights. The names of the twenty-three respondents have been fictionalized, and a few details about their lives have been camouflaged, such as the names of corporations for which they now work, or the colleges they once attended. To prevent easy identification by otherwise unacquainted neighbors, the makes of their automobiles have been changed, and, in a few cases, the sexes of their small children reversed. This minor scrambling of detail was undertaken to prevent an even greater intrusion upon the respondents' privacy through publication than had already occurred during the interviews. The written and spoken words of the respondents quoted in what follows are exactly as they were written or spoken, and I have been careful to avoid selecting quotations out of a context which would contradict the import of the quoted material. The words of the respondents are used here with their permission.

I also got to know many of the respondents' children, who ranged in age from infancy to post-doctoral study. The younger son of the Pavels participated in two interview sessions; the Kaubs' son joined in for half an hour, and the son of John and Martha Weeks supplied me with a spare microphone for the tape recorder, when I had forgotten mine, from his store of electronic parts. I found that there was no marked conflict between these particular children and their parents, but the political convictions of the children are developing in rather different channels from those of their parents. To study the political attitudes of young people approaching voting age in Orange County

[2]This literature is cited and discussed in Chapter Three. Its most capable summary and presentation is in Frederick M. Wirt et al., *On the City's Rim: Politics and Policy in Suburbia* (Lexington, Mass.: D. C. Heath, 1972).

would require a different data base and a different book; the result would further challenge the stereotype of ultra-conservatism in the area.

This book is dedicated to my three nieces, who have lived in Orange County all their lives, although they were born across the county line in Long Beach. They hardly typify the youth of Orange County— nobody does—but each, for her own reasons, fully deserves a book. (Perhaps I should add that their parents were not included in the microsample, nor do they live in Ramona Heights.)

The data from which the portraits of twenty-three people and their political convictions are drawn are quite extensive. There are some 6,000 pages of transcribed tape-recorded interviews, plus correspondence, questionnaires, reports of voting choices, attitude tests, and notes on telephone conversations. In spite of this rich foundation, it is possible that the characterizations of individual human beings offered in these pages may seem like caricatures. Even the best phenomenological intentions may produce an account that reads like fiction to its subject. Any picture drawn with words must be impressionistic, and the connotations of those words perceived by the reader may not be intended by the author. I can only insist that any resemblance between the twenty-three voters described in this book and any real, living persons is completely intentional.

Acknowledgments

Students of American politics will recognize my debt to Robert Lane. His book *Political Ideology*, based on depth interviews with fifteen men living in a New Haven public housing project, deserves its place among the modern classics of social science. Professor Lane kindly supplied me with a copy of his interview guide, and I based my own upon it. My work was thus inspired by his, but could hardly be called a replication, in part because different issues from those in the 1950s cry out for consideration now. Furthermore, because of a difference in training and temperament, I have been more hesitant than Professor Lane to utilize psychological interpretations.

The gathering and transcription of data was made possible by a faculty research grant from the Social Science Research Council and by a similar gift from the Relm Foundation. Data analysis was facilitated by a series of modest but timely grants from the Faculty Research Committee of the University of California, Santa Cruz, Academic Senate. None of these organizations attempted to guide my interpretations, nor can they be held responsible for the result, and I thank them profoundly for their disinterested support.

When drafting the research design, I benefited greatly from discussions with David Riesman and correspondence with Bernard Hennessy and Charles Page. A day in Palo Alto with David Riesman and Michael Maccoby did much to settle questions of research strategy.

Joel Barkan, then teaching at the University of California, Irvine, was hospitable to my project and proved a very stimulating colleague. He accommodated my interests in designing his own survey research, as mentioned above. Relations with the Irvine bureaucracy were handled smoothly by Mary Rezick of the School of Social Science at Irvine.

Several colleagues have sustained my long involvement with this work. The enthusiasm of William K. Muir for this project has been inspirational, even when expressed over the intercampus tie line from Berkeley. Peter Euben was most helpful in guiding me to the literature on civic religion and in criticizing my treatment of it. My debt to Maurice Natanson and phenomenology has already been delineated. Ivan Vallier's untimely death cut short a developing intellectual friendship which I valued highly. His uncompromising approach to the quest for sociological judgment could only be admired, if not successfully imitated. I burdened John Hummel with reading several chapters at a late date, as I had burdened him earlier with reports of progress and the obstacles to it.

The demanding task of transcribing the recorded interviews was performed by a series of typists of varying skill. Set among them like the proverbial rose was Gail Zifferstein of UC Irvine, whose long experience of transcribing recorded speech patterns made her regard the transcription of ordinary conversations into standard English as a kind of relaxation. Janet Nohner copied and repaired the work of some of the other transcribers with great efficiency. The eventual manuscript was typed largely by Charlotte Cassidy, who comes as close to perfection in rendering copy into type as any practitioner of the art. When Charlotte was not available, Judy Macri pitched in to type two chapters, even while following her team's march to victory in the World Series.

My closest associates in writing this book were Elaine Enarson Herring and Pat Shuler. They received a modest hourly wage as research assistants, which was very far from being a measure of their value. Theirs was the task of managing the data: indexing, searching, and charting; making endless trips to the library; tracking down footnotes; finding books that had fallen down behind the shelves in my office; supplying cups of coffee; and sustaining the momentum of the project. If I could have persuaded Elaine not to go off to graduate school, and Pat not to enter law school, the book might not have been finished earlier, but it would have been better. In what follows, when I use the editorial "we" or write of "our" microsample, the wording does not result from a pose of editorial pomposity. The plural pronoun refers to the triumvirate of Elaine, Pat, and me.

My editor at W. W. Norton has been Donald S. Lamm. I have known Don for twenty years; a friendship can either blossom or fade in the author-editor relationship, and I believe ours remains intact.

Since visiting Orange County, I have taught small seminars in the politics of suburbia at least once a year. After immersion in the psychological, sociological, and political science literature, I have asked students to look at some of the Ramona Heights transcripts. Their analyses have supplied a number of useful insights, and class discussions have done much to sharpen my own grasp of the subject. I am grateful to them for making me understand better what I have been talking about. The students involved were: Charles Adams, Laurie Arkin, Patricia Ayerza, Denise Ayres, Lance Bayer, Brian Beers, Ronald Blair, Roy Blokker, Bonnie Borowick, Bruce Briggs, James Bubar, Barbara Buhai, Margaret Corr, Karleen Crivello, Thomas Cruddas, Kent Dannehl, Franklin Dickinson, Michael DiDonato, Elaine Enarson, Pamela Fairley, Edward Feinstein, Martha Fitzmaurice, Lee Gaston, Glen Gertmanian, Dale Gray, Simon Haines, David Hanlon, Janet Hill, Bobbie Hoover, Patricia Ito, David Johnston, Cyrus Kavoosi, Gary Kitahata, Mindy Leiterman, Barbara Lopez, Michael Marx, James McAdams, Joseph Near, Paul Newton, James O'Callahan, Lise Peterson, Hector Salazar, Lois Schlyer, Katherine Seligman, Steven Shev, James Shuck, Thomas Siemsen, Steve Sims, Andrew Smedberg, Joanne Striley, Ellen Swanberg, Rodney Tanaka, David Tenzer, Karen Thomas, Jack Tomlinson, Louis Trager, Juan Valadez, Bonnie Vandesteeg, Cynthia Wall, Cathy Wertz, Steven Wesolowski, David Whang, Stephen Williams, and Kurt Yeager.

Finally, like other authors, I must thank the members of my family for sharing the burdens of authorship. They did not find living in Laguna Beach for a year to be a hardship; Marty learned to walk there, Amy learned to read, and Steve mastered sailing and skateboarding. They came to tolerate their father bolting down his dinner, evening after evening, and dashing off with the tape recorder. Much time spent on the book since then should have been spent with them. I owe thanks to the three of them, and to my wife, Sally, who has put up with a lot, during both the research and the writing.

The people and organizations listed here, and particularly the twenty-three voters of Ramona Heights, contributed whatever virtues the book may contain. I only wish I could blame them for its faults.

KARL A. LAMB

Santa Cruz, California
March 1974

PART ONE

A Neighborhood in Orange County

Orange County is suburban, prosperous, new, fast-growing, white, intensely orthodox, patriotic, church-going, often puritanical, often rootless, often heavily mortgaged, and often fearful that something unpredictable may happen—factory closures, space agency cutbacks, tax increases—to start its citizens sliding toward the poverty from which many of their parents escaped.

The White House staff does not come entirely from Orange County in fact, but they do so in spirit.

—*Michael Davie of the* London Observer

CHAPTER ONE

Orange County:
Stereotype, Prototype, or Mystery?

"As Maine goes, so goes the nation."

—*Political saying of the 1880s*

Orange County as Enigma

WHEN FRANKLIN D. ROOSEVELT'S smashing victory of 1936 was totaled up, James A. Farley, chairman of the Democratic National Committee, issued a new version of the old political saying: "As Maine goes, so goes Vermont." For only those two states had clung to their Republicanism in face of the rushing New Deal tide. Far away, on the West Coast, California joined the Democratic majority. And California was joined enthusiastically by Orange County, a still largely pastoral area that had achieved its independence from Los Angeles County in 1889 (it had formed the southeastern corner of that county). Orange County had not voted for a Democratic presidential aspirant until 1932, when FDR carried the county by 1,200 votes out of 50,000. Roosevelt also won the county decisively in 1936, but it has not supported a Democratic nominee since. Depression-era Democratic voting was an aberration that was soon forgotten; Republican domination of political affairs has been as pronounced since 1936 as it was before 1932. The population of Orange County has increased some 800 percent since 1936, but its Republicanism seems little affected by growth and change.

In 1968, Orange County voted overwhelmingly for its native son, Richard M. Nixon—63 percent for Nixon, only 30 percent for Hubert H. Humphrey. Although the county was now famous for its "extremism," only 7 percent of the voters deserted the two-party system to support George C. Wallace.[1]

In 1972, 68 percent chose Nixon, compared to the nationwide Nixon vote of nearly 61 percent. George McGovern won 27 percent of the Orange County vote, while 4 percent supported the former Orange County congressman, John G. Schmitz, candidate of the American Independent party.

The analysts of American political history agree that the majority coalition formed—but its nature obscured—by Roosevelt's overwhelming 1936 victory has ruled the nation since then. Not even the personal popularity of President Dwight D. Eisenhower disturbed this long-term trend.[2] Indeed, it survived the mass movement of Americans to the suburbs in the decades following World War II.[3]

The imminent collapse of this New Deal coalition has been predicted,

[1] By 1970, Republicans were 53.3 percent of Orange County's 612,006 voters, while Democrats numbered 41.3 percent; in 1972, Republican registrations declined to 50.2 percent, while the Democrats increased to 42.6 percent. Therefore, Orange County exemplified the suburban maxim "vote for the man, not the party" in overwhelmingly supporting Nixon. In 1970, 4.4 percent of the county's voters declined to state a party preference, denying themselves participation in primary elections; by 1972, with the eighteen-year-old vote, this proportion grew to 6.8 percent, marking a trend away from traditional party loyalty.

[2] The triumph of the Roosevelt coalition was presaged in 1928, when the candidacy of Alfred E. Smith weaned the northern cities away from their Republican allegiance, which had endured, in general outline, since 1896. See Samuel Lubell, *The Future of American Politics* (New York: Harper, 1952). For documentation of the persistent majority of Democratic attitudes, see the principal works of the University of Michigan Survey Research Center, particularly *The American Voter* (New York: Wiley, 1960); *The Voter Decides* (Evanston, Ill.: Row, Peterson, 1954); and *Elections and the Political Order* (New York: Wiley, 1966).

[3] The possibility that "the suburban vote" constituted a new force was considered early in the 1950s. See, for example, Louis Harris, *Is There a Republican Majority?* (New York: Harper, 1954), pp. 119–126, and Robert C. Wood, *Suburbia: Its People and Their Politics* (Boston: Houghton Mifflin, 1958), pp. 135–153. But the evidence was contradictory then, and it is now clear that Democratic suburbanites liked Ike but did not embrace his party; the new suburbanites who vote Republican were Republicans before they moved. For confirming data and a summary of the literature, see David Wallace, *First Tuesday: A Study of Rationality in Voting* (Garden City, N.Y.: Doubleday, 1964), pp. 47–57.

and even chronicled, for years—by political commentators, as well as by Republican candidates. The turmoil of the 1960s was bound to stimulate a desertion from the majority party, or at least create a new agenda of political issues.[4] In 1972, however, President Nixon was reelected in a lonesome landslide, with the Democrats returning a majority to Congress. The shape of America's political future remained obscure. The Watergate investigations, punctuated by the resignation from office of Vice President Agnew, indicated that the best laid plans of Republican strategy would come to naught. Beyond that, little was certain, except that the world had changed, and so had the voters. What did those changes portend?[5]

Orange County voters have been outside the mainstream of American politics since 1936. Yet they are studied here in the conviction that they offer clues to the nation's political future. Kevin Phillips, political adviser to former Attorney General John Mitchell and prophet of *The Emerging Republican Majority,* claimed that Orange County and its neighbor, San Diego County, were clear examples of a new "populist conservatism" which is largely centered in the areas of fastest population growth. These areas, he claimed, would lead the nation into a new era ruled by a Republican majority.[6] Phillips saw the 1968 candidacy of George Wallace as providing a way-station for voters embarking on a permanent journey from the Democratic to the Republican parties. He did not, however, adequately account for that growing force of political independence which leads voters to sever their ties with any party. This spirit of independence is among the new forces at work in American politics which are prominently displayed in Orange County. In the post-Watergate era, these new forces do not necessarily lead to a Republican majority. National voting patterns will be more like those of Orange County in the future than they were in the past. Orange County is not so much joining the mainstream as charting its new direction.

Political analysts usually deal only with cold statistics—population figures, voting returns, and the percentages generated by opinion polls. Having made a nod to such figures, let us consider the warmly held convictions of actual Orange County voters.

[4]See Richard M. Scammon and Ben J. Wattenberg, *The Real Majority* (New York: Coward-McCann, 1970), for one description of the new issues.
[5]The role of elections in the American political process, including the theory of critical elections, is examined in detail in chapter ten. Clearly, the critical election of our era did not take place in either 1968 or 1972.
[6]Kevin B. Phillips, *The Emerging Republican Majority* (Garden City, N.Y.: Doubleday, 1970), p. 445.

OF BIRTH AND TAXES

Fletcher Barbera, age thirty-three, is an electronics engineer. Educated in the Ivy League, and ambivalently proud of his New England ancestry, he spent his boyhood in Southern California and returned there after college to establish his career. He is a registered Republican, and calls himself a moderate conservative. The subject of taxation came up during the second session of our conversations.

Fletcher: Oh, I don't think the tax burden is oppressive . . . I'm sure there are areas where government is not as efficient as it might be, but on the whole I don't think our government—federal, state, or local— is grossly wasteful. I think most of the things that they're trying to do are worthwhile.

A moment later, however, Barbera modified this positive vote for government and taxation by mentioning his opposition to the progressive income tax; he'd prefer a fixed rate. He stated the standard incentive argument in personal terms.

Fletcher: I'm at a point where my incremental income tax, if you include both federal and state, is thirty-three percent. In other words, to make an incremental two hundred dollars of spendable income, I have to make an incremental three hundred dollars in gross wages, from the company I work for. And I'm still trying. . . . But if I went much further, okay, if I got up to, say, a fifty percent point, it begins to put a damper on my desire to increase my income, and I think that's very bad. . . . When you start to put an artificial damper on things, I think in the long run it could be detrimental to our economic growth.

But Barbera was not dogmatic about this, and his low opinion of the graduated income tax was not coupled with other attitudes, such as support of states' rights against federal school integration orders, a position found in the pamphlets of many ultra-conservative political organizations. It was simply a belief not necessarily connected by strands of logic or emotion to other convictions. A week later, Barbera referred to this apparent inconsistency.

Fletcher: I'm kind of opposed to the progressive income tax. But I don't worry about it every day. I mean, like, I'm not going to *do* anything about it.

And, shortly thereafter, he reaffirmed his conviction that the federal government is not oppressive; that it makes mistakes, just as private enterprise does; but that its motives are benign and most of its actions beneficial.

At the very beginning of our conversations, when I asked Fletcher Barbera to identify the major problems facing America today, he launched into a long discourse on the problems of ecology and the uncertain impact of technological development on the balance of nature. This led him to think of birth control, which he tends to oppose, not on moral grounds, but because birth control pills can have unsuspected and detrimental side effects, as happened with the wife of a friend. Therefore, he favors the legalization of abortions.

Fletcher: I don't see why an abortion couldn't be like removing a wart on your big toe. You pay the money and you get the fix.

His wife, Maureen, who was raised a Catholic, agrees with his general attitude. But she feels that the number of abortions performed on an individual woman should be limited, first, because of the danger of cumulative physical damage, and, second, because she fears that abortions would encourage promiscuity and spread the "hippie" life style.

Maureen: I think there ought to be a limit. I have visions of the same woman going in every month and saying, "I need one again." [She laughs.]

Fletcher: And your vision includes the fact that she's not married.

Maureen: Well, of course she's not! She's young, and she's got her sleeping bag over her shoulder! [Both laugh.]

Three blocks away from the Barberas' comfortable four-bedroom house is the equally comfortable but smaller home of Jan and Eldene Markus. They are second-generation Americans, his parents having been born in Czechoslovakia, hers in Poland. Jan Markus became an electrician through an informal apprenticeship in Illinois forty years ago. His last job in California was as maintenance supervisor in a small factory. He retired at age sixty-two, after a major operation for cancer. But it is a comfortable retirement, for both he and his wife have worked and saved most of their lives. They are childless, but their home is the summer headquarters for numerous nieces and nephews visiting nearby Disneyland. They are fiercely patriotic, but their allegiance is to the American government of here-and-now, not to some vague nostalgia for times past. Both are registered Democrats. They seem to be unusually eager taxpayers.

Eldene: We are always willing to pay our taxes, believe me. This country is worth paying taxes for.

Jan: One trouble is that people get a lot of services through the federal and municipal governments; they don't even give that a thought! Look at all the roads. You've got street lights, and things that you use every day. And they take too much for granted. And so of course we can't operate the governments without any money. Look at all the flood control. All that stuff costs money. And our government does things and spends money on things that people don't even realize. And it's things that we need. . . . We have to have those things. Otherwise we couldn't be a country like we are. But somebody has to pay for that.

Toward the end of our conversation, two weeks later, Jan Markus returned to the tax theme. "Actually," he said, "we get more out of government than we realize. And we just shouldn't complain about taxes so much." But the Markuses insisted that taxes should not be a burden on the poor, and that corporations should be required to pay more nearly their fair share.

Like the Barberas, the Markuses are concerned with population growth. On one occasion they signed petitions calling for sex education in the local schools, and on another they signed a petition supporting the legalization of abortion in California. Jan Markus makes clear his conviction that the best public measure would be the support of birth control clinics. Better to prevent conception before it occurs, he feels.

Several houses down the street live Arthur and Tina Roybal. Arthur was born in a Los Angeles *barrio* and was the first member of his family to attend college; his grandparents were born in Mexico. Tina is the daughter of a Lebanese rug merchant who immigrated to Ohio and moved to California when Tina was in high school. Both are registered Republicans. Their five-bedroom home easily accommodates their four children. They are both employed in the public schools—Tina as a teacher, Arthur in administration.

Arthur Roybal feels that suburban residents who work in a central city should be taxed (probably on income) to help maintain the facilities of the central city. If a person benefits from the city, even without living there, he should help pay for its maintenance. He also feels that the federal government should intervene more forcefully in the operation of the national economy, to guard against economic recession.

Arthur: I feel sometimes government is taking too big a hold, and yet I think we've come to the point where we have to allow them to, in certain instances, and I believe this would be one of those instances.

According to his wife, Arthur has become generally more liberal in recent years, but they both describe themselves as "middle of the road" in political matters. Their attachment to the Republican party is a formal one; since this is a Republican area, they feel their votes will have the greatest impact in the Republican primary election. They favor sex education in the public schools, and public support for the distribution of birth control information. Support for the liberalization of laws governing abortion is implicit in these expressed attitudes, although we did not discuss the matter specifically.

These are six registered voters of Orange County. None resents the burdens he bears as a taxpayer; the Markuses even pay taxes with enthusiasm. All express a willingness to pay increased taxes to alleviate major urban problems. No claim is made here, nor will it be made in what follows, that these six voters typify, in a statistical sense, the majority in either Orange County or American suburbia. But to select six persons at random and find them expressing such attitudes—particularly in Orange County—is at least a mild surprise. They do not match the presumptions about suburban political attitudes commonly held by political analysts.

What are the sources of the casual assumptions made about voter attitudes in a given region, or a particular legislative district, in the absence of a scientific opinion survey? One source is the opinions of their elected representatives. At the time of these interviews, the Barberas, Markuses, and Roybals were represented in the United States Congress by John G. Schmitz of Tustin, victor in a special election to fill the vacancy created by the death in office of James B. Utt. Mr. Utt was famous (or infamous) for his determined conservatism; he was once quoted as saying, "The federal government is like the child molester who offers candy before his evil act."[7]

The replacement of Utt by Schmitz occasioned little comment, for Schmitz had established an ultraconservative record in the California legislature. His stand against taxation was blunt: he promised he would not vote for any bill that would increase taxes, unless war were declared against North Vietnam. Schmitz fought vigorously against the legislation legalizing abortion championed by State Senator Anthony Beilenson of Beverly Hills. Schmitz guided a bill to passage which provides that any teacher admitting a student to a sex education class without written parental permission may have his teaching credential revoked. John Schmitz is also an avowed member of the John Birch Society.

We have before us a microcosmic case in which the opinions of six constituents contradicted the clearly announced positions of their con-

[7]Quoted in Sheldon Zalaznick, "The Double Life of Orange County," 78 *Fortune* 5 (October, 1968), p. 140.

gressman on two issues—legalized abortion and tax increases. If they were aware of the conflict and disturbed by it, they could have taken two actions: make the legislator aware of their opinion in hopes of changing his; or vote for his opponent at the next election. The first of these alternatives was, in a sense, taken by the Markuses when they signed a petition favoring the liberalization of abortion laws, although the petition was addressed to state legislators and the Markuses were not aware of Schmitz's position. But did these two issues influence their voting decision?

The Barberas, staunch Republicans, voted for Schmitz. They were not aware of any conflict between Schmitz's opinions and their own; when asked in August, 1970, if they knew anything about Schmitz that might lead them to vote against him, Fletcher Barbera replied that he did not. Neither he nor his wife was aware of Schmitz's affiliation with the John Birch Society, an organization they disapprove of. However, Maureen Barbera had seen pictures of Congressman Schmitz, and she jokingly said that she might vote against him because of his moustache. She simply did not like his appearance.

Maureen: I'm not terribly keen on Mr. Schmitz, but I guess it's because he looks like a ferret to me. That's physical appeal, and that's where Bobby Kennedy had it made! And I'm a woman.

The Markuses, staunch Democrats, did not vote in the primaries. In November, however, they voted for Thomas Lenhart, Schmitz's Democratic opponent. They were asked if they knew anything about Schmitz that made them dislike him.

Eldene: Oh, I think he's too much of a Bircher. And if he's a Bircher, they're—there's something, I don't know just how to say it. They're mistrusting. They mistrust people. They make bad opinions of people. He was a Bircher at one time, and Birchers supported him, and I'm just not for Birchers. The John Birch Society.

Jan: Well, I wouldn't vote for anybody that's a Bircher. Because they're revolutionaries. They want to take over the country. I'm not for anything like that. They're as bad as the communists, doing the same thing. But I don't hear much about them anymore. I think they fell by the wayside.

Eldene: Oh, they're still in existence, Jan. Maybe not as powerful, or maybe they're underground. [She laughs.]

The Roybals voted in the November election, but neither voted in the congressional contest. They could not support Schmitz because he was "too closely politically allied with the right wing," but they felt they had not learned enough about the Democrat, Thomas Lenhart, to decide whether or not they could support him. Their solution was to leave that portion of the ballot blank. (Or, more accurately, not to punch the computer card for that contest.)

These six voters live in the area served by the mass media of Los Angeles; they are bombarded daily with news of political events from around the world; it is no surprise that their congressman's positions on particular issues are not at the forefront of their political conscious-nesses. They fit the picture painted in one study of the linkage between public opinion and government policy.

> Far from looking over the shoulder of their Congressmen at the legislative game, most Americans are almost totally uninformed about legislative issues in Washington. At best the average citizen may be said to have some general ideas about how the country should be run. . . .[8]

The Barberas, Markuses, and Roybals do indeed have general ideas about how the United States should be run. And they can be placed among the average citizenry, for they are, in a much-quoted phrase, "unyoung, unpoor, and unblack"—adjectives used to describe the majority of American voters.[9] Furthermore, they live in the suburbs— along with the plurality counted in the 1970 census of the United States. If no violent revolution destroys the fabric of society, the American future depends on what kind of leadership this plurality will seek and accept; what forms of government activity it will encourage, or at least tolerate; and what level of taxes it will pay.

THE ECLIPSE OF CONGRESSMAN SCHMITZ

However, if Americans are "almost totally uninformed" about legislative issues in Washington and in their state capitals, how can this decisive role be assumed by the suburban plurality? What is the mechanism through which any group translates its "general ideas" into specific acts by its elected representative? The election, of course, is that mechanism. But its function will be imperfectly performed in an area

[8]Warren E. Miller and Donald E. Stokes, "Constituency Influence in Congress," re-printed in A. Campbell et al., *Elections and the Political Order* (New York: Wiley, 1966), p. 355. For a comparative study of representation in state legislatures, see J. C. Wahlke et al., *The Legislative System: Explorations in Legislative Behavior* (New York: Wiley, 1962).
[9]Scammon and Wattenberg, *The Real Majority*.

that votes so habitually for one of the two traditional parties that the opposition does not seriously support an alternative candidate.

This was the cause of the defeat of Thomas Lenhart, Schmitz's opponent in 1970. As Schmitz began his first regular term in the United States Congress, he seemed invincible. When district boundaries were redrawn by the California legislature in reapportioning congressional districts, Schmitz was assigned an area with an even greater proportion of Republican voters than before. (His most notable constituent lived in San Clemente; he was Richard M. Nixon, president of the United States.) Eventually, when Schmitz's disagreement with his constituents' values was brought forcefully to their attention, he was defeated. But it was not his position on taxation or abortion that defeated him; it was his opposition to Nixon's foreign policy.

John Schmitz entered politics in the state senatorial primary election of 1964, when Barry Goldwater carried Orange County decisively and won the entire state narrowly in the Republican presidential primary. Schmitz ran against a candidate privately backed by the established—and wealthy—Republican leaders of Orange County. Schmitz won because of a grass-roots campaign staffed by conservative campaign workers who were extraordinarily loyal to him. When he won the primary, Republican leaders were required to make their peace with him.[10]

On June 2, 1970, when Schmitz sought the congressional seat vacated by the death of James B. Utt, he faced six opponents, three Republicans and three Democrats, in a special nonpartisan election. Two of the Republicans were quite liberal, compared to Schmitz. The fact that three Republicans entered against Schmitz suggests that there was no concerted effort to locate an attractive candidate and finance an assault on Schmitz within his own party. A single liberal opponent might have defeated him, particularly since Democrats were able to vote for Republican candidates in that unusual election. With the liberal vote split between three Democratic and two Republican candidates, Schmitz won nearly half the June 2 vote, and he resoundingly defeated a single Democrat in the final election on June 30. After that victory, the enthusiastic group that worked for Schmitz seemed likely to dominate the Republican primaries in the foreseeable future, and the Democratic party would offer only formal opposition in the general elections. The

---

[10]California law prohibits formal party organizations, such as county central committees, from taking part in primary elections, yet requires them to support the primary winners. This is only one of the limitations on organizational activity, instituted as reforms by the Progressives, which make California parties unusually weak. The kind of organization recognized as a party in New York, Pennsylvania, Ohio, or Michigan simply does not exist in California.

limited electorate that participates in primaries is motivated more strongly by ideological considerations than are the members of even their own party who vote only in general elections.[11] Schmitz was easily elected to a regular term in November.

John Schmitz had built a career on anticommunism, and he early voiced his distress at the efforts of President Nixon to establish a détente with the Soviet Union and China. When asked by a reporter if he were upset by Nixon's trip to China, Schmitz replied that he would only be distressed if the president returned.

Viewing Schmitz as an embarrassment to Nixon, some wealthy Republicans of Orange County agreed to back the county tax assessor, Andrew Hinshaw, as a candidate against him in the 1972 Republican primary. The failure of Schmitz to support the leader of his party was made the central issue of the campaign, and Schmitz was soundly defeated.

The fact that Schmitz could be defeated by the county tax assessor —not the most charismatic position from which to run for Congress— led to speculation that Orange County Republican politics was becoming liberalized. A more likely explanation is that the campaign transcended the usual ideological concerns of a specialized electorate; most Orange County Republicans had never shared the convictions of the noisy activist minority, but they had never organized their own opposition. After George Wallace was retired from the 1972 campaign by the attempt on his life, Schmitz won the presidential designation of the remnants of Wallace's 1968 organization, the American Independent party. In November, 1972, Schmitz won only 28,262 votes in his home county.

Orange County as Stereotype

The 1970 Democratic decision not to support Thomas Lenhart against John Schmitz is understandable; scarce resources are best allocated to candidates with a chance of winning. Nevertheless, this kind

[11]This conclusion is congruent with the finding of McClosky et al., "Issue Conflict and Consensus among Party Leaders and Followers," 54 *American Political Science Review* 2 (June, 1960), p. 426, that national convention delegates are more ideologically committed than general party members, and the finding of Samuel J. Eldersveld, *Political Parties: A Behavioral Analysis* (Chicago: Rand McNally, 1964), p. 197, that middle-level party cadres show substantial political awareness. For examples of how primary elections threaten the power of party leaders, see V. O. Key, Jr., *Politics, Parties, and Pressure Groups*, 4th ed. (New York: Crowell, 1958), pp. 422–423.

of decision becomes a self-fulfilling prophecy. Certain that conservative candidates will win, liberals never test their strength. There are few certainties in the volatile atmosphere of California politics, but even casual observers are certain that Orange County not only is conservative in its voting habits, but provides a stronghold for organizations of the extreme right.

This stereotypical picture of Orange County may be supported by citing any number of political and social phenomena. Yet each of them may be contradicted. For example:

1. Orange County always elects Republicans. (But Orange County has two Democratic legislators, Congressman Richard T. Hanna and State Assemblyman Kenneth Cory, who seem well entrenched.)

2. Orange County has been the setting for numerous stories about the activities of the John Birch Society. (Orange County membership in the Birch Society was estimated at 3,000 in 1968—the last year anybody bothered to estimate—out of a population of 1.3 million. Even then, weeds were growing in the lawn of the American Opinion [Birch] Library in the city of Orange.)[12]

3. Ultraconservative groups managed to kill a much admired, pioneering sex education program in the city schools of Anaheim. (The Anaheim union high school district serves three of the twenty-five incorporated cities in Orange County, and parts of six others. None of the other districts has surrendered school programs upon attack by the right wing, although the county school board once removed John Hersey's *Hiroshima* from school library shelves. One of the other cities, Fountain Valley, has a school system considered a model for the nation, vigorously supported by the local citizenry.)

4. Orange County habitually gives a large majority to the most outrageously conservative candidates. (Wilson Riles, the black school administrator who defeated flamboyant incumbent Max Rafferty for the office of statewide superintendent of schools, held Rafferty's Orange County plurality to only 34,808 out of 445,846 votes. Senator George Murphy failed to win reelection in 1970 because of his surprisingly narrow margin in Orange County.)

5. Orange County votes on the conservative side of issues. For example, it led Southern California in supporting infamous Proposition 14 of 1964, an initiative measure repealing all fair-housing legislation, which was subsequently declared unconstitutional by the United States Su-

---

[12]Zalaznick, "Double Life of Orange County," p. 184.

preme Court. (An exhaustive analysis of the contrasting voting records of Northern and Southern California suggests that "the striking regional differences in California politics . . . are determined in good measure by the different political preferences of the leaders and activists in the two regions," while they are largely independent both of growth rates and of the gross differences in the population characteristics of the two regions.)[13]

6. Orange County is the home of Disneyland, the most notable marriage of indifferent American taste with superb American technology. (The values of Disneyland are pure Hollywood. It is marked by the realistic appearance of its mechanical fauna, ranging from parakeets to Abraham Lincoln, created through the process of "Audio-Animatronics," and by its compulsive cleanliness—drop a chewing gum wrapper, and a uniformed, crew-cut, teen-aged boy materializes to sweep it into a covered dustpan.)

7. Orange County also houses Knott's Berry Farm, presided over by ultraconservative octogenarian Walter Knott, Goldwater fan and leading Orange County Republican. It encompasses a movie-set western town; a railroad and other rides; a replica of Philadelphia's Independence Hall; and a bookstore loaded with John Birch Society material. (Knott's Berry Farm is a more relaxed place than Disneyland. Its stagecoach is drawn by real horses, and its mule-train ride provides mules. The stables smell like stables. It is altogether less totalitarian in concept and more human in scale than Disney's Magic Kingdom.)

8. A leading newspaper of Orange County is the *Santa Ana Register*, founded by the late R. C. Hoiles, who believed that no government was best of all: the schools, police force, and post office should all be operated by private contractors. (Readership of the *Los Angeles Times* increases in proportion to the individual's quantity of education and length of residence in Orange County.)[14]

9. Orange County is the fastest growing large county in the United States. Its population is unstable. As its residents restlessly climb the ladder of affluence and new suburbanites flock in from Los Angeles, one out of every four homes changes hands every year. Residents of the county have no chance to develop ties with their community or achieve the kind of identity with it that will lead them to support its purposes.

[13]Raymond E. Wolfinger and Fred I. Greenstein, "Comparing Political Regions: The Case of California," 63 *American Political Science Review* 1 (March, 1969), pp. 84–85.
[14]This was one finding of the unpublished survey conducted at the University of California, Irvine, in 1970, described in the Preface.

(Somebody has been doing the planning, providing water and sewers, building roads and schools, and voting for bond issues. Orange County residents enjoy a remarkably high level of municipal service.)

The stereotype of Orange County lives on, as journalists and scholars invoke it through force of long habit. A compact collection of popular clichés about suburbia, compiled by British journalist Michael Davie, offered "the Orange County spirit" as a label for the motivation of the Watergate conspirators' and of Nixon's staff assistants in general. He found them to be grasping, aggressive, insecure, conservative ideologues with a compulsion to prove themselves in the environment of the eastern United States. They applied the Protestant work ethic astringently to welfare applicants, at the same time seeking large government contracts for industries with which they were connected.[15] He found them suspicious of the civil servants they were required to deal with, and he implied that their dress and grooming bespoke their abhorrence of the relaxed life style favored by campus youth. All these traits could be traced to the pernicious influences of living in Orange County, yet they also infected the members of the staff who had never been in Southern California.[16]

How does Orange County exert its pervasive influence? Writing of Orange County political history on the basis of newspaper editorials and voting returns of the 1930s, a professional historian concluded:

> Even the tremendous population growth since World War II, which has wrought such fundamental changes in Orange County's economic life, has not significantly altered its fundamentally conservative political orientation. This basic conservatism, which has endured in the face of change and transition, seems to be an intrinsic facet of Orange County character, a faith that even outsiders adopt once they set foot in the area.[17]

---

[15]Kirkpatrick Sale has designated a broader geographical area. He finds that the Nixon Administration is dominated by America's "southern rim," stretching from Florida through Texas to Southern California, which he sees as the last frontier of rapacious laissez-faire capitalism. See his "The World behind Watergate," *New York Review of Books*, May 3, 1973.

[16]Davie's article was reprinted in the *San Francisco Chronicle*, April 28, 1973.

[17]Robert L. Pritchard, "Orange County during the Depressed Thirties: A Study in Twentieth-Century California Local History," 50 *Southern California Quarterly* 2 (June, 1968), p. 205. Pritchard feels that the county's lapse from conservatism in 1932 and 1936 was due to the economic suffering of the time, but that the return to conservative Republicanism resulted from the distress felt by the county's opinion leaders at the radicalism of Roosevelt's Second New Deal from 1935 on.

This is not only a reassertion of the stereotype, but an explicit suggestion of causation: perhaps there is something in the very soil of Orange
County, or perhaps in the air its residents breathe, that converts all
comers, regardless of past experiences or attitudes, into staunch conservatives.

The development of any stereotype is fed by elements of fact. Orange
County supplies many such facts—from Disney's fake Matterhorn rising
out of the flat land of Anaheim, to the "Orange County Mafia" re-
cruited for Richard Nixon's White House. The interaction of "common
knowledge" with supporting evidence is illustrated in the following
statement by two noted political scientists:

> The conservative tone of political life in Southern California is well
> known. Radical right organizations flourish in the area, which is the prime
> source of out-of-state rightist mail received by Congressmen and Senators.[18]

Of the three assertions made here, only the last one (concerning the
source of right-wing mail) is thought to require documentation. Of
course, if senators and congressmen are aware of receiving only right-
wing messages from Orange County, their image of the county is likely
to be correspondingly influenced, although the large bulk of letters to
public officials comes from a fraction of the population, which writes
again and again. Indeed, "of the total stream of such letters from the
grass roots, two-thirds are composed by about 3 per cent of the population," and this small segment is much more conservative, as well as
much more ideologically oriented, than the general public.[19] Similarly,
when journalists find activities of the right-wing fringe to be news-
worthy, their stories may unintentionally suggest that such activities are
typical.

But a stereotype also *creates* the reality when it is used as the basis
for judgments that become self-fulfilling prophecies. The convictions of
a representative like former Congressman Schmitz do not supply adequate evidence on which to judge the beliefs of his constituents. Each
of the stereotypes cited previously invites the same flaw in judgment:
accepting the superficial signs of conservatism in Orange County as fact,
without consulting the thoughts, dreams, and fears of the people who
live there.

---

[18]Wolfinger and Greenstein, "Comparing Political Regions," p. 74.

[19]Philip E. Converse, Aage R. Clausen, and Warren E. Miller, "Electoral Myth and
Reality: The 1964 Election," 59 *American Political Science Review* 2 (June, 1965), pp.
333, 334–336.

Orange County as Prototype

Quite a different conception of Orange County can be formulated.

Beneath its eccentric surface . . . Orange County is more interesting for its typicality than for its uniqueness. A great many suburbias across the United States share with Orange County the problems, preoccupations, and tensions associated with growth and change. They're exaggerated in Orange County, partly because growth has been so very rapid. But seen for what it essentially is, a kind of hypersuburbia, Orange County is, as a Southern California businessman recently put it, "a demonstration city for the world."[20]

It is not difficult to find characteristics of the Orange County population that are comparable to those of other suburbias. Median family income in Orange County, for example, is very close to that in Fairfield County, Connecticut, an affluent bedroom area serving New York.[21] The percentage of nonwhites in the Orange County population is less than half of the still small nonwhite populations of Nassau County, New York, and Montgomery County, Maryland, a suburb of the District of Columbia.[22] The rate of population growth in Orange County is half again as great as that in Suffolk County, New York.[23]

But such figures do not highlight what makes Orange County a showplace of America's future. That future is increasingly suburban. And every suburb exists in a society that is increasingly complex, its economic enterprises staffed and its government agencies managed by technical experts. The Orange County of today was created by, and in turn creates, advancing technology. Manufacturing industry in the area is dominated by leading sectors of American technology: aircraft, aerospace, and electronics. Employment in these firms during the height of the cold war era and the effort to place an American on the moon

[20]Zalaznick, "Double Life of Orange County," p. 139.
[21]Median family income in Fairfield County, $13,086; in Orange County, $12,245. Source: 1970 census.
[22]Nonwhite population of Orange County, 2.7 percent; of Nassau County, 5.0 percent; of Montgomery County, 5.5 percent. Calculated from 1970 census data.
[23]Population growth from 1950 to 1960: in Orange County, 225.6 percent; in Suffolk County, 141.5 percent. Source: 1960 census. Orange County grew from a total population of 703,925 in 1960 to 1,420,386 in 1970, an increase of 101.8 percent. In the same period, Suffolk County grew from 666,784 to 1,124,950, an increase of 68.7 percent. Source: 1970 census.

combined with the natural attractions of Orange County—its famous climate and beaches—to bring engineers, technicians, and a highly paid corps of hourly workers into the county. An earlier technological development, the automobile, made it possible for the newcomers to live in South Orange County, near the cooling breezes of the Pacific, and work in the expanding firms of North Orange County or Los Angeles County. Because of their positions in highly technical industry, therefore, an important component of the Orange County population may be described as an "affluent technocracy."

Suburban living is famous for encouraging a separation between life centered around the family and hours spent by the wage earner to finance family life. But is there any carryover of attitudes learned on the job—attitudes toward authority, or beliefs about how a large business enterprise should be organized, or feelings about the need for decision-making by experts rather than compromises produced by the political process—which may be carried home to influence the way the technocrat reacts to the problems of governing his suburb, or his nation? If the increasing specialization of the American work force is to have an impact on political attitudes and behavior, the trend may be more obvious in Orange County than in other areas.

Orange County is described as "hypersuburbia." Most suburbs gain identity from being satellites, within the metropolitan area, of a central city; the transportation web is not unlike a spider's, as the commuters stream from the periphery to their jobs in the center. But what is the center for which the Orange County communities are the suburbs? Los Angeles, growing to maturity after the development of the automobile, never really developed a center; it was destroyed by the voracious demands of the freeways for land. The population growth of Southern California has been decentralized before the fact; there never really was a center. Industry and commerce are scattered. An engineer determined to keep his family on the beach front at Balboa must drive fifty-five miles to his office in Los Angeles. Residents of Orange County all seem to know at least one commuting horror story—the man who lives in Newport Beach, for example, but works in Pomona. The helicopter line that was established to serve such needs has gone bankrupt, a victim of economic recession and public fears after two fatal crashes. What is the impact on political attitudes of living within an uncontrolled urban sprawl, where passage from one municipality to the next goes unnoticed on the freeway? Orange County must be a place to find the answer.

Students of suburban politics find that the farther people live from the central city and its established political habits, the less partisan they tend to be. New suburbanites may think they are returning to a kind of small-town democratic government practiced by their forefathers, with some such model as the New England town meeting in mind. Suburbanites take issue after issue "out of politics" by handing its management over to the professionals—the professional engineers of a water or sanitation district, or the professional city manager who poses as a scientifically trained bureaucrat while actually guiding his city council of amateurs through the shoals of politics.[24] Local government in California has enjoyed the dubious advantages of nonpartisan institutions since the Progressive era. Thus, local nonpartisanship antedates the modern development of the suburbs. What is the impact of this disdain of local partisanship on partisan attitudes concerning state and national issues? Orange County should provide a vantage point for seeking an approximate answer.

Suburbia is not monolithic; as decentralization proceeds, with industry, commerce, and entertainment seeking the periphery, different municipalities grow, each with a different character. Originally viewed as a looking glass into the uniformity and mediocrity of the middle class —the definitive locus of American values[25]—Suburbs now appear in many varieties; there are upper-middle-class, working-class,[26] and even industrial suburbs. Some suburbs consist mainly of bars and nightclubs banned by neighboring jurisdictions. By definition, a suburb is a municipality within a larger population area that retains control over the essentials of its own government; for good reasons or evil, the zoning codes soon establish some suburbs as more wealthy and exclusive than others.

Orange County exemplifies this pattern. The densely populated area nearest Los Angeles County seems but an extension of its sprawl of deteriorating, cheaply constructed residential areas, largely built in the early 1950s, relieved only by the garish "strip commercial" thoroughfares such as Beach Boulevard and Garden Grove Boulevard, which change character not at all as they cross municipal boundaries—except that one city often does not synchronize the timing of its traffic lights with its neighbors'. Anaheim, Garden Grove, Tustin, Santa Ana—the boundaries fade into each other, the mixture of industry, housing tracts, and unplanned development seemingly characteristic of all. In Santa Ana, there is a miniature ghetto housing the 1½ percent of the county's

[24]Wood, *Suburbia*, p. 84.
[25]*Ibid.*
[26]Bennett M. Berger, *Working-Class Suburb* (Berkeley and Los Angeles: University of California Press, 1960), p. 101.

population that is black. In Anaheim, tourism has been the main industry since the building of Disneyland. But Disney imposed order only within the walls of his own property; the neon signs of the motels and quick-order chain restaurants surround the Magic Kingdom with visual disharmony.

As distance from Los Angeles County increases, spun out at a mile a minute along the older Santa Ana Freeway or the newer San Diego Freeway, population density drops, and more exclusive residential areas are found along the beaches or in the hills that rise above them. Suburban sprawl in this part of Orange County has been limited and delayed because so much of the land area (one-third of that in the county) was once the Irvine Ranch, and more than 80,000 acres is still controlled by the Irvine Company. (James Irvine I, born in Ireland, came to San Francisco during the gold rush and made his initial fortune as a grocer. With two temporary partners, he formed the 110,000-acre ranch through purchases from the heirs of three of the great Spanish land grants. The Irvine Ranch stretched from the mountains to the sea; it became a diversified agricultural corporation, occupying a mid-point between the developing population centers of Los Angeles and San Diego.) The Irvine Company now functions primarily as a land developer; at the present rate of growth, its land holdings will not be fully occupied for fifty years. Many of the residential communities are built on land leased for long terms from the Irvine Company; the corporation will remain a powerful force in the area.

Many of the more wealthy residents of Orange County live in Newport Beach; Newport Harbor is one of the biggest and busiest small-craft harbors in the world. Orange County leads the movement to supply residential complexes for specialized clientele—Ross Cortesi's Leisure World and Del Webb's Sun City, colonies for the retired; and a chain of resortlike apartment houses for "swinging singles." Other communities are best described as upper-class suburbs, providing for the wealthy a comfortable shelter, far from the terrors of central ghettos (Watts) or the monotony of look-alike housing in the working-class areas. Emerald Bay and Irvine Cove, near the artists' and artisans' center of Laguna Beach, are exclusive in a literal sense. Surrounded by walls, they yield access only through guarded gates. The guard telephones the host to be sure that the visitor has been invited and is expected.

How do suburbanites who have fled the central city regard the political problems of such cities? Secure in their autonomous municipalities, where their property tax dollars support no integrated schools—there are no minorities to integrate—are they determined to look on idly as urban problems destroy the fabric of our national life? Part of the answer may be found in Orange County.

The stereotypical image of Orange County as a blend of rapid physical growth and political atrophy labels it a bastion of right-wing conservatism. This image is based on attributes of the area that may be fairly superficial; the extent to which they can characterize the voting population of the county deserves investigation. If there is evidence that the voters are not nearly as conservative as their representatives and the organizations that claim to speak for them, an important question remains: why have their liberal attitudes had so little effect? Are the voters apathetic, are they frustrated by some kind of institutional lag developed by the political parties, or are they told so often that Orange County is a conservative stronghold that they go down to enjoy the beach, rather than take up political arms in a lost cause?

Because of the pace of the area's recent growth, and the weakness of California party organizations (there is no Los Angeles "machine" reaching its tentacles across the county border), political and social forces are on display in Orange County that are more difficult to observe in other suburban areas. One of these is the impact of the nonpartisan local tradition on political attitudes and action, in a metropolitan complex loosely connected by the uniform output of the mass media, notably television. A key demographic factor is the concentration in Orange County of engineers and technicians and the professionals who serve their medical, educational, and governmental needs. This group may be labeled an affluent technocracy. In an increasingly technical society, the size and influence of this affluent technocracy are likely to grow—with political repercussions. The flight to the suburb is symbolic of a family-centered ethic; how are the parents influenced by the values of their children? Finally, with a suburban plurality in at least potential command of national politics, what are the chances for the resolution of America's most pressing domestic problems—racism, the failure of welfare programs, pollution of the environment, and the explosive tensions of the ghettos—which are largely urban problems?

These were the questions I took with me to Orange County. I sought answers by interviewing, at length, twelve families in a single suburban neighborhood.[27] The turning reels of the tape recorder became, for them, an audience. In most cases, I became their friend, despite my

[27]Selection of the families and other questions of methodology are discussed in the Preface.

curiosity about their most deeply held values and the life experiences that influenced them. Friendship, or at least contact, was maintained sporadically over nearly four years. I wrote to ask them how they voted in specific elections and often received reports on their children's activities. I returned to the neighborhood during the presidential election campaign of 1972 with a new agenda of intrusions on their privacy. In 1973, all twelve families returned lengthy questionnaires giving their reactions to the Watergate scandals.

As time went on, I became deeply involved with the problems of sorting some five thousand pages of transcribed conversations, while keeping up with my respondents' reactions to fresh political events. The task was lengthy and complicated, but it was immensely valuable, and I became convinced that these twelve families do, collectively, open a window on America's political future.

CHAPTER TWO

Twelve Families in Ramona Heights

When the Angel of Peace to Earth first descended,
    To bless with his presence the children of men,
'Mid the fairest of scenes his pathway e'er tended,
    And unto his smile the glad earth smiled again.
He joyed in the fragrance of oranges and roses,
    And loved 'mid their glances to linger or roam,
And he said: "Here in Tustin, where Beauty reposes,
    I also will linger or build me a home."

—Orange County real estate advertisement,
                        ca. 1887[1]

"A warm, protected place . . . so far, we can afford it."
                        —Maureen Barbera, 1970

I N MANY PARTS of the United States, Ramona
Heights would be called a subdivision. In California, it is
called a tract. This monosyllable can express profound
contempt, as in "You'll never catch me living in a *tract*
house!" Suburbanites who are sensitive to social and cultural status may load the word "tract" with many of the

[1]Quoted in Leo J. Friis, *Orange County through Four Centuries* (Santa
Ana, Calif.: Pioneer Press, 1965), p. 94.

negative connotations that the word "suburban" can hold for dwellers in penthouses overlooking New York's Central Park.

> ... the vocabularies of some recent left-wing critics of American society seem to have substituted the terms "suburb" and "suburban" for the now embarrassingly obsolete term "bourgeois" as a packaged rebuke to the whole tenor of American life. What used to be condemned as "bourgeois values," "bourgeois style," and "bourgeois hypocrisy" are now simply designated as "suburban."[2]

Ramona Heights

Ramona Heights, then, is a tract. It consists of nearly five hundred homes, all detached single-family dwellings, located on lots that are rather cramped, for the size of the houses. The houses are of a single architectural style—a kind of modified California rambling ranch—but of different design. The smallest has three bedrooms, the largest has five. But every house has a double garage, attached so its roof line meets that of the house, to make a more imposing structure. The entire neighborhood was constructed in an eighteen-month period beginning in early 1964, and all five hundred houses were sold and occupied by October, 1965. Since then, some owners have added swimming pools.

The classic two-stories-with-veranda design, which characterized homes of the upper middle class a generation or two ago, has vanished. The nearest approach to it in Ramona Heights is the five-bedroom split-level model, constructed on a slope: garage on the lowest level, with a bedroom wing directly above it, and a children's playroom behind; the public rooms (living room, dining room, kitchen, and a breakfast room) on the upper slope, a few steps above the garage level, a few steps below the bedroom wing. The front yard slopes with the natural contour of the land, but the back yard is divided into two level segments: the upper for adult lawn furniture and perhaps a barbecue pit; the lower for children's playground equipment, or an eventual swimming pool, just outside the playroom door behind the garage. Quentin and Deborah Elliott purchased this model in mid-1969 for $51,000. The house had two previous owners and was nicely landscaped, with a rose garden in the patio off the breakfast room,

[2]Bennett M. Berger, *Working-Class Suburb* (Berkeley and Los Angeles: University of California Press, 1960), p. 100.

and a rock garden separating the upper and lower levels of the back yard.

All the split-level homes in Ramona Heights follow this same pattern: split-level back yards with views. The streets were laid out following the ridges of the site; bulldozers then improved on the natural contours, so that the land was reshaped in advance to fit the split-level design. All signs of violence done to the natural landscape have vanished, and the uniformity of the neighborhood's architecture is obscured by the individual approach of each home owner to the challenge of landscaping. After a few years, trees are well established, some perversely threatening the Irvine Company's lease restriction on the height of trees, designed to protect the vistas from neighboring properties. A few rock gardens, featuring exotic varieties of cactus, have been installed in their front yards by wives whose commuting husbands have no time for yard work. But the more common pattern is green lawns broken by trees and bushes and the brilliant blossoms that flourish in Southern California, ranging from poinsettia to hydrangea. If enough topsoil is laid down and adequate water supplied, the gardens of Ramona Heights bloom with little further encouragement. The most common preoccupation is pulling up weeds.

In 1964, when the homes of Ramona Heights were first placed on the market, their prices ranged from $28,950 to $42,500. These amounts purchased the houses only; the lots were leased on a long-term basis from the Irvine Company. With the liberal credit terms and low interest rates then available, it was possible to buy with a cash down payment of as little as $1,600. (The distinction between "tract" and "custom built" home is real, not imaginary. Could any family with only $1,600 in savings buy a lot and then hire an architect to design a house for it?) Since 1964, the pressures of population growth on limited available land, coupled with steadily rising construction costs, have worked the magic of value appreciation—which Californians may regard as a right, not as good fortune—upon Ramona Heights. Homes for sale in 1970 carried price tags of from $40,000 to more than $60,000, and values have increased more than 5 percent annually since then.

The tract's name merits comment. Helen Hunt Jackson's romantic novel *Ramona*, originally published in 1884, did much both to create and to reinforce the myth of California's Spanish heritage. The myth is one of a noble Castilian culture existing beside the gentle monks of Father Junipero Serra's missions, which persuaded the Indians to abandon their heathen ways. The myth obscures the fact of conflict and bloodshed; of rapacious ex-convicts in the military ranks; of Mexican, Indian, and Negro racial strains in the Spanish surnamed families; of the massacres of Indian tribes and the ruthless stealing ("secularization") of the mission lands.[3]

In 1970, there lived in Ramona Heights about a dozen families who were at least distantly related to the Spanish-Mexican conquerors of California. Three of them are included among those interviewed for this study. Ramona Heights, with its expensive homes stretched out along the ridges overlooking Newport Bay, is a great social distance from the *barrios* of East Los Angeles, San Antonio, Texas, or Albuquerque, New Mexico, where many descendants of the original Mexican families now live. They exist on the borderline of the American culture and economy, segregated from full membership in American society by stubborn prejudice and a fading language barrier. Arthur Roybal and the two other Mexican-Americans interviewed in Ramona Heights give important insights into the nature and attitudes of middle-class Mexican-Americans. What psychological traumas are inflicted on those who climb up from the *barrios* into the bastions of Anglo affluence? What impact does the experience have on their political attitudes? Are they a natural source of leadership for their less fortunate brethren left behind in the *barrios?* Or do they, like the stereotypical suburbanite, turn their backs on the urban problems from which they have escaped?

One reason for the purchase of homes in Ramona Heights by affluent Catholic families is the presence, just a half mile from the border of the tract, of a new parish church and parochial school. The church takes its name from the English translation of the original *pueblo* of Nuestra Señora Reine de Los Angeles—Our Lady Queen of Angels. The buildings are new, the grounds nicely landscaped. There are also two Protestant churches nearby, equally new, each apparently trying to appear more modern than the other, at least architecturally, with great thrusting spires and glass-walled buildings. The nearest synagogue is five miles away.

If spiritual needs can be fulfilled quite close to Ramona Heights, so too can material ones. Across Alessandro Boulevard from the tract is the inevitable shopping center. Its largest structure, spacious enough to be a hangar for jet aircraft or to house a major factory, is the supermarket. It features a large section of gourmet foods, a bakery, and shelf after shelf of wines and liquors. In comparison to other markets in its chain, it is a veritable flagship. The residents of Ramona Heights say that its prices are also higher.

[3]For an account of the myth of California's Spanish heritage, and its exploitation in festivals and by commercial firms, see Carey McWilliams, *North from Mexico: The Spanish-Speaking People of the United States* (New York: Monthly Review Press, 1961).

Completing the shopping center are a variety store, a large drugstore, a dry cleaning establishment, and a separate small bakery. Major purchases (appliances, home furnishings, clothing, etc.) can be made just three miles away at Fashion Island, the regional shopping center being developed by the Irvine Company, and including the major Orange County branches of two department stores. These branches are as large as their counterparts in Los Angeles, and more carefully laid out.

But churches and department stores follow the growth of population; they do not explain it. Ramona Heights and half a dozen other nearby tracts were built and quickly occupied because of the natural attractions of the area. A partial list of the attractions which brought people to Ramona Heights would include:

—superb public beaches at nearby Balboa and Corona del Mar.

—the extensive yacht harbor at Newport Beach.

—the climate of Southern California, guaranteeing apparently endless summer days without rainfall, modified by the cooling breezes from the shore which prevent the buildup of oppressive heat (except when the hot Santa Ana winds blow from the East; they blew in the summer of 1970, carrying smoke and ashes that blotted out the sun, from a forest fire seventy miles away).

—the same breezes plus the low population density of the area make the smog which blinds and chokes Los Angeles a rare visitor to South Orange County.

—the Newport-Mesa consolidated school district, supported by a solid tax base in the wealthy dockside homes of Newport Beach and some light industry.

—a new campus of the University of California, established in 1965 at the new city of Irvine, and offering a full range of undergraduate degrees and some graduate work to 6,885 students by the fall of 1971. The university developed extension courses to serve the area's engineers and a program of cultural events to serve the community.

—convenient access to the Santa Ana and San Diego freeways for rapid travel throughout the metropolitan area.

—Orange County Airport, one of the busiest in the country for private and business use, with increasing service by commercial jet airliners.

—if the sunny days and ocean breezes become monotonous, real mountains can be reached in less than half a day's drive; "taking the children to the snow" is a common winter pastime.

Ramona Heights must rank as one of America's more favored places to live, in terms of climate, access to boating and other water sports, ready communication with the metropolitan area of which it is a part, and good public services. The most important political fact about Ramona Heights is that political involvement is not necessary to assure enjoyment of the amenities of life. The developer provided broad streets which, in the Southern California climate, seldom need repairs; street lighting; an abundant water supply; sewers; and a thoughtful layout of streets that provides the optimum number of views from picture windows at the same time that it slows the pace of automobiles negotiating the hills and curves. Police, fire protection, and refuse collection are provided by the municipality, and snow never falls to clog the streets. Ramona Heights is so far removed from the tensions that have produced violence in decayed cities as to seem the epitome of suburban law and order.

The services once supplied by political organizations in big cities either are handled by efficient bureaucracies or are not relevant to the residents of Ramona Heights. No ward committeeman need be contacted to wheedle a street light or the repair of potholes in the street. Lighting is adequate, and the streets remain smooth. The residents of Ramona Heights are in general highly educated members of various professions. Connections through City Hall are not needed to assure employment. If their jobs should vanish, they are eligible for unemployment compensation, but the matter is handled by a state bureaucracy, not a local influence peddler.

In a material sense, the daily life of those who live in Ramona Heights is of high quality. Municipal services are good; they came with the purchase of the home and require no political negotiation. There is no compulsion to become involved with, or even pay much attention to, local politics. Maureen Barbera says that she thinks of the neighborhood as a "warm, protected place," where tax revenues are used efficiently and the level of public service is consistently high—much higher than it was in Pomona, where they lived previously and paid higher taxes.

The only neighborhood issue mentioned by any of the respondents was the growing need for a traffic light at a busy intersection on Alessandro Boulevard. As adjoining subdivisions were built, the traffic at that corner increased, and it was difficult, during the morning rush hour, for a car from Ramona Heights to enter the rapid flow of traffic. There was one serious, but not fatal, accident. When asked if she knew anyone with influence to get such things done, Maureen Barbera said, "Gee, that sounds kind of dirty." This is in striking contrast to the attitudes of members of the lower class in cities dominated by political machines.[4]

But the needed traffic light—which was installed in 1971—symbolized the changes that disturb the residents of this "warm, protected place." For the attractive qualities of their paradise are threatened by the steady influx of people. The volume of commercial air traffic is growing, and the noise of jet aircraft with it. Controversy rages over the location of yet another freeway, which the state highway commission feels should go along the coast, bisecting some of the more attractive neighborhoods of Newport Beach. The Irvine Company wants to develop Upper Newport Bay, which some of the residents of Ramona Heights can see from their windows. One of the few tidal inlets remaining along the coast from Seattle to San Diego, it provides a sanctuary for birds and marine life. Its potential as a marina, with more of the same luxurious homes that line the water in the lower bay, is obvious. The plans of the Irvine Company were at least temporarily defeated by local conservationists.

In 1970, ecology and pollution—man's interaction with his environment—were established as important national political issues. The residents of Ramona Heights have examples close at hand—they need only look into the sky as jet aircraft swoop upward, trailing columns of black soot. The local impact of these issues is obvious. The area is growing, and not all the growth follows careful planning. When a suburban area urbanizes, how can it avoid the same characteristics—blight, ruined air, violence—that its residents left behind in the city? The voters of Ramona Heights needed no political organization to perfect the services they enjoy in their neighborhood. Yet they feel a sense of unease—a lack of control—over what changes may occur in their lives with the influx of more and more families into the still underdeveloped areas nearby.

Ramona Heights and the World Outside

I first got acquainted with the residents of Ramona Heights during the last eight months of 1970. The turmoil of the previous decade was fading, but national equanimity had not been restored. Richard Nixon had been president of the United States for two years, but American ground troops continued to die in Vietnam, although in reduced numbers. The true nature of that war was made more clear with the news

---

[4]Contrast, for example, the image of the local politician as an ambassador to a hostile outside world held by Italian slum dwellers in the West End of Boston in Herbert J. Gans, *Urban Villagers* (New York: Macmillan, Free Press, 1962).

of a massacre at the hamlet of My Lai. Construction workers attacked a group of students demonstrating for peace in New York City. That spring, when the invasion of Cambodia was announced, new trouble erupted on college campuses; four students were killed by National Guard bullets at Kent State University in Ohio. In East Los Angeles, a Chicano (Mexican-American) rally turned into a riot, and police brutality was charged. The Regents of the University of California were determined to fire UCLA Acting Assistant Professor Angela Davis because of her admitted membership in the Communist party. A bomb heavily damaged the Irvine campus branch of the Bank of America. In Los Angeles, Charles Manson and female members of his hippie "family" were on trial for the ritualistic cult murders of Sharon Tate, her guests, and the La Bianca family. Vice President Spiro T. Agnew attacked college students, television network executives, and other targets. President Nixon spoke often of a "silent majority."

In November, state, local, and congressional elections were held, with paradoxical results. Nationally, President Nixon was unable to win a Republican majority in either house of Congress, in spite of intensive personal campaigning. In California, Republican Ronald Reagan was reelected governor by a lesser margin than was predicted, and he was unable to carry a Republican majority into the legislature. Republican Senator George Murphy was defeated by a youthful Democratic challenger, John Tunney. And the arch-conservative superintendent of California's public school system, Max Rafferty, was defeated for reelection by one of his principal deputies, Wilson Riles, a black professional educator.

The 1970 interviews suggested reasons for the paradoxes of the 1970 elections, as voters with a declining loyalty to party and a growing belief in the corrupt nature of politics confronted individual candidates. To further test the hypotheses growing from analyses of the original transcripts, as well as to get reactions to the presidential candidates and to specific proposals for ameliorating urban-suburban conflict, I returned to Ramona Heights in the late summer of 1972. Public affairs were more calm then, and President Nixon was credited, by all but a few of the voters, with accomplishing the change. They acknowledged that many problems remained, but they felt that George McGovern could not do as well in resolving them. In 1973, when the Nixon Administration was shaken to its foundations by investigations of corruption, I again consulted the microsample, and found that a few had been equally shaken by the Ervin Committee hearings. The reactions of these twenty-three voters over a span of years offered hints for predicting the actions of similar voters in similar suburbs.

A Dozen Families

Before seeking such clues in their recorded words, it is necessary to introduce the twelve families. The Barberas, Markuses, and Roybals, mentioned in the last chapter, also deserve a more complete description.

Fletcher and *Maureen Barbera* live in a four-bedroom ranch house. Fletcher was born in 1937, Maureen in 1940. They have three small children—girls who were five and two in 1970, and a baby boy then four months. Both are registered Republicans, and cannot recall ever voting for Democrats, although they are willing, in theory, to split their tickets. They own two automobiles, neither of them new. Fletcher's income in 1969 was slightly over $20,000; he was vice president of a small electronics manufacturing firm, in charge of finance and management. He changed jobs in 1971 and again in 1973.

Fletcher is one-eighth Italian; a grandfather was responsible for his family name. But the women of the family—members of the Daughters of the American Revolution—quickly recovered their composure, and Fletcher takes his first name from the surname of a great grandfather who was a ship chandler in New Bedford, Massachusetts. An oil portrait of this worthy gentleman graces the mantel of their living room fireplace. He is a stern-faced merchant with mutton-chop whiskers, but his lively eyes betray the sternness, and the quality of his amused glance seems to dominate the room. Maureen Barbera's parents were also from New England, and the Barberas frequently refer to their Puritan heritage—sometimes jokingly, sometimes in earnest. They are the only couple of the twelve who express strong, positive ties to a family tradition formed long ago, and far away from California.

Maureen Barbera is a handsome woman. Her regular features and high cheekbones seem to come directly from the society page announcing some debutante ball or hunt club meeting. Although she attended high school in Southern California, she was sent to Vassar for college; her natural idiom is the speech of an eastern upper-class girl's finishing school, and she expresses strongly held opinions with clarity and humor. Her father removed her from Vassar at the beginning of her senior year to prevent what he considered an unfortunate marriage; Maureen accepted this judgment and did not attempt to return to the East and her fiancé, or to complete her education. She worked as a model in Los Angeles before her marriage to Fletcher Barbera.

Fletcher is quick-minded and articulate. He expresses opinions with a dogmatism that is rivaled only by his wife. He is almost completely bald; both his father and one grandfather were bald by their mid-thirties. The air of maturity lent by baldness is negated by a number of almost boyish mannerisms, particularly the way his eyes dart around the room from person to person and object to object. Son of a family of substantial wealth, he attended high school in Southern California, and then went to college in the East, at Amherst. Although Maureen was at Vassar during the same period, they did not meet until Fletcher had returned to California and was established in his career.

Maureen Barbera's main activity outside the home is her membership in the Junior League of a nearby city. She is completely happy with this charitable organization and its social status. The Barberas had undeniably wealthy parents. In Maureen's family, that wealth extended back for several generations. Such parental status, together with educational experience, provides commonly accepted indicators of membership in the American upper class.[5] Both Fletcher and Maureen had nursemaids when they were small. Asked if there were any possessions or activities they would like to add to their style of living, Maureen unhesitatingly replied, "Live-in help."

The Barberas are remarkable among the twelve couples for the nearly dialectical quality of their conversation. When a question is posed, they discuss the answer between them, exchanging ideas, often making slight jokes at each other, until a joint answer is agreed on. And they are very methodical. I brought my tape recorder every Thursday evening at 7:45 for six weeks. Our conversations usually continued until 1:00 A.M.

Quentin and *Deborah Elliott* are relative newcomers to Ramona Heights and to California. They moved there from a Chicago suburb in September, 1969, when Quentin was transferred by his firm, a rubber company well known for its automobile tires, to serve as regional manager for the industrial sales division. Quentin had been employed in the firm's international division and had served in Sweden and Chile. Coming to Orange County was their eighth move in twelve years with the company, and Quentin made a three-day trip to California to select a house. They picked the area of Ramona Heights from a map because of its proximity to the ocean; Deborah was intrigued with the possibility of living in a home with a seascape vista. (Ruefully, she showed me the

[5]Indicators of upper-class status are described and utilized in G. William Domhoff, *The Higher Circles* (New York: Random House, Vintage Books, 1971).

view from their back yard: the water of Upper Newport Bay was visible, but only at high tide.) Quentin commuted fifty miles to his office in Los Angeles every day.

The Elliotts have four children: boys who were eleven and nine in 1970, a two-year-old girl, and a baby girl adopted to provide a companion for the two-year-old. To accommodate the interests of the family, they joined a local tennis club, and Quentin committed himself to becoming a scoutmaster in late 1971. The second Sunday after they moved in, the Elliotts joined the nearby Episcopal church. This was a familiar pattern; whenever they moved into a new home, the Elliotts joined the nearest Protestant church (more or less regardless of its denomination) as an entree into the community and as a means for Quentin to express a deep-seated interest in religion.

But Ramona Heights was not destined to become just another way-station in the climb up the corporate hierarchy. Over a period of six months, the dissatisfaction Quentin had felt with his way of life for several years crystallized. He felt his work was unrewarding, and so much time spent commuting left little for his family. Deborah agreed, feeling it was time for the family to put down some permanent roots. Quentin resigned from the rubber company and accepted a position as a fourth-grade teacher in a working-class suburb twelve miles away from Ramona Heights. His salary dropped from over $20,000 to less than $9,000, but the family had $5,000 per year income from investments, and Quentin's father, an eastern industrialist, helped pay off the two mortgages on their five-bedroom split-level house. In 1970, Quentin attended summer classes at a local college to earn the provisional California teaching credential needed for his new position. He received his regular credential after a year's experience and was fired, for his school district could not afford the higher salary commanded by the credential. Quentin found a position in the Ramona Heights school in the fall of 1971.

In terms of family origin, education, and wealth, the Elliotts could be viewed, like the Barberas, as members of the upper class. In the early 1950s, Quentin Elliott graduated from Princeton, where his main interest was the hockey team, and entered the executive training program of a large insurance firm. During the Korean War, he was drafted and sent to Germany as an infantryman. On the strength of a long-standing interest in religion, he was able to transfer to the chaplain's corps, serving as an office clerk. After his military service, he reentered the corporate world and married Deborah, whom he had first met on a student tour boat during college. After their marriage, he worked for two other corporations before settling into his position with the rubber company.

In politics, Quentin considers himself an independent and a moderate. In Illinois, he admired the style of Republican Senator Charles Percy and did volunteer work in a Percy campaign. But Quentin found the Democratic candidates most attractive in California, and he registered as a Democrat in 1971. In 1972, he supported George McGovern with the greatest enthusiasm of any member of the microsample.

Quentin is friendly, articulate, and bubbling with jovial good humor. In 1970, he seemed a compulsive talker, for his responses to my inquiries resulted in pages of monologue. Deborah Elliott was painfully shy, and she participated in the 1970 conversations only after long urging by her husband. She deferred to Quentin's judgment in political matters. Born in the United States, she was educated in Canada, and she pleads ignorance of American political institutions.

Their personalities seemed quite different in 1972. Quentin was subdued, almost hesitant, in some of his answers. He said that changing from salesman to teacher had taught him "to engage my brain before opening my mouth." Deborah was more relaxed and comfortable, her shyness largely forgotten. She described her work as a counselor for an organization that mans a "hot line" telephone to give emergency advice to troubled teen-agers. In 1973, Deborah found the Ervin Committee hearings the equivalent of a civics course. She was able to catch up on all the American history she had missed in school.

In the spring of 1972, the Elliotts' oldest boy became interested in a fundamentalist congregation meeting in a tent in a nearby city. Quentin accompanied him to Bible camp, where he experienced a revelation of the insignificance of his intellectual concern for theology, compared to the experience of faith. The entire family now attends the tent meetings.

Arnold and *Judith Garcia* also live in a five-bedroom split-level, which he valued at $56,000 in 1970. It is immaculately landscaped; the interior is professionally decorated and kept in spotless condition. Mrs. Garcia has time, as well as hired help, to accomplish this. Their younger son, nineteen years old, was in 1970 a student at a nearby college, while their older son had just entered dental school.

Arnold Garcia was born in a *barrio* in Dallas, Texas, a few weeks after his parents entered the United States from Mexico. His father was an affable, energetic man who eventually became chief salesman in the furniture department of a large chain store. Arnold remembers his father with admiration, saying, "He had the world by the tail."

Arnold's own career is fascinating. Trained as an accountant, he failed the oral portion of a City of Los Angeles civil service examination because, he felt, of his name and accent. This was one of many incidents of discrimination which he experienced. But this particular one, denying him civil service status, made him a capitalist and, eventually, a rich man. Arnold served throughout World War II as an army supply sergeant, gambling judiciously to build up the capital that he would take into the world of business. He now owns an auto parts supply firm in East Los Angeles and extensive rental properties in Los Angeles and North Orange Counties, from which he has so far been able to exclude black tenants.

When asked about his income, Garcia was reticent, claiming that his accountant keeps track of such matters, and that he himself doesn't care to know how one year's income compares to another. But as he recalled a favorable transaction he had made in 1969, he said, "You wouldn't believe that a Mexican could make that much money."

Arnold Garcia has made it in a competitive world. He despises those who challenge the rules of that world, for he feels they lack ambition. His wife, Judith, may be a symbol of his success. Now in her mid-forties, her blond good looks advertise her Nordic ancestry. Arnold's automobiles are another symbol of success. He commutes one hundred miles a day in his air-conditioned Mercedes-Benz 300 SL. His wife drives a 1971 Chrysler. Each of his sons has a new Volkswagen. But Arnold Garcia expresses contempt for his sons. He feels they are too soft to succeed in a harsh world.

Several calls were required to persuade Garcia to be interviewed. He would not permit the tape recorder to be used nor notes to be kept. Perhaps because of this, his conversation was exceptionally frank; we spoke for nearly three hours on a Sunday morning, until his wife insisted for the third time that they had to go to the nursery for a sale of fuchsias. As a result, quotations from Arnold Garcia will not be his exact words, except for memorable phrases, but the notes dictated immediately after our 1970 conversation run to sixteen single-spaced pages.

Arnold spends six days a week at his place of business, and Judith feels that he should save Sundays for the family. Mrs. Garcia had no interest in talking to me; thus the twelve couples of Ramona Heights include only twenty-three voters. In 1972, I interviewed Arnold in his office in East Los Angeles, again without the tape recorder, but in a very cordial atmosphere. I declined an offer to join the card game in progress in the back room.

Arnold Garcia is registered as a Republican, but his sons have registered as Democrats. Arnold pays little attention to elections, claiming cynically that the candidate with the most money will win. He voted for

Richard Nixon in 1968, but he would have voted for George Wallace if Wallace had shown he had a chance. He claimed that Wallace's racism was a pose adopted for the political needs of Alabama and did not express the core of Wallace's inner convictions. Arnold voted for Nixon again in 1972.

Harry and *Jacqueline Johnson* live three blocks from the Barberas, in a similar four-bedroom house. One of the bedrooms has been converted into a den and TV room. It has an added fireplace; an antique musket hangs over the mantel. Harry Johnson collects antiquated firearms and also owns a modern rifle. Their home is luxuriantly carpeted and filled with color-coordinated colonial furniture. The Johnsons' two daughters have grown up, married, and moved away. Their first grandchild was born early in 1971.

Harry Johnson is the sole owner of a business that manufactures machine tools. There are two plants, one in Orange County and one in Los Angeles County. Both Harry and Jacqueline were born in California of working-class parentage, and the education of both ended in high school. But Harry worked hard in a machine tool shop and rose quickly through the ranks. His work was essential to the war effort, so he was not drafted into the armed forces during World War II. Shortly after the war, he was able to go into business for himself, and his business prospered along with the cold war aircraft industry boom in Southern California. In 1969, his personal income was more than $50,000. Federal, state, and local taxes consumed nearly $30,000, but this fact does not particularly distress the Johnsons. Their life is nicely organized, extremely comfortable, and they find fulfillment in it.

Harry Johnson was born in 1920; his wife is eighteen months younger. Both are deeply tanned; Jacqueline Johnson seems the prototype of the Southern California sportswoman. trim figure, features unlined by approaching age, and clear blue eyes. The Johnsons' passion is golf. They owned a twenty-four-foot cabin cruiser berthed in Newport Harbor for more than two years, but they found that golf prevented them from using the boat fully, so they sold it. They belong to the Roman Catholic Church, but they attend mass only on major holidays. Their weekends are given over to golfing; they travel half the length of California, from Carmel to Palm Springs, playing various courses. They have traveled to Europe, but they prefer California life.

The Johnsons have always been registered Democrats. They describe themselves as middle of the road. They voted for John Kennedy in 1960 and for Lyndon Johnson in 1964. They aren't certain, but they think they voted for Hubert Humphrey in 1968; they chose Ronald Reagan for governor over Democratic incumbent Pat Brown in 1966; in 1970, they supported both Ronald Reagan and Republican Senator George Murphy for reelection. They voted for George McGovern in the 1972 primary but did not vote for president in November, being out of the country.

Harry Johnson travels over his modest business empire in a 1972 Porsche; his wife shops, and they visit golf courses, in a 1970 Cadillac. They bought their home in 1964 for $35,000 and made a number of improvements in it; Harry Johnson valued it at $55,000 in 1970. He reported that the 1970 recession in the aerospace industry did not hurt his own firm particularly, for most of their business was no longer done for defense contractors.

The Johnsons are pleasant, hospitable people. Nothing much seems to excite them.

Kenneth and *Marie Kaub* have lived in Ramona Heights since their house was completed in 1964. It is also a four-bedroom model, featuring a fenced front yard with a flagstone patio and a narrower patio in the cramped back yard, with a dramatic view over the roofs of the houses below. They share the house with Mrs. Kaub's son, who was thirteen years old in 1970, and five dogs (a mother wirehaired terrier and her litter, now grown as large as the mother) which they can't bring themselves to dispose of, although a local ordinance prohibits more than three dogs per household. The boy also keeps a mouse, a snake, and an iguana as pets.

Kenneth Kaub is a medical doctor certificated in neurology. He works at a state mental hospital, where his salary in 1970 was just under $26,000. He mentioned, without rancor, that this made him one of the less well paid members of his profession. He expressed great bitterness, however, about the effect of the Reagan Administration's budget cuts on the state mental health program. Kenneth was born in a small Lutheran farming community in eastern Kansas and attended one-room schools before going on to the consolidated high school. But his early schooling was delayed by hospitalization for the surgical repair of a damaging birth defect. Even after the repair, his face was left asymmetrical, and his speech has a flat, nasal quality. When asked about his memories of the school years, he replies simply, "The other kids made fun of me a lot." Kenneth wears a neatly trimmed beard, perhaps to conceal the irregularity of his face. He seems painfully shy, and his voice seldom rises above a whisper, but he has a wry, self-deprecatory sense of humor. When he completed medical school at the University of Kansas, he returned to his home town and attempted to establish a general practice. But the practice was never successful; he says, "I guess they still thought of me as the kid from next door." He came to California for his residency in neurology. Marie was an X-ray technician at the same hospital. They have been married for ten years. Kenneth was born in 1930, Marie in 1935. Kenneth's parents have died, and he never goes back to Kansas. He has not been inside a Lutheran church for twenty years.

Marie Kaub is the daughter of a family that traces its origins to the Mexican settlers in what is now New Mexico. One of her ancestors, she says, was a general, Kenneth adds, "A lot of them were bandits, too." Her childhood was harsh, as the family lived in a succession of two-room shacks in the *barrio* of Albuquerque. She vividly remembers food being brought by welfare workers. She knew discrimination in the public schools, but it seemed even more fierce in the parochial school she attended for a time, when both of her parents were working. The nuns were strict disciplinarians and very conscious of social status. Nevertheless, Marie has found her religion a solace, and she placed her own son in Our Lady Queen of Angels parochial school.

Marie's first marriage was a disaster. Her young husband, who was frequently in trouble with the police, deserted her soon after she became pregnant. Working as a power company lineman a year later, he failed to follow the prescribed safety procedures and was electrocuted. By that time, Marie was learning X-ray technology at a local college, and she moved with her son and parents to California soon afterwards.

Marie's complexion is olive, and her rich brown eyes dominate a face that still bears traces of the slender beauty of her teens. But she has grown heavier and confesses that she is a compulsive eater. Kenneth is developing a comfortable middle-aged spread. The kitchen is Marie's kingdom, and she glories in it. Marie likes giving dinner parties for her neighborhood friends, and she greets her guests at the door with a bubbling gaiety that masks a lingering insecurity.

The Kaubs seem to be two people who were deeply wounded by life but have found in each other, and in Ramona Heights, a generous measure of relief from, and compensation for, that early suffering. Marie remains active in two neighborhood clubs that were formed when the tract was first occupied as vehicles for the wives to get acquainted with each other. She has won status and respect in a social circle that does not extend beyond the borders of the neighborhood. And Kenneth, the shy physician, is quite happy to claim his wife's friends as his own.

Marie is registered as a Democrat, Kenneth as a Republican, following the partisan identifications of their childhood. Like the other couples with mixed registration included in this study, they claim that it is an advantage. They receive the propaganda of both parties, they say, and are thus better informed, although Marie defers to Kenneth's more complete education in discussing political matters. In contrast to their registration, Kenneth tends to favor Democratic candidates and Marie Republican ones (although neither could stomach Ronald Reagan, Max Rafferty, or John Schmitz). Perhaps in overidentification with the social class she has achieved, Marie's attitudes are increasingly conservative. As an employee of California's imperfect welfare state, Kenneth finds that his attitudes conflict more and more with those held by the medical establishment, and he has long since resigned from the American Medical Association.

Jan and *Eldene Markus*, the enthusiastic taxpayers, live in the smallest model house built in Ramona Heights. It has three bedrooms, an enormous combined living-dining room, and the inevitable two-car garage. When I first visited them, odors of garlic and spices permeated their home as they made sausage with an electric grinder in the breakfast room.

Both Jan and Eldene have firm opinions and no reticence at all in expressing them, although some subjects were more favored than others. Jan would not disclose exact figures concerning his income, but he was eager to discuss the most minute details of his recent operation. Eldene discussed sexual matters in frank terms. She has read in the field of popular sociology, and she uses awkwardly terms that are part of her reading, but not of her speaking, vocabulary. She pronounces the term "elite," for example, as "ee-*light.*"

Jan Markus was born in East St. Louis, Illinois, in a neighborhood that is now a black ghetto. Eldene was born and lived through her high school years in a smaller town some fifteen miles away. They did not meet until each had graduated from high school and spent half a dozen years in the world of work—Jan as an electrician, Eldene as a seamstress. Jan by then had spent two years in California, following an older brother who founded a construction business in the less grandiose Los Angeles of the 1930s. Consciously or not, Jan returned to East St. Louis to find a bride in the same way that his own father, after working for seven years in America (and becoming a citizen) had returned to the old country for his bride. But the return to California was delayed by World War II because of the war industry boom. Jan was working in an electronics plant in St. Louis that quickly shifted into war production. He had already been deferred from the draft because of a spot on his lungs. Eldene remained at her sewing machine, making parachutes. The move to California came only in 1948. By then, both of their families were headed to the West, and they have more than a dozen nephews, nieces, and a few grandnephews and grandnieces living within a hundred-mile radius of Ramona Heights. A nephew was stationed at the nearby marine base, Camp Pendleton, and visited them nearly every weekend during the summer and fall of 1972.

As noted before, the Markuses are fiercely patriotic; their opinions on law and order place them easily within the "hard-hat" stereotype; but some of their other attitudes do not fit that pattern. They knew discrimination in their youth, and Eldene describes vividly the sneers of third-generation Irish-Americans directed at first-generation Polish-Americans. But they won their way through, by dint of ambition and thrift; and they do not sympathize with the complaints of black or Chicano spokesmen who would change the system. At the same time, they resent the greed displayed by large corporations and exhibit a sophisticated understanding of economic monopoly. They feel that a little more socialism would be good for the country.

Because of their own savings, a modest pension from the electrician's union, and social security payments, Jan Markus was able to retire early —he is not yet sixty-two—after he had spent half a year recovering from a cancer operation. Their income from these sources is more than $10,000 per year—far from lavish, by Ramona Heights standards, but comfortable. They paid cash for their home and so are not burdened by mortgage payments. Eldene spends much of the day in the yard, which is a profusion of blooming colors. Jan's hobby is repairing automobiles, and they own two aging cars themselves. He also does auto repair work for members of the family.

The Markuses were both raised nominally as Catholics, but they no longer practice a religion. If pressed, they might confess to atheism, but that would imply a more certain attitude toward religious questions than they exhibit; they really pay little attention to such matters, other than to note the wealth and hypocrisy of religious leaders. They are much more interested in politics; Eldene reads the newspapers avidly, and clips or underlines articles for Jan's attention. Lifelong Democrats, they follow the fortunes of Orange County's tiny Democratic party with almost proprietary concern, but they are proud of voting for "the man, not the party."

Frank and *Mary McGee* live in the four-bedroom house they bought when the tract was first built. The makeup of their family has changed in the intervening years: the older son has joined the navy; the daughter attends the University of Oregon; only the younger son, who was twelve in 1970, remains at home.

Francis Xavier McGee was born in 1921 in a coal mining town in West Virginia. His father was manager of one of the town's two small mines. The town suffered with its region and the nation during the depression, but the family situation remained fairly comfortable, and Frank was hardly aware of the economic turmoil. His father remained a Republican, and Frank later registered Republican as a matter of course. But the passion of the town, and of Frank's father and two brothers, was baseball. Looking back, Frank McGee thinks he regarded his public schooling primarily as a convenience arranged to permit him to play on the school baseball team, and he sometimes regarded the panoply of saints recognized by the church as supernatural agents who could be petitioned for aid in winning tight games. For the only career Frank could conceive of for himself was as a professional baseball player.

By the time he completed high school, Frank acquired the nickname "Fibber," after the husband of radio's Molly McGee. But it did not stick. A greater source of chagrin in the 1970s is that he shares the name, but not the political opinions, of a television news commentator.

Frank attended Pennsylvania State College (as it was then called) from 1938 to 1942. His principal interest was baseball, but his academic major was in foreign languages. Knowing he would be drafted in any case, he enlisted in the army upon graduation. He was engaged to Mary, his high school sweetheart, but they decided to postpone marriage. After completing basic training, Frank was sent to Puerto Rico, and again he was able to play some baseball. The months passed slowly, and he felt that he was stationed on the sidelines of both the war and life itself. By late 1943, he felt that the war in Europe was drawing to a close. In order to return to the mainland, and to Mary, he volunteered for infantry officers' candidate school. They were married during a brief leave. Completing the course at Fort Benning, Georgia, and receiving his commission as a second lieutenant, Frank arrived in Europe in time for the Battle of the Bulge. Wounded in his third day of combat, he was in the hospital when Germany surrendered.

Recovered from his wounds, Frank returned to a tryout with the Philadelphia Phillies. He was accepted, completed spring training, and was assigned to a farm team in upstate New York. He completed the 1946 and 1947 seasons at shortstop, with a respectable batting average.

But the war years had delayed his development as an athlete, and he realized he would never make the major leagues. In the winter of 1948, he hitchhiked to California with a teammate who was a Californian. The teammate's mother had a beach cottage which she was happy to rent. Frank sent for Mary and the baby and embarked upon a series of jobs. He worked in a fish cannery, next in a factory, then as a carpenter, and eventually became a subcontractor, doing the framing of houses under construction. In 1958, he passed the real estate salesman's license examination, and sold part-time, when carpentry was not available. He soon became a full-time real estate salesman, settling into a permanent position as one of four salesmen in a small broker's office. He specializes in investment properties, which he prefers, Frank says, because he can deal with facts about the earning potential of invested capital, rather than a housewife's emotional reaction to the colors of a kitchen.

In 1960, Frank and Mary began to hear whisperings about an organization called the John Birch Society. They attended meetings in living rooms and soon were holding meetings in their own living room. Neither had been particularly active in political affairs, although Mary had done some campaign work for John Kennedy—and had been appalled when youthful Kennedy enthusiasts seemed to insult the American flag. Birch Society study sessions and literature provided answers for questions that had troubled them, and raised new ones. That same year, 1960, they were impressed by the anticommunist teachings of a local priest, and they attended an adult education course about the communist menace taught by John Schmitz. They became friends of and loyal campaign workers for Schmitz, and Mary changed her registration from Democratic to Republican. Gradually, their Birch Society section dissolved as its members devoted their energies to particular causes and candidates.

In his early fifties, Frank McGee is spare and muscular, still very much the athlete. His iron gray hair was closely crew cut until his daughter persuaded him to let it grow in late 1971. He is a veteran of a number of political campaigns; he's been on the winning side of some, the losing side of others. But he finds the very process of political involvement rewarding for its own sake. And this involvement includes his wife, Mary. Although she is basically retiring and introspective, her political concern has made her bloom into an effective public speaker. Frank himself has become active in service clubs, but in 1970 he was denied a seat on the board of directors of his own club because a portion of the membership felt that his Birch Society affiliations might adversely affect the club's image.

In 1968, Frank and Mary changed their party registration from

Republican to American Independent to help assure George Wallace a place on the California ballot. They changed their registration back in time for the 1970 Republican primary. The year 1972 found them back in the American Independent party, working for John Schmitz. Mary McGee feels that Watergate revealed the corruption of the two traditional parties.

As Frank is essentially self-employed, his income is proportional to the time and energy he devotes to his work, but he gives much time to volunteer political activity. In 1969, he earned about $19,000. He is the only voter interviewed for this study whose concern for the public welfare is so compelling as to limit his private income.

The McGees are traditional Catholics. They are distressed at the ferment in the contemporary church. Since mass is now celebrated in English at Our Lady Queen of Angels, they drive twenty miles every Sunday to attend a Latin mass.

Piotr and *Myrna Pavel* live four blocks away from the McGees, not far from the Barberas. The cultural distance that separates them is hardly hinted at in the fact that the Pavels are Democrats. Piotr Pavel was born in Russia, driven out by the revolution, and educated in France and Germany as an electrical engineer before coming to the United States in 1938. His wife's parents were also born in Russia and were active in the anti-Czarist movement before 1905. Myrna's father was a union organizer and remained active in New York socialist circles for many years, but he felt that the vision of a better society was betrayed by Joseph Stalin. Myrna has been fascinated by politics since childhood. The Pavels' ancestry is Jewish but they are not religious in a formal sense. Piotr Pavel speaks five languages and regards American society from the perspective of a foreign-born citizen. He is an intellectual of formidable interests and accomplishment; in 1970, he was on medical leave from his position as research engineer with an aircraft manufacturing firm, after suffering a heart attack. After recovering, he worked sporadically as a consulting engineer.

Piotr and Myrna are proud of their sons' accomplishments. The eldest, recently married, was in 1970 a postdoctoral research student in psychology; the younger son had entered medical school in the fall. With the boys gone, their four-bedroom house is larger than they need. But they regard the investment in their steadily appreciating home as their only shield against inflation during retirement.

Piotr Pavel's father was a lawyer, his mother a physician. He vividly recalls traveling by sleigh with his mother during the famine and epidemics of 1917. After Bolshevik power was consolidated, Piotr applied for permission to enroll in a technical institute, to study engineering. Crucial to admission was an examination in political science, administered by an army officer. Asked to demonstrate the inevitability of proletarian triumph, Piotr Pavel recited Marx verbatim. But his own bourgeois background had not been well enough concealed. The officer wagged his finger, saying, "Comrade, I can't pass you."

A few months later, Piotr was able to leave Russia for official reasons of poor health. He never saw his parents again. His mother died a few years later as a result of overwork, and his father vanished during the Siege of Leningrad.

After completing his education in Germany and France, and working for a French electrical engineering firm for several years, Piotr saw the signs of a new war approaching Europe. He emigrated to the United States under the arrangements provided for the White Russians—as an emigrant with no home country. He found employment in the American equivalent of the French firm he had worked for. During World War II, he assisted in the perfection of radar and other radio-electronic devices. He met Myrna at a party, and they were married the same week that he became an American citizen.

During her New Jersey childhood, Myrna had bitter experiences of anti-Semitism and formed a cynical opinion of the party machines that dominated local politics in the area. A girl of many interests and talents, she studied opera and became acquainted with some of the great names of the American theater through her involvement with a WPA theater group. She was caught up in the excitement generated by the social experiments of the New Deal, which seemed for a time the culmination of the reformist cause for which her father had worked so long. Unable to pursue her operatic training for financial reasons, she sought work that would be relevant to social change. She was a social worker when she met Piotr.

Following the war, Piotr was employed on a succession of projects by a succession of companies, usually in the most advanced frontiers of electronic technology. He was involved in planning communications for the testing of the hydrogen bomb at Eniwetok Atoll; he later contributed to the design of the Lunar Excursion Module used by the Apollo astronauts. In the 1950s, while employed as an engineer and consultant by the Agency for International Development, he had the experience of being approached by Senator Joseph McCarthy's investigative henchmen for testimony against his supervisor. He refused.

The Pavels moved to California in the early 1960s, living first in

Beverly Hills. They purchased their four-bedroom home in Ramona Heights in 1964. They have two middle-aged sedans, and their younger son drove a battered Volkswagen bus which he plastered with bumper stickers supporting Democratic candidates and action on a variety of ecological issues.

The Pavels are generous, hospitable, and articulate people. Myrna Pavel seems the prototype Jewish mother, for as soon as a guest enters their home, she begins bustling in the kitchen. But this does not interrupt conversation, for guests are usually brought to the adjoining family room. Myrna is a superb cook; both she and Piotr show its cumulative effects in their substantial waistlines.

Piotr Pavel is proud of his American citizenship and praises some national characteristics. But he turns a cold outsider's eye on many of its social and political oddities. He was startled, for example, to find that many American engineers attend church, including some quite fundamentalist sects. In Europe, he reports, professional people regard religion as a matter for the masses. He was appalled at the sheer waste of technical manpower resulting from the phasing out of space and defense contracts, as trained engineers became stock and bond salesmen or opened franchised restaurants. And he was deeply disturbed by the negative mood of the student political activists of the 1960s. He recalls the terrors of McCarthyism.

In the fall of 1970, the Pavels were able to fly to Europe for Piotr's first visit in over thirty years. As their reservations for a group flight were not confirmed until the last minute, they made no arrangements for absentee ballots. They noted upon returning that their two votes would not have produced a winning margin for most of their candidates, although they were delighted by the election of Wilson Riles and John Tunney. They voted for George McGovern with little enthusiasm in 1972. Their long-standing mistrust of Richard Nixon was confirmed by the Watergate hearings.

Ralph and *Caroline Porfilio* live in a five-bedroom split-level home with a swimming pool. In 1970, their five children ranged in age from twelve-year-old twin boys to a six-year-old girl. Ralph was born in 1936, Caroline in 1937. They paid $44,000 for their home in early 1967, and in 1970 valued it at $55,000. They own two Chevrolets; Ralph drives fifty miles a day to his job in the home office of a large conglomerate California industry with concerns ranging from farming to food processing to the manufacturing of house trailers. Ralph is involved in designing and equipping the new food processing plants that his firm is building in the area. His annual salary is more than $22,000.

Both Ralph and Caroline were born and reared in Southern California. They met while students at the University of Southern California in Los Angeles. Upon their marriage, they decided to seek adventure in the harsher climate of "the East." Joining the corporate world, they moved first to Wisconsin, then to Ohio, and finally to Illinois. They now regard that period of their lives as an exile, rather than an adventure. The twins were born less than a year after they married, and Caroline says, "It took me seven years to get back here and get some help from the in-laws with these kids!"

The Porfilios are members of Our Lady Queen of Angels Church. They approve of the trend toward modernization of the church ritual, but they disapprove of any involvement by priests or nuns in political affairs. Rarely attending mass themselves, they send their children to an hour's religious instruction every week. Caroline is more critical than Ralph of the church leadership, which she describes as being out of touch with the times. Caroline was raised as a Protestant, and she favors the legalization of abortion more strongly than does her husband.

Caroline is an eager joiner of organizations. She serves as an adviser to the organization of teen-age girl hospital volunteers. She is a member of the board of directors of a Junior League-style organization being formed in the area; she has been a Girl Scout leader, and she remains active in her sorority alumni group. The family holds membership in one of the expensive clubs which offers tennis courts, swimming pool, restaurant and bar, sailing instruction, and a boat launch. The Porfilios own a small sailing dinghy which they store in a rack at the club. Ralph is much less involved than his wife in civic organizations, following the classic pattern of the suburban breadwinner. He belongs to some professional engineering societies but is not active in them.

Ralph Porfilio is relatively small in stature; his skin is fair (although it becomes deeply tanned in the summer), his hair and brows are dark. His motions are quick and he talks eagerly, the words spilling out over each other. He seems to contain an unlimited amount of nervous energy. Inner tensions animate his conversation and his political attitudes. Caroline is quite like her husband in appearance, but seems somehow more in control of her life.

Ralph is registered as a Democrat, Caroline as a Republican. The parents of both were Republicans, and Ralph changed his registration, he says, in order to assure receipt in the household of the campaign material supplied by both parties. Caroline says he became a Democrat in order to spite his mother, who is a dedicated Republican. However, they regularly vote in their separate primaries. Both the Porfilios voted for Barry Goldwater for president in 1964; for Richard Nixon in 1968 and 1972; for the reelection of Governor Ronald Reagan and the reelection of School Superintendent Max Rafferty in 1970. In the 1970 senatorial contest, Democrat Ralph voted for the Republican incumbent, George Murphy, while Republican Caroline voted for the Democratic challenger, John Tunney. In the congressional contest that year, Ralph voted for John Schmitz, stating that the seniority advantages of the incumbent should be protected. (He did not mention that Schmitz had only a few months' incumbency.) Disapproving of Schmitz's ties with the John Birch Society, but unable to support his Democratic opponent, Caroline Porfilio—like the Roybals—left the ballot blank.[6]

Richard and *Alice Rinehart* have lived in their three-bedroom home since Ramona Heights was first occupied. Their son left the family in 1965 for military service, followed by college and marriage. Their daughter completed high school in 1966 and went to the University of Southern California, her parents' alma mater. In 1970, she had finished at USC, completed a European tour, and was back in Ramona Heights, looking for a job.

Richard Rinehart is a senior engineering executive with the Southern California Edison Company, a firm he has served for his entire working life. During high school summer vacations, he worked as a meter reader; after army service and graduation from USC, he began as a junior rate engineer and climbed the corporate hierarchy with a slow but steady pace. He expects that the pace will continue until he retires. His 1969 salary was $19,000; he forecast that with promotions and cost-of-living salary increases, his 1974 income would be between $27,000 and $30,000. When his cooperation in this project was sought, Richard Rinehart recalled reading *The Organization Man*, by sociologist William H. Whyte, Jr.,[7] and asked if the present effort was of similar nature.

[6]Three of the twenty-three adults interviewed in Ramona Heights (13 percent) declined to vote in the 1970 congressional contest, because they could not support John Schmitz, yet did not feel they had enough information to support his Democratic opponent. Was this a common phenomenon in the thirty-fifth congressional district? If so, a more lively Democratic campaign could have had a significant effect on the outcome. In fact, 5,961 fewer votes were cast for the congressional candidates than were cast for governor, and 5,162 fewer than were cast for United States senator. However, this represents less than a 2 percent drop in the total vote cast, and John Schmitz won with 67 percent of the vote. A similar but less extensive drop was experienced in neighboring congressional districts.
[7]William H. Whyte, Jr., *The Organization Man* (New York: Simon & Schuster, 1956).

Months later, I thought to ask what Rinehart thought of *The Organization Man.* He replied:

Richard: My impression, ten years later, is that it portrayed pretty well how people lived in the housing developments he described back East. . . . I was not overly impressed at learning anything I did not know already, and thus I believe that it had little effect on my later behavior. I guess I felt that I was part of the same scene, Southern California division, and hence not looking at anything strange.

As Richard was moving up the corporate hierarchy, the family moved cautiously from a Los Angeles residential neighborhood (where they settled upon Richard's return from the army), to the San Fernando Valley in 1948, then to the city of Tustin, in Orange County, in 1955, and from Tustin to Ramona Heights in 1965. They plan no further moves, but they hope to buy land in the mountains on which they can construct a retirement cottage. Their children's education was financed with loans against the shares of blue-chip stock they own, and the loans are being repaid on a regular basis.

Richard Rinehart's father was a German-speaking Swiss who came to the United States as a young man in 1905 and married the daughter of Norwegians. He established a farm, and later entered the farm machinery business near Seattle, but was lured to Southern California by a business boom shortly after Richard was born in 1925. Meanwhile, Alice's parents left their family ties in Connecticut and came to San Diego in 1915, where Alice was born twelve years later. Alice and Richard met at a sorority dance when both were undergraduates at the University of Southern California, and they were married during the summer of 1941. Richard joined the navy, rather than be drafted, early in 1942, and served in the Pacific theater until the conclusion of the war.

Much of the Rineharts' social life revolves around their status as alumni of USC. They are active members of the Alumni Association; they hold season tickets to the football games; and every month they play bridge with seven other couples they met at USC. In addition, Alice Rinehart has made something of a career of membership in civic organizations. When the children were young, she was a troop leader in the Brownies and then the Girl Scouts, and Richard was an assistant scoutmaster; Alice was an officer in the parent-teachers organization. But Alice has recently completed a term as president, having moved up through the lesser offices, of a Junior League–like organization that places teen-aged girls in community service work and later sponsors their debutante balls.

The Rineharts are keen gardeners. Plants flourish both in their yard and inside their house, where various walls display climbing vines, and a library shelf is filled with books on gardening.

The Rineharts are registered Republicans. Richard had been a Democrat, following the lead of his immigrant parents and the appeal of Franklin D. Roosevelt, but, disenchanted with Harry Truman, he became a Republican. In their usual methodical manner, Richard and Alice agree in advance how they will vote and take their marked sample ballots to the polling place. They are a two-person political machine. Although they consider themselves somewhat independent in outlook, the Rineharts voted for the Republican candidate in every election I asked about. They supported John Schmitz because of his integrity, well aware that they disagreed with many of his positions. Although they know some "fine people" who have belonged to the Birch Society, they are repelled by the inflexibility of the society's pronouncements. They do feel that the organization has been made into a liberal whipping boy, and they feel it took courage for Schmitz to confess his membership. They are also admirers of Max Rafferty, and followed his leadership of counterattacks against the leftist and pacifist student groups on the UCLA campus in the 1930s.

The Rineharts label their political convictions, in general, as conservative.

Arthur and *Tina Roybal*, who felt unable to vote in the congressional contest, live in a five-bedroom split-level house. They have been married twenty years. Their oldest daughter was eighteen in 1970, a freshman at a local community college. They bought her a three-year-old English sports car to enable her to commute to her classes. Arthur drove a 1964 Buick; Tina kept the family station wagon, a 1966 Ford. But they don't regard automobiles as indices of prestige; they drive their cars until they are ready for the junkyard. There were three other children, aged fifteen, eleven, and nine. With her youngest child well established in school, Tina completed a refresher course and returned to the classroom, after nearly twenty years' absence, to teach third grade. Arthur spent fifteen years as a high school teacher and athletic coach. He accepted an invitation to participate in a federal program in educational planning which led to his present administrative post as principal assistant to the county superintendent of schools. Arthur says the program was one of the remarkable events of his life. Their combined income in 1970 was about $28,000.

As noted before, Tina Roybal is the daughter of Lebanese immigrants. Her father was a rug merchant, and they were living in Shaker Heights, Ohio (an affluent suburb of Cleveland), when Tina was born. But the call of a better climate brought them to California soon afterward; Tina attended Beverly Hills High School, where she was active in campus activities. She then attended the University of California campus at Santa Barbara, a then small institution formed on the base of an existing teacher's college.

Arthur's parents grew up in Mexico but moved to California after their marriage. The sixth of ten children, Arthur was born in 1925, and grew up in Watts, in an area then largely Mexican that is now occupied by blacks. He attended high school in Watts, where he played varsity football and was elected an officer of the senior class. Confronted by the draft, he enlisted in the navy and served in the Pacific during the final years of World War II. He became a pharmacist's mate, and he considered entering medicine as a career. He says that the navy taught him that he was able to compete successfully with the Anglos in fields other than athletics. He enrolled at Santa Barbara and met Tina. By his sophomore year of college, he was anxious to get on with the business of living. He married Tina during their senior year, completed a master's degree in education in a single year at UCLA, and began his career.

With her family obligations, Tina has gotten involved in little work outside the home except for becoming an adult leader in the Girl Scouts. Arthur has joined service clubs as a result of assignment by his employers, and he holds office in some professional educational organizations. But he regards such memberships as a duty, rather than an opportunity. They do not belong to a church.

Both Arthur and Tina have fair complexions and dark hair. Arthur seems to have little of the Indian ancestry that is often considered an attribute of the Chicano. And he steadfastly refuses to identify himself with the Mexican-American community. He states that he has climbed up out of a cesspool, and he doesn't care to be reminded of its smell.

The Roybals are both registered Republicans. They consistently vote for the more liberal (or "moderate") candidates in the Republican primary elections, see their candidates defeated, and then vote Democratic in the general election. They voted for John Kennedy in 1960, Lyndon Johnson in 1964, incumbent Democratic Governor Pat Brown (running against Ronald Reagan) in 1966, Hubert Humphrey in 1968, and Democratic Assemblyman Jess Unruh (running for governor against Reagan) in 1970. As educators, they had strong opinions about Max Rafferty, and they fervently supported Wilson Riles, Rafferty's opponent. They did not vote in the Schmitz-Lenhart congressional contest.

However, true to their belief in supporting the man, not the party, Arthur voted for Dennis Carpenter, the Republican candidate for the California State Senate. Arthur had heard good reports of Carpenter from friends, and these favorable impressions were confirmed on the one occasion he met Carpenter. In 1972, Tina voted for George McGovern, but Arthur voted to reelect Richard Nixon.

Like many former athletes, Arthur in middle age has grown stocky. His shoulders are still powerful, but his hips are probably thicker than when he was a linebacker. His mind is quick, however, and his opinions definite. Tina is of slight stature and in her early forties retains flashing good looks. In political matters, she defers publicly to her husband. One feels that she has a good deal of private influence over family decisions, but that her husband makes all the public announcements.

John Wesley and *Martha Weeks* also own a five-bedroom split-level, which they bought when Ramona Heights was first occupied. They came to the tract because of its proximity to John's work; he is a research aeronautical engineer with an aerospace firm located in the industrial park next to the Orange County Airport. The Weekses had been living in Long Beach, and commuting was a burden; John can now reach his work in less than ten minutes. The family maintains three cars: a 1961 Volkswagen, for neighborhood shopping, a 1965 Plymouth station wagon, and a 1969 Mercury Cougar sports car that is shared by John with his son, who drives to the Irvine campus of the University of California. John's income in 1969 was approximately $21,000.

Although they moved to Ramona Heights to be near John's work, the Weekses feel that it is the most pleasant neighborhood they have ever lived in. Martha is active in three of the Ramona Heights women's clubs; through that association, she is acquainted with Marie Kaub. Martha says that Ramona Heights has many of the friendly qualities of a small town. At the beginning of our first interview, Martha said that the central orientation of their lives is "home and hearth," and that they are most concerned with what is good for the family. They had wanted a large family; due to a series of miscarriages, they have only two children: a boy born in 1950 and a girl born in 1961. Their son is a serious, hard-working boy who managed two part-time jobs while attending UCI; he also led hikes, sponsored by the local Audubon Society, into the marshes of Upper Newport Bay. He wears a precisely trimmed beard and has had a greater effect than he realizes on his parents' outlook on American society.

John Wesley Weeks is one of those persons who amaze Piotr Pavel:

an engineer who takes religion seriously. In Long Beach, the Weekses helped to found a new Methodist congregation. John was superintendent of the Sunday school; Martha was church secretary and, with John, a member of the board of trustees. Their social life for a number of years revolved around that congregation, which had the small-town friendliness that Martha Weeks has so often found and responded to. They were forever attending church potluck dinners, and the monthly square dances held by the young married group in the church social hall. John had been raised a Methodist, but Martha's denomination had been rather more severe, requiring total immersion to accomplish baptism. John persuaded her that sprinkling was adequate for their children.

The Weekses are devotees of aircraft and flying. When he was six years old, John was taken for a ride in a biplane by an uncle. The uncle asked if he wanted to become a pilot. John replied that he'd rather become a man who designs airplanes. This remained his goal and identity throughout his education and into his present job, where he supervises engineers designing electronic equipment for aircraft. Martha and John met in high school in St. Louis; they return for class reunions. When John entered the army in 1943, Martha became an airline stewardess. They do not join in the neighborhood criticism of the Orange County Airport; they like the sound of aircraft, and say the sky would seem empty without them.

John Weeks likes his job, but as his company's life depends on defense contracts, he has a sense of impermanence. Because his office is so close, he sometimes returns there to work on unsolved technical problems after hours or on weekends. He also attends classes at UCI to prepare for alternative employment in the computer industry. Less involved with church activities than when they lived in Long Beach, John now devotes his weekends to golf. When I first met him, John was practicing putts on his living room carpet. In his late forties, John has grown quite stout, which is a source of worry to Martha. He smokes several miniature cigars a day, and on social occasions he drinks cocktails, his Methodism being modernized to that extent. John is jovial by temperament and fond of small practical jokes. His life style seems to have been largely influenced by his midwestern upbringing and membership in an engineering fraternity at the University of Kansas following World War II.

John and Martha Weeks are interested in a number of causes, one of which is international understanding. They have worked with the American Field Service, inviting foreign students into their home. They are both registered as Republicans, but they are not intensely partisan; if California had open primaries, they would register as independents.

In 1970, they voted for Ronald Reagan and most of the Republican ticket. But they voted for Democrat Thomas Lenhart instead of John Schmitz, for they found Schmitz's ties to the John Birch Society despicable. And they voted for Wilson Riles rather than Max Rafferty for superintendent of public instruction. They supported Nixon and Agnew enthusiastically in 1972. John Weeks was devastated by the Watergate investigation; he felt something like a sense of personal betrayal.

Technocrats and Their Neighbors

One characteristic of Orange County that makes it a fruitful vantage point for viewing America's future is the substantial portion of its population that may be numbered among the "affluent technocracy." Status as an affluent technocrat depends primarily upon employment which provides an income significantly above the average for gainfully employed Americans. There are three additional, and important, characteristics: specialized education or training, position in a bureaucratic organization, and involvement in the application of technological advance. The training for specialization may be both extensive and formal, such as attaining a college degree in engineering; it may be less extensive, such as attending the executive training program of a large firm; or it can be relatively informal, consisting largely of experience gained on the job. A given individual may experience any or all of these types of preparation for specialization. But the outcome of all three types is the same: the individual is prepared for a specialized role in a relatively large and complex organization. This organization will exhibit the characteristics of bureaucracy, as defined by Max Weber: division of jurisdiction, a hierarchy of authority, the maintenance of records, and management according to rules.[8] And the role of the technocrat will involve him in the design, manufacture, or marketing of the products of advancing technology, although "technology" should be broadly defined: Dr. Kenneth Kaub, as a physician in a state mental hospital, serves society by providing the advances of medical technology to patients who are the wards of society.

The affluent technocrat has much in common with Whyte's "organization man." But certain differences are important. The affluent technocrat has achieved a certain level of income, for which the organization man may only be striving. Additionally, in Whyte's conception,

[8]H. H. Gerth and C. Wright Mills, ed. and trans., *From Max Weber: Essays in Sociology* (New York: Oxford University Press, Galaxy Books, 1958), pp. 196–198.

[the organization men] are the ones of our middle class who have left home, spiritually as well as physically, to take the vows of organization life, and it is they who are the mind and soul of our great self-perpetuating institutions.[9]

Perhaps because of his achieved measure of affluence, the technocrat of Ramona Heights has not necessarily internalized the values of his organization. He may perceive a separation between himself and his organizational role. This difference is important; the ability to define oneself apart from one's occupational role has important political implications.

The Ramona Heights sample contains twelve family heads. Only two are clearly ineligible for designation as affluent technocrats. They are Frank McGee and Arnold Garcia, both small, independent businessmen who can, if they choose, easily practice concepts of individualism. Unlike the technocrats, they need not adapt their work attitudes to a hierarchy of authority in which they have only a middle position.

Four of the twelve fit our criteria easily: Pavel, Porfilio, Rinehart, and Weeks. All are graduate engineers; all work for large and complicated organizations, performing specialized roles.

Three are marginal cases: Elliott, Kaub, and Barbera. Quentin Elliott was very much a part of the technocratic, organizational world until he renounced it in favor of teaching. His attitudes towards his former work life may illuminate the feelings of those who remain happy in their similar positions. But in becoming a schoolteacher he has only moved from one kind of bureaucracy to another. Kenneth Kaub exercises considerable independent judgment within the boundaries of his medical specialty, but he is aware of the constraints imposed by the bureaucracy within which he works. Fletcher Barbera began his career as an engineer in a massive electronics company, but he was unhappy with the sense of small personal influence over the total performance of the company. He has since held three other jobs, each in a smaller firm than before, with correspondingly greater responsibility for himself. Fletcher has tried the large, bureaucratic organization, and he cannot stand it.

Finally, there are three special cases: Johnson, Roybal, and Markus. Harry Johnson is the proprietor of his own firm and thus a small businessman in the same sense as Garcia, but his firm makes machine tools and therefore is involved with the application of technological advance. Jan Markus's career has been as an electrician, one of the highly paid hourly workers of the technological society, but he has never absorbed

---

[9]Whyte, *Organization Man*, p. 3. Whyte has been criticized for his romantic defense of individualism and his corollary assumption that individual personality is necessarily absorbed by the organization.

an identity, or even feelings of ambivalence, from an organization that paid his wages. He identifies himself as a working man (although an independent, skilled tradesman), with interests naturally contrary to the motives of any employer. Arthur Roybal has specialized training, including a graduate degree, and he holds a management position within the educational bureaucracy, but it may be inappropriate to conceive of an educational bureaucracy as having a "product" comparable to that of an aerospace firm.

Thus, if any of the ten remaining breadwinners do not qualify as affluent technocrats, they are certainly the neighbors of affluent technocrats, and Ramona Heights provides a kind of natural habitat for the affluent technocracy. The political life histories of the twelve families provide rich data for investigation, as well as a challenge to the explanatory powers of social science. For we are presented with persons of similar status and background but contrasting political attitudes and actions, as well as quite different reactions to the crises of our times. Consider, for example, the Barberas and the Elliotts. Both are, or have been, marginal members of the American upper class: private schools, servants in the home, Ivy League educations, and employment by technocratic industry. Yet, while the Barberas vote Republican almost automatically and are distressed by the anticonformity of the hippie life style, the Elliotts are buying their way out of the corporate world, and Quentin sometimes asks his children to think of their home as "the Elliott commune."

The three Mexican-Americans of our sample provide another example. All experienced discrimination in their youth, and they share the characteristic of selecting someone not a Chicano for a spouse. But Arnold Garcia is a ruthless materialist, attracted to the candidacy of George Wallace; Arthur Roybal has become a Republican, but only to "defend" himself against conservative Republican candidates; and Marie Kaub remains a Democrat, although her loyalty to the party is shaky.

Among the four respondents whose status as affluent technocrats is unquestionable—the four engineers employed by large companies—there is a broad spectrum of political conviction and attitude. Piotr Pavel is a cosmopolitan, liberal intellectual; John Wesley Weeks is a moderate Republican who prizes his independence and retains an aura of his provincial background; Richard Rinehart is a staunch and articulate conservative. Ralph Porfilio seems less sure of his status than any of the four, and expresses hostilities that might surprise his occupational colleagues.

Of the twenty-three adults interviewed at length, four—Quentin

Elliott, Piotr and Myrna Pavel, and Alice Rinehart—have been involved, at one time or another, in partisan political activity beyond voting in primary elections. Yet the candidates supported have ranged from Adlai Stevenson through Charles Percy to Ronald Reagan. The McGees are involved in fairly constant political activity, stimulated by membership in the John Birch Society.

It may be useful to summarize the twelve families according to standard categories. This will indicate the social similarities which provide boundaries for individual divergence. In every case, the husband has been the principal breadwinner. Except for Eldene Markus, who is childless, the wives have remained at home to attend to child-rearing, and any reentry into the world of work makes a relatively modest contribution to the family income. The more common pattern is for the wife to devote some energy to the work of volunteer social, religious, or charitable organizations.

All but three of the twelve families had annual incomes in 1969 of $20,000 or more. The median family income was $23,000; because of the Johnsons and Garcias at the top of the scale, the average income was about $26,000.

In terms of education, fifteen of the twenty-three respondents are college graduates, but only Kenneth Kaub and Arthur Roybal hold postgraduate degrees. Five additional respondents completed some college work but did not receive a degree, while four (the Markuses and the Johnsons) completed only high school.

At the time of the 1970 interviews, the ages of the respondents ranged from thirty (Maureen Barbera) to sixty-two (Piotr Pavel). The median age was forty-five and a half. Clustered around this median were Martha Weeks, John Weeks, Richard Rinehart, and Arthur Roybal.

Of the twenty-three, ten are Protestant, seven are Catholic, and two (the Pavels) are Jewish. But the Pavels' Jewishness is a matter of cultural tradition, rather than formal practice. Four respondents (the Markuses and Roybals) are not members of any organized church, although Jan and Eldene Markus and Arthur Roybal were raised as Catholics.

Their ethnic origin is diverse. Three respondents (Arnold Garcia, Marie Kaub, and Arthur Roybal) are Mexican-American. Piotr Pavel was born in Russia, and his wife's parents were Russian. Richard Rinehart's father was Swiss; Francis McGee's Irish ancestry lives on in his name, as does the Italian ancestry of Fletcher Barbera and Ralph Porfilio. But this ancestry is remote in every case except Rinehart's. Poland, Czechoslovakia, and Lebanon were the birthplaces of the parents of Eldene Markus, Jan Markus, and Tina Roybal, respectively. Although she was born in the United States, Deborah Elliott spent her girlhood in Canada. Exactly four (the Johnsons and the Porfilios) of the twenty-three respondents were born in California.

They all live in Ramona Heights.

PART TWO

Work, Play, and Politics under the Sun

Unless consciously diffused, the tug-of-war between the inner cities and suburbs of this country could erupt more fiercely in the coming years than did the struggles between the farmers and city-dwellers in earlier periods. The two present antagonists are joined together more closely by technology, geography, even the air they breathe, than the opposing forces in those earlier economic and political tugs-of-war; but the proximity only aggravates the rudeness of their rivalry. The balance of power already lies with the suburbs, lessened in effect somewhat by their decentralization and preoccupation with "privatism." Even with those limitations, however, the political styles, symbols, and substance of the seventies are likely to be heavily influenced by the neo-agrarianism, heavily gadgeted modernity, and personal strivings that are the essence of suburbanism, a way of life and outlook already more influential politically than either doctrinaire liberalism or conservatism.

—Frederick G. Dutton, *in* Changing Sources of Power *(New York: McGraw-Hill, 1971), p. 135*

CHAPTER THREE

Republicans, Democrats, and Independence

Not only the increase but the absolute proportion of independents has become increasingly identified with the comfortable urban-suburban middle class. . . . The political parties are progressively losing their hold upon the electorate. A new breed of independent seems to be emerging as well—a person with a better-than-average education, making a better-than-average income in a better-than-average occupation, and, very possibly, a person whose political cognitions and awareness keep him from making identification with either old party.

—*Walter Dean Burnham*[1]

"I revel and rejoice in my independence."

Quentin Elliott

Do Suburbs Make Republicans?

THE STEREOTYPE of Orange County is based in fact. Along with similar areas of Southern California, it has produced a political record strongly tinted by conservatism. In the middle- to upper-middle-class areas like

[1]Walter Dean Burnham, *Critical Elections and the Mainsprings of American Politics* (New York: Norton, 1970), pp. 128, 130.

Ramona Heights, the Republican party dominates; and within the Republican party the more conservative candidates win primary elections. (If John Schmitz is an exception, the explanation must be that Schmitz finally placed himself outside the spectrum; his views were simply not within the American political discourse of the early 1970s.) Since this conservatism in voting is a striking aspect of the area's history, we must seek an understanding of its cause. Is there something unique to Orange County that propels its voters to the right, or does that compulsion result from influences that are not based in geography?

A version of the notion that conservatism infuses the very air and earth of Orange County has been supplied by Walter Knott. As an explanation, it is neatly packaged, with the same touch of old-time flavoring as the boysenberry jelly featured at Knott's Berry Farm. Knott is reported as delivering it with a chuckle.

> People get out here and associate with people who understand this conservative philosophy. They become homeowners, have a little piece of America. They begin to think a little differently toward government. They become Republicans.[2]

Knott's suggestion is not very nourishing as an explanation. How does owning "a little piece of America" modify one's attitudes towards government? Presumably it could stimulate a surge of patriotism; but, since the implication is that it also compels one to seek limitations on the scope of government, that patriotism may be applied only in the international sphere. In domestic politics this new conservatism could mean little more than a resistance to paying taxes for government solutions to domestic problems. Knott offers a second clue: "associate with people." One of the earliest hypotheses put forward by students of suburbia was that the political integration of newcomers into suburban life will in many cases result in their conversion into Republicans. William H. Whyte, Jr., claimed that entry into the suburbs signified entrance into at least the middle class and usually the world of the organization man. Democratic allegiance was an attribute of the life and status being abandoned; "acceptance" by one's peers in the new surroundings was furthered by becoming a Republican.[3] Acquaintance with David Riesman's conception of the "other directed"[4] quality of the modern person-

---

[2]Quoted in "A Little Piece of America," *Newsweek*, November 14, 1966, p. 37. This article identifies Orange County as "the great right-wing vote reservoir of the U.S. West."
[3]William H. Whyte, Jr., *The Organization Man* (New York: Simon & Schuster, 1956); in the Doubleday Anchor reprint, p. 332. "Acceptance" was a conscious goal of many of the new suburbanites Whyte interviewed.
[4]David Riesman, *The Lonely Crowd* (New Haven: Yale University Press, 1950).

ality led to an assumption that the adoption of the new party represented a basic change of mind, as a result of absorbing the convictions of one's peers.

Whyte's hypothesis was formulated, and supported to an extent by other researchers,[5] in an effort to explain a very real phenomenon: in spite of an influx of new residents from cities that had normally voted Democratic, the suburbs voted heavily for Dwight Eisenhower and the Republican party. But repeated examinations of suburban voting have negated the hypothesis. The individual's identification with a political party is formed before his move to any particular suburb, and it is an aspect of his identity and self-esteem that is not casually changed. The voters of Ramona Heights bear this out. But they add a local observation: they are not aware of subtle or unsubtle pressures toward political conformity on the job, in the neighborhood, or within their circle of friends. And they find the level of political interest, activity, and discussion no higher in Orange County than in other places they have lived. However, they define "political conformity" in the narrowest of terms: its absence means that they feel no social pressure to change their party registration from Democratic to Republican, or vice versa. A noisy conversion to anarchism or communism could well generate a negative reaction from friends and associates, as Richard Rinehart points out. But none of the twelve couples contemplates such a conversion, and most identify themselves with the political middle of the road. Frank McGee, of course, is the exception; he feels that his connections with the Birch Society are not necessarily a business asset, and did lead to his being opposed in the usually pro forma election to the governing board of his service club.

Fletcher Barbera could be speaking for most of the men interviewed in Ramona Heights when he talks about pressure toward political conformity at his place of business.

Fletcher: We have some pretty staunch conservatives, and we have some pretty liberal people, and you know, occasionally we'll have fairly active debates at lunch time, or occasionally even during the working day; you know, two or three guys in an office or a hall get into some kind of discussion. There is a wide range of opinions, and in general I think that most people will at least listen to the other guy, but I don't think there is any social pressure to be one thing or not be another.

[5]The Whyte hypothesis was given qualified support by Louis Harris in *Is There a Republican Majority?* (New York: Harper, 1954). But Harris emphasized that Eisenhower's victory was a personal one, which did not necessarily presage a new partisan majority.

Dr. Kenneth Kaub says there are political discussions at the state hospital where he works, but he feels that the civil service status of the staff precludes any active campaigning, particularly during working hours. The cuts made by the Reagan Administration in the budget of the state hospitals has caused a plunge in Reagan's never great popularity, and Kaub can recall only one colleague who argued in favor of Reagan on ideological grounds. Marie Kaub is known to be a Democrat by most of her friends, many of whom are Republicans, but this is not generally a source of strain in social relationships. She does recall one exception.

Marie: I have a very good friend who will start to say something, and then she'll say, "Oh, I'd better not say anything because you're not of the same party I am," and she will drop it. . . . There are times when I try to bring her out more and say, "Well, go ahead and say it," but she says, "Oh, no, no." There's a stone wall there and there's no use pushing.

This Republican friend apparently forgives Marie for being a Democrat much as she forgives her for being Mexican-American: it's an accident of birth for which Marie is not personally responsible.

Similarly, the Democratic Pavels, in many ways the prototypical eastern urban liberals, report there are two couples among their close friends with whom they simply do not discuss certain political questions—campus unrest, the drug problem, or racial integration.

Piotr: They say, "We didn't do this when we had very little money. We studied; we didn't demonstrate." You know, the same old stuff.

The main point about the voters of Ramona Heights is that, like most people, they do not base their social lives or their work lives upon partisan politics. (Frank McGee, again, very nearly qualifies as an exception.) Political agreement is not a prerequisite of friendship; meaningful social relationships do not require matching political attitudes, although friendships are occasionally enriched by political discussion. Some relationships must be protected from the disruptive power of intruding partisan considerations. The Republican Rineharts recall changing the subject when political discussions with friends of long standing became overheated. John and Martha Weeks have similar recollections. At some point it is best to agree to disagree, and a positive value is attached to the ability to disagree. Eldene Markus sums it up.

Eldene: No one has put any pressure on us, and we express ourselves and they express themselves. . . . The relatives are split, and friends are split, and that's what makes this country so wonderful. You get to vote the way you want and for who you want.

In short, these residents of Ramona Heights do not live lives that are dominated by political thought or discussion. Their political actions are "so much a part of nonpolitical life that they can be captured only in a view that embraces almost all social life."[6] The "distinctive political style" of Southern California has been labeled as "extremist, paranoid, and hortatory."[7] But the voters of Ramona Heights do not see politics in this way; they discount the exhortations of candidates and office-holders, and get on with the business of living. They are amused by the notions commonly held about Orange County. The Rineharts report that old friends in the San Fernando Valley assume that anyone seen on the street in Orange County is not only a Republican, but a conservative Republican, "and it just isn't so." The Johnsons insist that people in Orange County are the same as people anywhere. Quentin Elliot was aware of the area's ultrarightist reputation but is pleased that his new neighbors seem to be moderate or liberal. The respondents are not aware of social pressures toward right-wing conformity; some of Frank McGee's associates view his right-wing connections with disfavor. Furthermore, if the respondents were aware of such pressures, they would resist. As Arthur Roybal puts it, when asked about pressures toward conformity:

Arthur: No, I haven't noticed. Maybe they know better than to approach me that way. About that time somebody'll pick themselves up off the seat of their pants, and I mean it.

Moving into Orange County does not make voters into Republicans. Neither does moving into Westport, Connecticut (which is even higher on the economic scale than Ramona Heights). A study of 829 Westport voters concluded that "there is little indication of a suburban swing to Republican voting that cannot be explained by the 'Eisenhower effect' in the national elections of 1952 and 1956."[8] The suburbs-make-Republicans hypothesis can be laid to rest.

[6]Robert E. Lane, *Political Ideology*, paper ed. (New York: Macmillan, Free Press, 1962), p. 447. Lane's book is based on depth interviews of fifteen working-class men from a Connecticut public housing project.
[7]Samuel C. Patterson, "The Political Cultures of the American States," 30 *Journal of Politics* (February, 1968), p. 203.
[8]David Wallace, *First Tuesday: A Study of Rationality in Voting* (Garden City, N.Y.: Doubleday, 1964), p. 271.

The inescapable lesson is that Republican suburbs attract Republican newcomers, or enough of them to maintain a high Republican percentage. . . . Suburban living does not change voting behavior; the behavior is determined long before the move to suburbia.[9]

Party Identification

Ramona Heights was not "a Republican suburb" in 1964; it was a new tract, its contours reshaped by bulldozers, full of bright new homes and unplanted yards. By 1970 it was well established as a neighborhood and provided for many of its residents an active social life. Two voting precincts were contained within its boundaries. Its residents, by and large, retained the political affiliations they brought with them: 62 percent of the couples were both registered as Republicans; 22 percent were both registered as Democrats; and the registration was mixed (with one spouse in each major party) in the other 16 percent of the cases. One college student was registered in the Peace and Freedom party, and a retired naval officer in the American Independent party. A dozen declined to state their party preference. This preponderance of Republicanism is less than that found in the more exclusive, wealthier precincts of the area, but it gives a larger proportion of Republicans to Ramona Heights than to Orange County·as a whole. This is exactly what would be expected from the economic and occupational status of the tract's residents.[10]

Republicans in Ramona Heights are not Republican because of their place of residence. And the Markuses and Pavels of our sample did not become Democrats through perverse reaction to the Republican majority surrounding them. Party identification is absorbed from one's parents and other aspects of the childhood environment. A sense of association with one of the great political parties becomes an attribute of self, so that stimuli which challenge the validity of that association are resisted. Instead, it is reinforced through friendship with one's fellow partisans.[11]

These attributes of party identification in America have been much

[9]Scott Donaldson, *The Suburban Myth* (New York: Columbia University Press, 1969), p. 154.
[10]This generalization is supported by the major studies of American voting behavior. See, for example, A. Campbell et al., *The American Voter*, abr. ed. (New York: Wiley, 1964), chap. 6, 11, and 12.
[11] Wallace, *First Tuesday*, p. 272.

praised. They give each of the two major parties a dependable base of support, so that a party can recapture a majority after dismal defeat, when the public has in turn wearied of the opposition. In 1964, Barry Goldwater led the Republican party into temporary obscurity; within four years, public reactions to the failure of the Democratic administration to restore peace abroad and maintain order at home placed Richard Nixon in the White House. The relative permanence of partisan identification on the part of the individual voter, therefore, helps to assure the stability of the two-party system.[12]

Recognizing the psychological power of party identification, scholars and campaign managers placed it at the center of their explanation of voting behavior. Party identification was seen as the most certain determinant of voting behavior, and party identification, in turn, was closely correlated with occupation, income, education, religion, and race or ethnic origins, with some modifications due to regional (e.g., southern or midwestern) political history. Issues and ideas, therefore, had little impact; voting was largely determined by factors external to the voter.[13] Voting was nonrational rather than irrational.[14]

This vision of the electorate was largely formed during the Eisenhower era, a period of relative political calm. One of its results was to dethrone the hero of the old civics textbooks, the independent voter. Rather than employing cool reason to judge issues, untainted by partisan prejudices, the independent voter was seen as less involved in politics, less well informed, less attentive to campaigns, and less likely to recognize the importance of political issues. The investment of psychological energy in party identification seemed to go hand in hand with awareness of political questions and concern for their resolution.[15] According to this image, the voter who disdains attachment to a party is likely to be retreating from the issues of public life.

More recent work has suggested a more complicated explanation. During periods of relative political calm, both parties appeal to the same undecided middle-minded voters. The parties sound quite alike, as both seek to serve the dominant interests of society. Only in periods of rapid

---

12 Lane, *Political Ideology*, p. 453; Campbell et al., *American Voter*, p. 287.

13The best summary of this viewpoint is Campbell et al., *American Voter*. Its application to the strategy of an actual campaign is recounted in Ithiel de Sola Pool, Robert P. Abelson, and Samuel L. Popkin, *Candidates, Issues, and Strategies* (Cambridge, Mass.: MIT Press, 1964).

14 Wallace, *First Tuesday*, p. 272.

15For the most influential description in this vein of the independent voter, see Campbell et al., *American Voter*, p. 83.

social change do issues between the parties force themselves upon the consciousness of the voter, as the parties are forced toward a realignment.[16] The phenomenon of party identification thus has crucial ramifications in a time of social change. If partisans continue to shield their political outlook from change by selective perception of the environment, and by selective association with fellow partisans, a gap may widen between party leaders and followers. This will ease the work of a George Wallace, or similar protest candidate. But the opposite effect is also possible—voters may be more aware of change and the demands it imposes than are party leaders, who pursue issues and alliances that once yielded partisan advantage but will not do so again. For the policies of social institutions to lag behind the perceptions of their individual adherents is a common phenomenon. There is no reason for political parties to be immune from such a pathology—particularly if the ordinary voter should prove to be rather better informed and more eager to exercise his rational powers than he is usually pictured as being.

"Rational Independence" in Ramona Heights?

The voters of Ramona Heights certainly do not picture themselves as helpless atoms controlled by impersonal social forces, or as subjects of successful manipulation by political advertising experts. They are as aware as the behavioral scientists of the role played by their family backgrounds in establishing their partisan inclinations. According to Caroline Porfilio, her husband, Ralph, registered as a Democrat only to rebel against his mother, who is a Republican precinct worker. John Weeks recounts his family background, but he hastens to add a philosophical justification for his Republicanism.

John: I suppose, being a realist, that a lot of it comes from being raised in a Republican family. And while I don't vote a straight Republican ticket, I do lean heavily towards the Republican side. I think that my inbred feelings about it, or my environmental feelings about it, they're probably the largest influence. . . . In the broad sense I feel that many, many changes are made just to make changes, and I don't believe in changes done in that fashion. I believe changes are continuing, and are a necessary thing. I mean, you can't have anything unless you

[16]The historical pattern of party realignment and the possibilities for a critical election in the present era are discussed in chapter ten.

continuously update your system. But change just to be changing something is wrong. You've got to think about the changes and make sure that they are actually an improvement, and I feel that, by and large, the Republicans tend more in that direction than the Democrats do.

But John is aware that this generalization is true only in the broadest sense, and he points out that there are many individual Democrats who are superior to individual Republicans. He reserves the right to make up his mind anew in each electoral contest. Martha Weeks agrees. She really considers herself an independent, and she would register as one, except that she would then lose the right of participating in primary elections.

The impulse to identify oneself as an independent, quite apart from formal party registration, is strong in Ramona Heights. It is more than the cliché, "Vote for the man, not for the party"; it is a declaration of political independence, a determination to see matters with unblinkered eyes. Quentin Elliott, moving to Ramona Heights in 1969, brought this attitude with him.

Quentin: I revel and rejoice in my independence. Now, I probably know less about politics as a result of this, because I just say that when the time comes, and I decide whether I'm going to vote for this guy Schmitz or not, then I'm going to ask about him. And I just hope that, through the really quite limited sources of information we have, that I will make a more mental than emotional decision. Right now he has— and we're talking specifics—a Bircher label. Now, I talked about not accepting labels, and yet here I am accepting. So this is a dilemma for anybody.

Harry Johnson, who has been registered all his political life as a Democrat, but has voted for several Republicans in recent years, agrees. The important thing, he says, is to vote for the candidate "who is best qualified." He feels most voters are no longer constrained by their party affiliations.

Harry: There are a few people I happen to know who are Republicans or Democrats, and they would vote for a Republican or a Democrat come hell or high water! But I believe they're few and far between anymore; I think you would find maybe perhaps two percent of the people live by this anymore; the rest are pretty flexible.

On the other hand, some voters recognize the strength of their own partisanship. Fletcher Barbera states that he would have voted, in 1968, for any presidential candidate the Republican party nominated, and he cannot imagine anything that would have caused him to change his mind. Furthermore, a president deserves support from his own party, so Fletcher will vote for the Republican candidate for Congress. His wife, Maureen, says that she will split her ticket when the circumstances warrant, but Fletcher says that he is unlikely to split the ticket until he gets pretty far down it.

The Markuses exhibit an interesting variation on the theme of independence. Believing in its values, they identify independence with their fellow Democrats and project on their political opponents an affinity for unthinking straight-ticket voting.

Jan: I think it's a mistake when people just vote for the party.
Eldene: And not for the man.
Jan: Not for the man, and not for the things the country needs.
Question: So that your own tendency is to vote for the man, really, more than the party?
Jan: Yes, that's right. I would never vote just for the party. Of course, we're registered Democrats, but that doesn't mean we vote—
Eldene: Well, a Republican will never change—mix votes. They'll vote straight Republican; if he's a good man or not a good man, they vote party. Where a Democrat will swing.

This dialogue by the Markuses suggests what is indeed the case, that party identification may be a more powerful psychological force than the voter admits, even to himself.[17] It is entirely possible for a voter to be convinced that each election day he selects the best-qualified candidate, regardless of party, and the fact that the best-qualified candidate is always nominated by his own party is seen as an accident. Nevertheless, the Markuses are as independent as they claim. Feeling that the maintenance of law and order is a primary requirement of public affairs, both Jan and Eldene voted for Ronald Reagan for governor in 1966 because of the Brown Administration's delay in calling in troops to quell the riots in Watts, a black suburb of Los Angeles. In 1970, Jan voted for Reagan's reelection, but Eldene supported Jess Unruh. In 1972, Jan voted for the reelection of Richard Nixon, although he had in 1968 supported Hubert Humphrey. Eldene remained loyal to their party and to George McGovern.

Does this evidence of independence—the weakening of party labels—among Ramona Heights' voters indicate new voter responsiveness to

[17]The concealed partisan preference of self-declared independents is discussed in Campbell et al., *American Voter*, pp. 68–71.

pressures for social change? Not completely, since their declarations of independence of judgment do not extend to a complete disdain for partisan attachment. They have all registered in a party, and they usually vote in party primaries. In a later discussion of his independent attitude, Quentin Elliott explained that an independent may feel that it is "dangerous to overidentify with one side." He explained that an independent would never be comfortable urging a straight-ticket vote.

Quentin: The independent voter can't go down to a Republican headquarters and say, "Gee, I like Man X. I want literature on him so I can hand it out," and avoid the party's other candidates. I don't think you can do this very easily. Though I haven't looked into it.[18] I think the independents—and I'm an independent—aren't the ones who get involved. Though the issues of the times are going to smoke us out!

In similar manner, the Weekses have strong feelings of involvement that include their insistence on independence. They are registered Republicans, but they did not vote for former Congressmen Utt or Schmitz. They disliked Schmitz's Birch Society affiliation, feeling that Birch Society members are "misguided." Furthermore, they were offended by questionnaires he sent to his constituents that were, they felt, worded in a biased manner to create the illusion of widespread support for Schmitz's policies. John Weeks characterizes those policies as the resistance to all change. One of our conversations took place on June 30, 1970, the night of a special runoff election. Martha Weeks said they usually vote early in the morning, soon after the polls open, but they had delayed, knowing that—as the newspapers announced—the election was strictly pro forma, and Schmitz would win easily. Martha said she wondered during the day whether she should vote simply against something when she had nothing positive to vote for. When John came home from work, they walked to the polling place.

Question: May I ask who you voted for this evening?
John: I voted against John Schmitz.
Martha: I voted against John Schmitz too.

The Weekses are far from being blind partisans. They consider themselves fairly conservative, but they feel that some of the Orange County

[18]Because of the weakness of party organizations in California, candidates tend to conduct campaigns that are independent of the party to a greater extent than the other states Elliott had lived in. A party campaign headquarters is likely to have brochures for individual candidates for obscure offices such as controller, secretary of state, and the like.

Republican candidates have gone beyond conservatism to extremism. As they have explicit reasons for identifying with the Republican party, the fact that their perceptions are in advance of the Orange County Republican candidates will not lead them to change their registration.

The Ramona Heights voters are suspicious of political parties, including their own. In their own minds at least, they have good reasons for whatever degree of partisan attachment they have developed. Does this mean that they have a special kind of partisan allegiance, or nonallegiance, chosen more consciously than we might suspect? If so, it could be called "rational independence," to contrast it with the older image of the independent voter as a liability to the political system. Let us consider some of the evidence: not only the reasons given for adherence to the present party, but the reasons offered for a change of party in the past.

Although they declare their independence in strong terms, the Markuses' party identification is based on perceived class benefits. They identify themselves with the working class and feel that the Democratic party is definitely the working man's party. Tied to this is a perception of party position on specific issues. Eldene Markus sums up their feelings at one point by stating that Republicans "ignore the poor people, and they're not too good on education, and they lean towards big industry." The Markuses hesitate to label themselves as "liberal" or "conservative," but they are aware of what the terms mean.

Jan: I wouldn't say that I'm too liberal. I wouldn't be conservative all the way to the right, but I want things to be so that everybody has an advantage, and not the thing be too one-sided. . . . We should do things to make it better for everybody, to live better in this country, not just a few. . . . And I think that's something of a problem, when people who control all of this wealth, they don't need all of that money. . . . After all, if you want prosperity you have to put it into the working man's hands. They found that out during the New Deal.

The Markuses have just as definite justifications for their political attitudes and partisan attachments as any voters in Ramona Heights. These attitudes are expressed in direct, earthy language. The voters with more education use more abstract expressions, with no necessary gain in clarity.

Myrna Pavel has always thought of herself as a liberal; her father was a union organizer and social reform activist.

Myrna: I had a father who was just wonderful. His friends were people like Norman Thomas, and Eugene Debs. So how could I grow up otherwise? Though a lot of children of liberal parents have grown up to be quite conservative.

Piotr Pavel came to this country as an adult. Choosing a party was for him a conscious act. He approached it as a European intellectual would be expected to do—on the bases of ideology and of class interest.

Piotr: I thought of myself as a liberal and tried to fit that into the best possible place—not necessarily because it was the Democrats. As I see it, the overlap is, I don't know, it's quite substantial. . . . I tried to find out this way: I said, "I'm going to find out which way do the people vote who I could come closest to, you know, to their views." And labor votes preponderantly, if I'm not mistaken, Democrat. Big business votes preponderantly, if not exclusively, Republican. That was the answer, since I was more akin to labor than I was to the president of the board of U.S. Steel.

The Pavels became Democrats in the time of Franklin D. Roosevelt, and their dedication to the party has never wavered. They did volunteer work for the candidacy of Adlai Stevenson, and one of their sons walked the precincts in 1968 for Eugene McCarthy. Piotr Pavel cited the economic record of the Nixon Administration in 1970 as ample justification for remaining a Democrat, and they both voted for McGovern in 1972.

John Weeks, on the other hand, is less willing to accept broad general izations about the class basis of American politics; he questions them on the basis of his own experience. He was asked if he regarded the Democrats as the party of labor and the Republicans as the party of business.

John: I don't think that's really true. It may work out that way when you break them down that way, but I've got friends that are on the same level as I am, you know, economically speaking and socially speaking, and some of them are Democrats, and we have differences of opinion. On the other hand, I have some very good friends that, you know, are in the so-called blue-collar work force that economically they don't make the same thing. They're strong Republicans. My family was lower middle class. My father started out as a salesman, and he ended up in later years as a machinist. . . . And he was a very strong Republican.

Fletcher Barbera feels an ideological affinity in the same manner as Piotr Pavel—but with opposite results.

Fletcher: I guess really in my view the Republicans could have the label "conservative"; that's what I think I am, and I guess that's why I vote for the Republicans.

Arthur and Tina Roybal have quite a different outlook. They are registered as Republicans in Orange County for defensive reasons. Only through voting in the Republican primary are they likely to have an impact on the electoral result.

Arthur: Both of us have a real concern with the candidates that have been promoted by the Republican party in several election campaigns. And I'm not too sold on some of the candidates and the backing they're receiving. In fact, I think I originally registered as a Republican primarily to protect myself against certain people running. I certainly did it with that in mind.

Republican registration by the Roybals, then, constitutes action based on rather sophisticated understanding of the local political situation. But why the Roybals should attempt to exert some small influence through the Republican primary, while the Pavels (whose political understanding is no less sophisticated) remain members of the Democratic party, is a question not answered directly in their own words. Discrepancies of this kind remind us that any discovery of "rational independence" in Ramona Heights must remain tentative, qualified, and uncertain.

A similar discrepancy is presented by the case of the Johnsons. Raised in Catholic working-class families, they became Democrats as a matter of course. They now enjoy a very high economic position, and Harry Johnson owns a substantial private enterprise. They remain registered Democrats, although they have tended in the last few years to vote for Republican candidates. Harry was asked how he can reconcile his concern for the encroachments of socialism with his Democratic registration.

Harry: I think in the last five years there's been a drastic change in that. If anything, I think perhaps the Democrats are becoming a little more against the giveaway type program. . . . You seem to catch an equal amount of this from both sides of the fence nowadays. [He laughs.] I believe Governor Reagan has stated what he proposed to do in regard to the elderly, and made quite a campaign on this. Perhaps five years ago this would be almost unheard of for a Republican to make a statement like this. So I believe both parties are very parallel. I think you could take the individual who says he's a Republican or a Democrat, and you could talk to them, and I think it would be quite difficult to determine whether he was a Republican or a Democrat from his statements.

The Ramona Heights microsample contains four voters who have changed their registration from one party to the other. They are Richard Rinehart, Quentin Elliott, and the McGees.

Rinehart admired Franklin D. Roosevelt. He speaks in glowing terms of FDR's ability to lift the nation out of the psychological depths of the depression by the sheer force of his personality. Rinehart (born in 1916) was young then, and he compared FDR's appeal to the youth of that era with John F. Kennedy's appeal to a later generation. Richard cast his first presidential vote for Roosevelt in 1940. He registered at that time as a Democrat. By 1944, however, he registered as an independent, voting for Thomas E. Dewey, and he became a Republican around 1950. Asked to explain the change, he recounted a growing dissatisfaction with Roosevelt based on the third- and fourth-term candidacies, his obvious ill health in 1944, and the disadvantages resulting from the agreements Roosevelt negotiated at Yalta.

Richard: I guess somewhere along the line I kind of lost faith in the man, and then after the war, when we got back, you might say Mr. Truman kind of irritated me. But anyway I was no longer a Democrat. I was already a formulated Republican—because of leanings back in Mr. Dewey's time, or earlier, I don't know. But there was a falling out, I think, with the Roosevelt philosophy of deficit spending at that time. And then, when not registering one way or the other, it occurred to me, I think on the first election, I couldn't vote in the primaries, that next time I voted I would register as a Republican.

Asked a moment later to describe the differences between the two parties, Rinehart replied that the most important difference in their attitudes is on the question of fiscal responsibility. The Republicans, he says, are more likely to produce a balanced budget, and this will produce a healthier economy, at least in the long run. Alice Rinehart, laughing at her husband, said, "I would never guess that you were ever a Democrat!"

For her part, Alice Rinehart first registered as an independent but gradually drifted toward the Republican party, and she has become a dedicated Republican during the last fifteen years as a result of working in Republican campaigns. Getting to know her fellow partisans, she feels that she agrees with their ideas.

Alice: I have felt that the Republican party has had the better candidates, or what I think is best.

In the standard voting studies, the Rineharts would now be labeled as "strong Republican identifiers."

Quentin Elliott first registered as a Republican, and he found the Republicanism of Charles Percy congenial when he lived in Illinois. In California, he quickly decided to be a Democrat, for he could not support the conservatives who led the California Republican party.

The McGees, the only "right-wing activists" interviewed in Ramona Heights, have worked in the very movements that give Orange County its reputation. Their change from being voters with no more than an average interest in politics into political activists has some of the marks of religious conversion. It is conversion to activism in the cause of a specially defined patriotism, not a simple change of party. In the service of that cause, Mary changed from Democrat to Republican in 1960; they both changed to American Independent in 1968 to get George Wallace on to the California ballot; they changed back to Republican for the 1970 primary, but changed once more to the AIP to support John Schmitz in 1972.

Mary McGee explained that she originally became a Democrat because of her father's powerful example. He was a mechanical engineer who worked all his life for various large organizations (an affluent technocrat). As an Irish Catholic, he had always been devoted to the party of Al Smith, and this identification was reinforced during the depression. After being unemployed for many months, he found work on a succession of projects administered by the WPA (Works Progress Administration, a New Deal agency). His admiration for Franklin D. Roosevelt was undiminished until the early 1960s when, Mary claims, he began to understand the magnitude of FDR's concessions to communism.

Mary's own rejection of the Democratic party began during the presidential campaign of 1960, when she saw some youths at a campaign rally "insult the American flag." She complained to party officials, but the complaints were never acted upon. (This was at a time when Frank and Mary were beginning to attend Birch Society meetings, Schmitz's class on the communist menace, and talks by a priest on the nature of communism.) Her experience at the campaign rally acted as the catalyst for her conversion.

Mary: That was the great eye-opener into politics, and I began to become very interested in what was going on and why it was going on. And which ended in my reregistration.

Frank McGee also adopted the partisan faith of his parents, for reasons that remain obscure to him.

Frank: Well, I wasn't as much involved in politics then as I have been in the last ten years, and I was an automatic Republican and I don't know why.

He explained that his loyalty to the party was much greater then; the ten years of his involvement in politics have served to weaken his ties to any party. His political activity has been in the service of important causes, or of a specific candidate he knows and admires—particularly John Schmitz. Both Frank and Mary therefore think of themselves as independents who make their decisions without reference to party labels. However, the causes they have supported have been endorsed by conservative candidates in Republican primary elections and, like the Roybals, they know that their greatest voting influence within Orange County lies in the Republican primary contests.

The McGees' actions show a sophisticated understanding of the political process, as well as a willingness to dedicate considerable time and effort to political activity oriented toward specific goals, such as securing a ballot position for Wallace. Many would find fault with their goals and premises and argue that the world view of the John Birch Society is seriously flawed, if not irrational, but it is clear that they choose the political action most likely to advance their goals. At this level, then, their independence (or their registration in the Republican party when it suits their purposes) could be called "rational." To what extent may the same label be applied to the voting patterns of our other respondents?

THE LOOSENESS OF PARTY TIES

In their own minds, the voters of Ramona Heights do not make voting decisions haphazardly or at random; they regard voting as a conscious choice and a serious duty; and they are able to justify their decisions after the fact. In most cases, loyalty to one of the traditional parties is a significant, but not determining, factor. And party loyalty may take strange forms. The Johnsons remain registered Democrats but often vote Republican, perceiving Republican candidates in the past few years as providing the policies they feel best. Failure to change parties is justified (or rationalized) with the claim that the two major parties are quite alike, and that most voters are essentially nonpartisan in any case. The Roybals are registered as Republicans, in hopes of influencing the outcome of the Republican primary elections. When—as usually happens—the moderate candidates are defeated by conservatives in the primary, the Roybals vote Democratic in the general election. The Weekses identify themselves with the fiscal conservatism they perceive as a thread in Republican policies, but they declared their independence by voting against John Schmitz and Max Rafferty, conservative extremists they could not support. The Rineharts are also keen on fiscal conservatism, and Richard Rinehart cites that issue as his main reason for changing from Democratic to Republican registration twenty years ago. But they support Schmitz and Rafferty because of the qualities of courage and honesty they see in these candidates.

These voters, then, have reasons for voting the way they vote. If they change their party registration, it is for clearly perceived reasons; when —the more usual case—they retain their habitual party, they cite reasons for the continuation. None can be accused of blind partisanship, and all but Fletcher Barbera praise the independent voter's stance.

Not only do the voters of Ramona Heights praise independence, they practice it. Of the dozen families, only three are fairly unshakable in their partisanship. The Barberas and the Rineharts are dedicated Republicans, while the Pavels must count as habitual—but hardly unthinking —Democrats. Seven other couples—the Elliotts, Johnsons, Kaubs, Markuses, Porfilios, Roybals, and Weekses—have voted split tickets, and/or voted in the general election against the party in which they are registered, as well as praising independence as a quality. Arnold Garcia and the McGees were prepared to abandon their traditional parties to follow the banner of George Wallace, but Garcia finally decided that he would waste his vote in doing so, and voted for Nixon in 1968.

Far from being ill-informed, inattentive, or unconcerned, these independent voters are marked by a relatively high level of information and concern, which matches their higher economic and educational levels. According to Walter Dean Burnham, there is a "new independent" American voter, and his number is growing. The new independent has higher status, more education, and greater sophistication than the "old" independent. Burnham cites poll data concerning changes in party identification over a period of years to support his findings.[19] Dramatic support for his thesis was published in a 1971 Gallup Poll, which compared party identification to occupational level; for the first time in the history of the Gallup organization, more voters categorized as "professional and business" listed themselves as Democrats than as Republicans.

[19]Burnham, *Critical Elections*, pp. 120–132. The increase in "decline to state" registrations in Orange County is congruent with Burnham's findings. The figures are summarized in chapter one, n. 1.

Change in Party Identification, 1940–1971

OCCUPATION	1940			1971		
	REPUBLICAN	DEMOCRAT	INDEPENDENT	REPUBLICAN	DEMOCRAT	INDEPENDENT
Professional and Business	47%	29%	24%	31%	34%	35%
Clerical and Sales	37	41	22	25	43	32
Manual Workers	32	50	18	19	48	33

Gallup Poll, *San Francisco Chronicle*, October 18, 1971.

More remarkable than the decline of Republican support is the failure of Democratic identifications to increase by a comparable magnitude. In the thirty-year period, those declaring themselves to be "independent" have increased by 11 percent in the highest stratum, by 10 percent in the middle, and by 15 percent in the lowest. Both the Republican and Democratic parties are becoming less relevant, no longer able to function as vehicles for change in behalf of the people, no longer adequately serving the collectively powerless in their contest with the centers of power and special privilege.

INDEPENDENCE: PRELUDE TO DISASTER?

The growing independence of voters like those in Ramona Heights is therefore of crucial significance for the health of the political order. And their competence as citizens is important. We may readily conclude that the Elliotts, Roybals, and Weekses of our sample indeed perceive that the California—and Orange County—Republican party cannot meet the challenges of the modern era. But we must ask more of our data. What will these citizens—and millions like them—seek from national political leaders? Can "rational independence" become an asset to the political system, or must it be only a prelude to disaster?

V. O. Key, Jr., the late Harvard political scientist, studied opinion data generated during presidential elections from 1936 through 1960. He divided voters into three categories: switchers, who voted against their habitual party; standpatters, who voted with their habitual party; and new voters, who had no habitual party. He found, in each presidential campaign, that the issue attitudes of the switchers were congruent with those held by voters in the party the switchers were joining; the issue attitudes of the standpatters were congruent with the attitude of voters in their habitual party; and the attitudes of the new voters were congruent with those held by the voters in whatever party they joined. Professor Key concluded:

In American presidential campaigns of recent decades the portrait that emerges is not one of an electorate straitjacketed by social determinants or moved by subconscious urges. . . . It is rather one of an electorate moved by concern about central and relevant concerns of public policy, or governmental performance, and of executive personality.[20]

Basing our judgment on their own words, we can say that the voters of Ramona Heights fit Key's description. There are, of course, two important differences: our sample is not statistically significant, so it cannot be used to buttress generalizations about the entire electorate, without the kind of corollary support Key provides. Second, we reach this judgment on the basis of our respondents' views and voting on a full range of matters—national, state, and local—whereas Key's data was limited to presidential elections.

Finally, Key's judgment was based on the analysis of responses to questions posed in Gallup polls, and ours is based on depth interviews with a few voters.

It is possible that the strongest influences on voting and other political acts are social and psychological factors that are either buried so deep in the unconscious that voters do not indicate an awareness of them or are so much a part of their basic premises, their world view, that they are taken for granted and not consciously referred to. If this is true, is our case for "rational independence" thereby weakened?

No voter can exercise his rational powers (or his free will) in a vacuum. Limits are established by his past cultural and educational background, as well as by his present sources of information. Yet the microsample contains voters of similar status and experiences with sharply contrasting convictions. Quentin Elliott and Fletcher Barbera share a common social position (marginally upper class) and many common experiences (Ivy League education, work in technological industry, and Republican parents), yet their political attitudes and voting behavior show striking differences. The three Mexican-Americans of the microsample share similar childhood experiences in the *barrios* and presently live in the same affluent neighborhood. But their attitudes and behavior are markedly different.

Notions of causality derived from large samples are based on correlations which are tested mathematically to determine their significance and, therefore, their power to demonstrate that there is indeed an association between various characteristics of the population, such as

[20]V. O. Key, Jr., with the assistance of Milton Cummings, Jr., *The Responsible Electorate* (Cambridge, Mass.: Harvard University Press, Belknap Press, 1966), pp. 7–8.

religion and partisanship. But no correlations are perfect, and the relationship does not hold for every person in the sample. The search for understanding of the voters of Ramona Heights cannot ignore the possibility that they may be "straitjacketed by social determinants or moved by subconscious urges." Among other matters, we must pursue Frederick Dutton's casual assertion that "neo-agrarianism" and "personal strivings" constitute the essence of suburbanism.

CHAPTER FOUR

The Lessons of Work

It cannot be nothing to men how they spend all their working days. It is not really possible to treat the relations between men in their working day as though they did not affect their social relations.

—A. D. Lindsay[1]

"Now you could say, am I an engineer because I am conservative, or am I conservative because I'm an engineer? I think it's a little of both."

—Fletcher Barbera

IN RAMONA HEIGHTS, what is the impact of the way men spend "all their working days" on their attitudes toward the larger political order? Are any lessons they learn at work applied directly and immediately, or do they simply reinforce existing conceptions of society and how it does, or should, operate? The voters of Ramona Heights would probably answer the last question, "a little of both." They mention the political implications of work experiences, special knowledge gained on the job, or in training for the job. Some feel that specific policy attitudes have been modified; others feel that the impact is more general, verging on the philosophical.

[1]A. D. Lindsay, *The Modern Democratic State* (New York: Oxford University Press, 1962), p. 186.

Dr. Kenneth Kaub feels that his political attitudes were well established before he began working at the state hospital, but his work there has liberalized his opinions about social welfare, simply because he is now more aware of human needs in American society.

Kenneth: Perhaps I'm more liberal on the welfare and mental hygiene aspect because I see so many people that need help from some agency, whether it's the Department of Welfare or some vocational rehabilitation. I'm sure I see more of that than I would have if I hadn't been working in a mental hospital.

Asked to comment in more general terms, Kenneth noted that the modern trend in psychiatry is toward more liberal treatment of patients in such matters as grounds privileges and home visits, and that this relaxation of the traditional rules seems to have a favorable effect on the patients. This implies that modern permissiveness may not be a disaster. Asked to think of any insights he had gained at the hospital that might be transferred directly to the political realm, Kenneth replied with a laugh:

Kenneth: Well, I know we don't have all the mentally ill in the hospital. And I'm sure some of them are in politics.

Quentin Elliott mentioned special knowledge gained in his former industrial position that increased his awareness of ecological issues, as well as convincing him that more stringent governmental regulations are required.

Quentin: Having been in business, I know that there are factories and plants that are burning scrap metal at night, that can't be burned during the day because that scrap metal has colored paint on it, which is a much greater contaminant in the air than unfinished metal. And I won't name any names, I've already said too much probably, but this is done at night, see, when the inspectors aren't around. . . . Government could be doing far more, and they won't do it unless people like ourselves holler. And I'm not hollering yet. So I accept responsibility for what's not being done.

Arnold Garcia also cited business experience as the basis for his opinion on specific policies. He is a small businessman, proprietor of an auto parts store, and a landlord with major rental properties. In 1970, his main concern was the state of the economy, and he was particularly worried about inflation. He stated that the only possible remedy would be a wage and price freeze. He stated that he knew of many businesses that had raised their prices artificially (not in response to lessened supply or increased demand) to put them at a level the business would consider satisfactory if the freeze should be imposed. But the freeze had not yet come, and inflation continued on a new spiral. Arnold made this statement nearly a full year before the imposition of Phase I controls by the Nixon Administration. In 1972, he said that the freeze came too late and did not last long enough. He was displeased with Nixon's management of the economy but happy with the overtures to Russia and China. Without George Wallace on the ticket, he had decided to support Nixon's reelection. He knew nothing of John Schmitz's candidacy on the American Independent party ticket.

A more striking example of the direct impact of work experience upon opinion on a specific issue was provided by Fletcher Barbera and John Weeks, when asked in 1970 if additional antiballistic missiles (ABMs) should be deployed, as the Nixon Administration had begun doing, to protect the Minuteman missile silos. As engineers, neither thought the ABM was practical. Barbera went on to express confidence that the threat of retaliation would prevent both sides from initiating an exchange of missiles, making the ABM unnecessary. Maureen Barbera interjected that he should not talk of just two sides, but should include Red China. Fletcher replied that the retaliation argument was also relevant to China. "I don't think," he said, "that the people who are running Red China are madmen." Fletcher was delighted, six months later, when the rapprochement with China began.

When John Weeks was asked about deployment of the ABM, he grinned.

John: That's an unfair question, because I may have to work on that project. . . . Well, something that I have said all along is that it is about as good as a fly swatter against an air force. . . . From a practical standpoint, I don't think it would do anything except perhaps give a segment of the population a little peace of mind. . . . But the ABM to me is good from the psychological standpoint, and it's good from the government spending standpoint. This to me is a make-work kind of thing. Now, I'm not saying that it is felt this way in the government, because it isn't. They think, indeed, that it will do a very fine, limited job. . . . But I don't think the ABM is all that hot.

Like Barbera, Weeks felt that the threat of retaliation would deter both Russia and China from initiating a nuclear attack. He also felt that the Chinese leaders are not stupid. Weeks was pleased with the arms limitation talks then in progress. He discussed the safeguards built into the American system to prevent an accidental launch, expressing certainty that Russia and China had developed similar precautions, so that the chance of an accidental launch would be statistically highly unlikely. He finished on an emotional note.

John: If they did it, you can scratch one world, you know. It's just going to be all over, it's just a matter of hours, it's just *all over.* You know, the holocaust would just be unbelievable, what they can do. I've seen some of the tests that have been conducted, and you know, it makes no sense for either side. [Pause.] Well, it would take a complete group of idiots, and I don't think you can collect that many idiots together anywhere in the world.

If John Wesley Weeks, moderate Republican (who views the ABM as a public works project), Methodist, native Kansan transplanted to Ramona Heights, can speak for his colleagues, we may conclude that aerospace engineers are not insensitive to the consequences of their work. Yet, if such men become completely disenchanted with their labors, unable to bear the moral burden of contributing to the national capacity for irrational destruction, what are they to do? In a technological society, the specialist's maximum status and reward come from practicing his specialty. In a stagnant economy, the cost of quitting one's job may be not finding another one. As we shall see, one escape from dilemmas like these is to suggest that the coming generation not face them. Piotr Pavel counseled all young men to avoid the engineering profession, and expressed gratitude that his sons are entering other fields; John Weeks hoped that his son would avoid engineering.

Weeks and Pavel have viewed the relationship of their profession to society, and the stresses placed upon its individual practitioners by the organization of their profession. Both are genial and hospitable men; discussing this question, they express uncharacteristic bitterness and insecurity. It is not a generalized feeling; they are well aware of the causes of their frustration. At the close of this chapter, we shall explore more fully what may be called a crisis of individualism—the traditional American faith—among American engineers, particularly among engineers who have served the goals of the so-called military-industrial complex.[2] For the moment, let us observe that the work life of Ramona Heights voters indeed has implications that are far reaching; some re-

[2]The late President Eisenhower used this phrase in his farewell address; the classic case for its existence and influence is put by C. Wright Mills in *The Power Elite* (New York: Oxford University Press, 1957). The extent, or even the existence, of such an entity is a question beyond the scope of the present study. But the phrase has meaning and content for Ramona Heights voters, particularly including the affluent technocrats: Elliott, Pavel, Weeks, Barbera, Rinehart, Porfilio, and Johnson.

spondents are aware of these implications and attempt to explain them; in other cases, they are hardly even perceived.

> What men learn as they work for a living reaches far beyond their occupational interests; they learn a style of life, a manner of dealing with others, a habit of subordination or assertion. . . .
>
> Democracy, in a unique way, requires the ordinary man to develop skills of judgment and criticism of leaders. These must be responsible, moderate, sensible; that is, they must fall within the bounds of a commonly accepted framework of values. Such skills . . . come only with practice and experience. . . . Men must respect their own judgment before they exercise initiative or agree to share power.[3]

In his study of fifteen working-class residents of a New Haven housing project, Robert E. Lane found that the Marxist stereotype of the alienated factory worker was not particularly applicable; most of his workers were not the simple "machine tenders" portrayed by the Marxists and in Charlie Chaplin's movie *Modern Times;* he concluded that, by and large, work life does teach lessons of some value for a democratic society.[4] But these lessons are learned largely at an unconscious or subconscious level.

The breadwinners of Ramona Heights articulate attitudes toward their work using abstract concepts, including those of the social sciences. The most obvious example is Quentin Elliott, who abandoned the corporate life at age thirty-eight to begin a teaching career. His corporate job did not provide the satisfactions he wanted. Both Quentin and Deborah recognized that the corporation provided them a kind of maternal care—an established career pattern, help with moving to new places, and assurance that they would not suffer financially when having to sell a home and move on. They spoke of Quentin's former company as a kind of "movable womb." Over a period of years, however, Quentin grew unhappy with the exploitative aspects of his work as an industrial salesman, and he sought work that would permit him to establish a "giving relationship with people." In the middle 1960s, he investigated schools of social work. But then his company offered him a position in personnel, which he viewed as "industrial social work." It seemed to promise many of the satisfactions he missed, without a sacrifice of income. Still later, his superiors decided that he was better in sales (perhaps because, as a personnel manager, he was too empathetic with

---

[3]Robert E. Lane, *Political Ideology,* paper ed. (New York: Macmillan, Free Press, 1962), pp. 228–231.
[4]*Ibid.,* pp. 246–249.

employees and did not keep company interests foremost in his mind) and offered him the position of sales manager for Southern California, which was a kind of testing ground before moving into the higher echelons of company management.

Quentin: It is quite easy to overextend oneself in commercial selling in the USA today. The profit and tonnage drives being what they are, there are long and hard hours, which mean that when you arrive back, if you didn't like what you were doing in the first place, plus the strain of the job, it doesn't leave much vitality for you and your family. . . . I didn't see great rewards for me if I was able to succeed and move up in the company into higher management. . . . I felt that the status and prestige and so on, the things that people work for in addition to the money, didn't have enough appeal to me.

Fearing that he would be unwilling to change his career after passing the "psychological barrier" of age forty, Quentin became a teacher in 1970. One reason for the change, or at least a reason used to justify the decision after it was made, was the family's need "to put down roots." The Elliotts felt that the pressures of Quentin's former job were the wrong kind of pressures, and that the lessons of his work were the wrong lessons. His own health, and that of the family, would be better conserved if he became a teacher, working closer to Ramona Heights, although for a lesser salary. Their decision was easier to reach because they had $45,000 available to pay off the mortgage on their house, which eliminated a drain on their newly reduced income.

For Jan and Eldene Markus, the lessons of work have had a direct political meaning. He was an electrician, she was a seamstress, and both belonged to unions. They did not view their union membership uncritically; Eldene remembered that the leadership and much of the membership of the International Ladies Garment Workers Union were Jewish, and that the union sent large sums of relief money to Israel without a membership vote, a practice she felt was at least questionable. She was pleased that the ILGWU leadership eliminated communists who were seeking influence in the union. The Markuses feel the union movement has benefited the nation, but Jan volunteered his opinion that nobody is worth the wages electricians now earn in Orange County.

During Jan's career as an electrician, electronic technology burgeoned, equipment became increasingly complex, and greater technical knowledge was required. Jan took night school and correspondence courses to keep abreast of change, but he felt he really needed formal training in electrical engineering. Jan cited this experience as a major reason why he and Eldene have always supported education through such actions as voting for school bond issues. Their hopes for a better future society are pinned to education.

The Markuses feel that the Democratic party is most likely to protect the interests of working people. They admit that their savings, plus the very fact of living in Ramona Heights, might permit them to claim membership in the middle class. But they identify with "working people" and always will.

John Weeks and Fletcher Barbera both feel that their attitudes toward politics, particularly including social change, are influenced by their training as engineers. Yet those attitudes, and the voting behavior that follows, are rather different.

Fletcher: Being an engineer is a conservative profession. . . . Now, you could say, am I an engineer because I am conservative, or am I conservative because I'm an engineer? I think it's a little of both. Engineers are taught that, when you build a building, if you err any way, err on the side of safety. And check out your design thoroughly before you build too many of them. And a lot of principles which you could call kind of conservative in their philosophical overtones . . . it gets back to what is the real definition of a conservative, and the conservative is the guy who says, "Until I'm pretty damn sure that the change is positive, I won't make it."

If Barbera can be believed, then, engineers are naturally opposed to social experimentation, for it can have unforeseen consequences. But John Weeks expressed a different attitude. Because engineers work in the area of technological advance, he said, they are accustomed to the need for "updating a system," and they are, as a result, ready to accept social change. Or, if he should not presume to speak for other engineers, this at least summarizes his own attitude.

John: The type of conservative I am is one who believes in progress. I believe in making changes, progressively as we go along, to keep the society up to date, the systems up to date. I suppose I am biased because I come from a technological field where we are always advancing, and making changes, and you see a need for them, you must face them, and you make certain changes.

Because these attitudes are different, it is tempting to claim that engineering has had no conscious political impact on these two men; they only use their job experience to justify opinions formulated in response to other influences. But, while both are aerospace/electronics engineers, their jobs are not alike. Weeks is a research engineer in a very large firm, responsible for examining assigned problems, often farming out the drudgery of specific calculations to subordinates. He says that he will always remain simply an engineer, that management holds no attractions whatever. Barbera, on the other hand, was in 1970 the vice president of a small firm, specifically charged with assuring that the firm made a profit. He was responsible for curbing the imaginations of the engineer-salesmen who offered custom designs to clients. Fletcher had to be sure that their designs, no matter how elegant, could still be built at a profit. He said that many engineers have the temperament of artists and are not motivated by considerations of profit, and that the president of his company was such a man. Fletcher quit that job in 1971.

Determining the impact of work experiences upon their political attitudes is fairly complex. Barbera says that a leading attribute of his conservatism is financial: he and his wife do not buy much on credit; he was temperamentally suited to his 1970 job as watchdog of the company's profit. Barbera is a habitual conservative Republican in his voting behavior. Weeks, as a research engineer, is something of a hand maiden of technological change; and he refuses to support Republican candidates whom he perceives as opposing all social change. There is a congruence between work responsibility and political attitude, but it would be difficult to establish a causal relationship, at least on the basis of the influences perceived by the respondents themselves.

Hidden Costs of the Organizational Life

If social criticism of the last century is an appropriate guide, we have no reason to expect that individuals will be completely aware of the effects of their work experience on their lives, attitudes, and personalities. The concept of alienation, a recurrent theme in the metaphysical writings of Hegel, was developed by Karl Marx into a key concept for the analysis of industrial society.[5] Since then, political commentators writing in the Marxist tradition have held that the relationship of man to his work is crucial; that this relationship determines much of the structure of society; and that it further determines the individual's sense

[5]For an account of Hegel's use of the term, its adoption and modification by Marx, and its modern formulation by Erich Fromm, see John H. Schaar, *Escape from Authority* (New York: Basic Books, 1961), pp. 172–192.

of wholeness and worth, his very mental health. But the laborer does not necessarily understand the anxieties produced by his estrangement from the product of his labor. Industrial society has robbed him of meaning and purpose, but he does not even comprehend the terrible human cost required to increase commodity production. According to the Marxist critics,[6] man in modern society has internalized false values. He is never able to fulfill his native abilities, but must live as the market requires. Writing amidst the horrors of early capitalism, Marx did not have to search far to find examples of the exploitation of human beings and their reduction to the status of commodities. Since the phenomenon of alienation does not seem to have decreased, in spite of an increase in the working man's material welfare, contemporary writers claim that the crippling of man by society is as real as ever, but far more subtle. According to C. Wright Mills:

> Under the system of explicit authority, in the round, solid nineteenth century, the victim knew he was being victimized, the misery and discontent of the powerless were explicit. In the amorphous twentieth-century world, where manipulation replaces authority, the victim does not recognize his status. . . . Many whips are inside men, who do not know how they got there, or indeed that they are there. In the movement from authority to manipulation, power shifts from the visible to the invisible, from the known to the anonymous. And with rising material standards, exploitation becomes less material and more psychological.[7]

If people are indeed imprisoned by society, particularly by the large, impersonal organizations in which they spend their working days, but are hardly aware of their imprisonment, the implications for their political actions are very great indeed.[8] However, the presence of an *unconscious* sense of powerlessness in people may be hard to detect, just by talking to them.

Some interviews with the voters of Ramona Heights do contain hints of powerlessness or alienation. Furthermore, standard objective questions have been developed for the purpose of detecting these feelings, even when they are not directly expressed. One set of questions, which has been used extensively in opinion research with large national sam-

---

[6]For one account of this criticism, see John Plamenatz, *Man and Society*, (New York: McGraw-Hill, 1963), vol. 2, pp. 375–378, 404–407.

[7]C. Wright Mills, *White Collar* (New York: Oxford University Press, 1956), p. 110.

[8]For a description of voters as "alienated automatons" who are powerless at work and powerless in politics, but may be unaware of this powerlessness, see Erich Fromm, *The Sane Society* (New York: Fawcett, 1969; first published 1955), pp. 160–170.

ples, is the "political efficacy scale," first devised by the University of Michigan Survey Research Center when studying the 1952 election.[9] A version of this scale was mingled with forty-six other items on a questionnaire completed by the Ramona Heights voters.

The Survey Research Center authors found, not surprisingly, that a greater sense of political efficacy meant a voter would be more likely to go to the polls; the more years of education completed, the higher the sense of efficacy—as a result of beliefs gained in the educational experience about the way the democratic process operates. College graduates tend to vote, even when they seem indifferent or cynical about the outcome, presumably because of greater pressures to vote in the upper social milieus.[10]

Even though the members of the Ramona Heights microsample live in the same neighborhood and share relatively high educational and economic status, as individuals they vary greatly in their position on the scale of perceived political efficacy, from "perfect" (20 of 20 possible), scored by Frank McGee, to 9 of 20 possible, scored by Piotr Pavel. (The "score" is made up of values assigned to each of four possible responses to five different questions.) These data may be used to substantiate clues picked up in the transcripts themselves, and it may be noted that they are roughly congruent with behavior. Frank McGee is the political activist, because he was out of the country, Piotr Pavel did not vote in the 1970 election.

How is the sense of political effectiveness related to the experiences of work? Marx's view was based on the image of the assembly-line factory worker who, in serving the needs of a machine, is himself reduced to a machine. This image is not obviously applicable to the affluent technocrats of Ramona Heights. According to the British political theorist A. D. Lindsay:

> The factory worker cannot sell his labour without at the same time selling to his employer the right to govern and discipline him in the factory. It is this fact which makes men talk of wage slavery. Many professional workers find such expressions hard to understand. A professional worker normally sells his services without selling to any one else the right to order him about as he is performing them.[11]

[9]A. Campbell, G. Gurin, and W. E. Miller, *The Voter Decides* (Evanston, Ill.: Row, Peterson, 1954).
[10]A. Campbell et al., *The American Voter*, abr. ed. (New York: Wiley, 1964), pp. 252–254.
[11]Lindsay, *Modern Democratic State*, p. 183.

But Lindsay's view is also archaic. The worker in the Ford Motor Company is unlikely ever to meet, much less receive instructions from, his employer personified, Henry Ford II. He works for a bureaucratic, capitalistic organization. His dealings with it are mediated by the grievance procedures of his own bureaucracy, the United Automobile Workers, and relations between these two bureaucracies are based on a written contract.

The affluent technocrat may be in a more vulnerable position. He also works for a bureaucratic organization—Elliott's former rubber company or present school district, Kaub's state hospital, the aerospace firms of Pavel and Weeks, the power company of Rinehart. But, as a professional, he is not a union member. He is likely to disdain union membership as beneath his professional dignity. The technocrat deals as a lone individual with the employing bureaucracy; he is an organization man.

The residents of Ramona Heights show a variety of reactions to the values and pressures of the organizations for which they work, and these reactions influence their political attitudes. How can this influence be defined and explained?

Three Patterns of Adaptation

The explanation begins with a realization that the role of a professional in a complex, modern organization is not autonomous. He may feel so surrounded by constraints that his job seems little different from that of an assembly-line worker.

> Even at professional and managerial levels, technological change has made work more like factory production. . . . Alienation from work that has become routinized, yet demands manipulation in the "personality market," is visible in both [blue-collar and white-collar] groups.[12]

It was this very "personality market" manipulation of others in his role as salesman that led Quentin Elliott to reject his role in the corporation. He spent his working days attempting to sell himself as a prelude to selling his product, and this created a false personality that he then carried home to his family. He realized that, as a teacher, he would need to modify his "professional nice guy" approach and attempt to exhibit some firm authority. (His first classes found ingenious ways to exploit Quentin's inexperience. At one point they even persuaded him to buy ice cream bars for everybody during recess.)

[12]Robert Presthus, *The Organizational Society* (New York: Knopf, 1962), p. 219.

In selling his services to the organization, the professional does sell to others the right to "order him about" as he is performing them. Bureaucratic organizations are operated by a management hierarchy according to a set of rules. Human relationships are structured in a way that creates a potential conflict between authority based on position and authority based on skill.[13] How do the members of such organizations react when they become aware of the pressures of organizational life, with the attendant threats to personal autonomy and self-esteem? The technocrats of Ramona Heights have reacted in three distinctive ways. Richard Rinehart and Arthur Roybal have adapted to organizational pressures by internalizing some of the values of their particular bureaucracies, somewhat on the pattern of Whyte's organization men. Ralph Porfilio has compartmentalized his life, treating his job as nothing but a forty-hours-a-week inconvenience needed to finance the pleasures of his "real" life, which is a life of leisure. The remaining technocrats of the microsample —Barbera, Elliott, Kanb, Pavel, and Weeks—are unable to make either of these clear-cut adjustments. They feel the psychic costs of organizational life, but they want to maintain an achieved standard of living, and work they can take some pride in is important to them. Therefore, when they find that they cannot respect the rules and hierarchies governing their work lives, they attempt to change the circumstances of their employment.[14] (Four heads of families are not accounted for, because they do not work in large, bureaucratic structures. Jan Markus is retired. Frank McGee is a salesman in a five-man real estate office. Arnold Garcia and Harry Johnson own independent small businesses; rather than adapt to imposed bureaucratic rules, they write new rules.)

The life histories of these few voters suggest a modest hypothesis: people who find meaning in their work, who accept its rules, respect both their superiors and subordinates, and feel that their own work role is appreciated, tend to view the political system as an ordered system in which they can exert meaningful influence. A satisfactory adaptation to the pressures of organizational work life will contribute to a sense of political efficacy, and the sense of political efficacy will make the individual more likely to participate in political activity.

The evidence begins with Richard Rinehart, who has worked for the

---

[13] *Ibid.*, p. 11.

[14] These modes of adaptation are roughly equivalent to the three personality types which Presthus labels as "upward-mobiles," "indifferents," and "ambivalents." Presthus sees the indifferents as the uncommitted, even alienated, majority who are trapped in their jobs and can only bolster their sense of self-esteem through outside activities. But Presthus's analysis lacks the time dimension required to recognize the efforts of unhappy workers to change their lives.

power company for more than twenty years. His present position is comfortable, and he feels certain he will continue to advance at a slow but steady pace. Unlike the organization men who strive upwards in novels and movies, he has no sense of exhilaration through conquest. This is due both to his rather placid outlook on life and to the fact that he works for a public utility company which has no competition. Its business (and the opportunities for advancement of its employees) grows as steadily as the population of Southern California. One can imagine different firms, whose survival depends on technological breakthroughs, or the winning of contracts in fierce competition with other firms, that would treat their employees much more ruthlessly—and the aerospace firms indeed treat their engineers more ruthlessly, while paying them better.

Richard Rinehart, whose 1969 salary of $19,000 per year placed him just below the average for our microsample, certainly does not feel exploited by his employer. He plans to work there until sixty-five, the compulsory retirement age. Retirement is optional at sixty, but he doesn't expect he can afford to retire then, or that he would even want to. He described his job:

Richard: I think I like it because it's very challenging. When I get down there, there is always something new, or something more that needs doing. I can never finish in a day. . . . I think the big part of this job is that you recognize that you are doing something that is vitally needed in the community, and you can see that you have made a contribution to the growth of the community.

Rinehart's position is managerial; although he tries to keep up with relevant technological advances, his engineering training is not utilized daily. He says he may get out his slide rule once a month to check a subordinate's calculations. He has been an interested participant in management training courses provided by the company. One topic he studied was the typology of managerial organizations.

Richard: Well, there are two theories, and I guess you've heard of the X and Y theory of how you operate a business, and the military is the X theory pretty much, and it comes from decisions made on top and then communicated downward. The Y theory is the one that has come into vogue more lately, and there are some companies that try this, more or less.

He explained that, in the Y theory, members of the organization supply motivation from within themselves, for they are encouraged to participate (or at least feel they participate) in decision-making and goal-setting. His company has been operating for about two years on a variant of the Y theory, "management by objectives," in which managers meet with superiors and subordinates to determine their objectives. And it seems to be working. But Rinehart does not feel that a "pure" Y theory would be practical in most organizations.

Richard: Now, I don't know if you can ever get to a full, what you'd call a democratic, type organization like this. I have heard and seen and read of examples where they have gotten some fantastic things done this way, particularly in R and D [research and development] firms, or even in regular manufacturing firms where they have a profit sharing motive, and this kind of thing. But, in the ideal firm, I believe that it would be a blend of the X and the Y. If you're going to make a profit, you may have to recognize that not everybody in your company is really that involved in making a decision.

Most of them would like to feel that they are being recognized, and are making a contribution, and that further they have something to contribute, and I firmly believe that in my organization [the department he heads] it works this way.

What are the techniques of "management by objective"?

Richard: The underlying principle is that the subordinate cares in determining his own objectives, and that in turn the boss communicates what support he's going to give and whether or not he approves of it. . . . The idea is that it gives the subordinate a chance in managing his part of the business. But it's also a communication device so that each one knows what the limitations are on both sides.

Pressed to say whether there were disadvantages to working in such a large organization, Rinehart replied that the size of an organization depends on its tasks, and it is not possible to deliver electric power to Southern California with a small, intimate firm. Pressed further to say what he likes least about his job, he confessed that he feels that he doesn't control as much as he could wish, that his own contribution to the overall organizational purpose is relatively modest. Some days, he feels "frustration at not being able to do more towards achieving the goals we've set up."

Richard Rinehart clearly identifies with the grand purpose of the bureaucratic organization for which he works; the electric power company supplies a vital service to the community. Far from finding his work routinized, he enjoys the challenge presented by "something new" nearly every day.

Rinehart's company employs the currently accepted theories of busi-

ness administration, which are designed to overcome the psychic alienation from the job which occurs in rigid, authoritarian enterprises.[15] The
Marxist, who views labor in any capitalist enterprise as alienated by
definition, would dismiss "management by objectives" as yet another
example of "false consciousness" instilled by the work relationship.
Richard Rinehart has not developed a sense of powerlessness, either
conscious or unconscious. As for politics, he is a dedicated voter who
methodically confers with his wife and marks a joint sample ballot, so
that none of their votes will cancel each other. He participates in party
work to a limited extent and supports his wife's more time-consuming
participation. He scored 19 out of 20 possible on the political efficacy
scale, a score identical to his wife's (They did not confer on their
answers).

We can hardly claim that Rinehart's sense of political efficacy results
from his adaptation to the pressures of organizational life. Feelings of
efficacy were established by his educational experience and the general
socialization process, both childhood and adult. But his work relationship has not destroyed that sense; rather, the lesson of work has been
to reinforce it.

Arthur Roybal has made a similar adjustment to the pressures of
bureaucratic work. Roybal recalled two points in his occupational history
that changed his life: his service in the navy in the closing years of World
War II, and his attending a federally financed training program for
school administrators. Both, of course, were points at which he was in
contact with operations of the national government. Since both were
positive experiences, they may have stimulated a generalized positive
feeling towards government. However, this did not result in a compelling sense of need for political involvement, beyond seeing voting as a
duty.

Arthur served as a pharmacist's mate in the navy, and then went to
college on the GI bill, initially intending to complete premedical studies
and go on to medical school. But, becoming engaged to Tina, and
feeling delayed by the war years, he abandoned that ambition and turned
to education. The change seemed natural because of his long-standing
love for athletics. He moved easily into teaching academic subjects,

[15]See Douglas McGregor, *The Human Side of Enterprise* (New York: McGraw-Hill,
1960). McGregor's typologies and "management by objectives" are discussed in Richard
Todd, "Notes on Corporate Man," 228 *Atlantic* 4 (October, 1971), pp. 88–89. Todd
points out that these essentially manipulative techniques have little impact on unionized
workers but are very important for "management's relations with itself."

combined with coaching high school football and baseball, and worked in three different high schools over fourteen years. He then became the director of athletics for a school district of substantial size, his first taste of administration. Unification of that district with an even bigger one led him to accept an administrative assignment that was not related to athletics. This, in turn, brought him to the attention of the administrators of the federal training program. He described that program in glowing terms:

Arthur: Each district was to select certain numbers of candidates for participating in this program. Seventy-five from Southern California, and twenty-five from Northern California, were selected, and I was one of the hundred. And I would say that was the most significant event that ever occurred to me, because I received an education that no university or college could ever grant. We had specialists from the University of Michigan, Ohio State, and USC. . . . We had specialists from private industry, like Rand Corporation and TRW Systems Analysts, using the systems approach to educational management. Anyway, I think that that had a profound effect on my outlook on education, and, as a result, I gained quite a bit from it.

Participation in this program brought him to the attention of the county school administration, and he is now one of three assistant superintendents, with responsibilities for the development of new programs and curricula. The job is a challenge, and his predecessor was a remarkable man whose record will be hard to equal, but Roybal finds the job both stimulating and fulfilling.

Arthur: I don't think I've repaid education for what I got out of it yet. I hope to some day.

Like Rinehart, Roybal believes in the social utility of his occupation —providing a needed service for society. He is comfortable with his role in the bureaucratic hierarchy, and he feels a sense of permanence and security. The county office of schools is comparable to Rinehart's public utility company in that both are monopolies (presumably regulated in the public interest) and are not subject to the sudden reversals of fortune that may happen to organizations that compete in a free market. Again like Rinehart, Roybal has a smaller salary but a greater sense of security than his neighbors who are aerospace engineers. Roybal's training in the systems approach to educational management may be comparable to Rinehart's training in "management by objectives," and the sense of holding a significant place in the management of their respective bureaucracies could translate into the sense of political efficacy. But the objective measurement of Roybal's political efficacy is not available. As an educator with considerable experience in attitude testing, he was quite familiar with the kind of exercise he was asked to complete, and he felt that it constituted an unwarranted intrusion upon his privacy. He returned the test only partly completed, with objections to the wording of some items written in.

In politics, Arthur Roybal registers as a Republican and votes for the liberal candidates in the Republican primaries. When his candidates are defeated in the primaries, he votes Democratic in the general election. In the congressional elections, his Democratic candidates are also defeated, but this is not always the case on the state or national level. In 1970, for example, the Roybals supported Norton Simon against incumbent Senator George Murphy in the Republican primary, then voted for the Democrat, John Tunney, in the general election. This voting pattern indicates both sophisticated knowledge of the political process and some sense of political efficacy. We can hardly claim that Arthur's work experience was the only source of this efficacious feeling, but we may observe that his work experiences have not crippled it.

Ralph Porfilio is the only member of the microsample who has completely failed to internalize bureaucratic values. He seeks his personal fulfillment elsewhere, and separates his work life from his "real" life.[16] Psychologist Kenneth Keniston writes that such men turn their backs on careerism and opt for familism. Yet neither work nor family life (as they exist in modern America) is likely to provide an "organizing principle" that will assure healthy wholeness for an individual life.[17]

Ralph designs and equips food processing plants for a large California conglomerate. When asked whether he likes his job, Ralph replies simply, "It's a job." Asked specifically whether he regards his position as a source of satisfaction in itself, or whether its main importance is as a source of income, he answers:

Ralph: Oh, I find it interesting at times and rather boring at times. I think it's like any other job, really.

But Ralph is unwilling to describe any work day at all; his occupation is simply not a matter that interests him very much as a topic of

[16]For a hyperbolic description of this frenzied hedonism—"a life oriented to leisure is a life oriented to death"—described as a tragedy of California living, see Kenneth Lamott, *Anti-California: Report from Our First Parafascist State* (Boston: Little, Brown, 1971), pp. 53–54.

[17]Kenneth Keniston, *The Uncommitted: Alienated Youth in American Society* (New York: Harcourt 1966), p. 268.

conversation. Asked to think about problems of decision-making and authority in his own organization, or in the ideal business enterprise, he can only conceive of bureaucracies that are operated on a rigid, hierarchical principle.

Ralph: All decisions are really revolved down to one individual, who is, of course, the chief operating officer of the company. They are all basically his responsibility, and he has to have capable people underneath him, but he is the ultimate responsible party. . . . It's gonna be that way, that's just the way it is, and there's no other way to do it.

Question: Well, if you could design the ideal place to work, what would you do? Would you want it to be your own enterprise, or would you be more happy as a specialist in a large organization?

Ralph: Oh, I think everybody would prefer making, or at least I would prefer making, my own decisions. [Pause.] But then, again, I wonder if I would really be happy with the responsibility, or the blame, so to speak, for those decisions.

This, then, is Ralph Porfilio at age thirty-four. A success, in conventional terms—steady job, a five-bedroom home valued at more than $50,000, five children, a wife who is active in social and community affairs. They enjoy the "good life" of Southern California, belonging to an expensive club that provides tennis, swimming, and a launching dock for their small sailboat. Both Ralph and Caroline were raised in Southern California and are glad they have returned to it.

But Ralph commutes ninety minutes a day to a job he doesn't enjoy. And he didn't enjoy his previous two jobs in the Midwest either. He is glad to have had the experience of living in a different part of the country; he feels that the family's outlook was broadened by the experience of travel. But the jobs themselves offered no particular reward.

What is the impact on Ralph Porfilio's political attitudes of his never having found a sense of mastery, fulfillment, or even particular meaning, in his work life? He scores 16 out of 20 on the scale of political efficacy —which places him at the midpoint of the Ramona Heights microsample. Registered as a Democrat, he frequently votes in the primary election, but he has few strong feelings about the candidates, and he is accused of registering as a Democrat in order to spite his mother, a dedicated Republican. In general elections, he is more likely to vote a straight Republican ticket than is his wife, who is registered as a Republican. In 1970, Ralph voted for Republican Senator George Murphy and Congressman John Schmitz. Caroline voted for Murphy's challenger, John Tunney, and declined to vote in the congressional contest, because of her aversion to Schmitz's right-wing affiliations. They tease each other about their partisan differences, but neither regards them as particularly important. Indeed, they do not seem to regard voting as terribly important. It is a duty they perform, rather than an opportunity they take to influence the course of events.

And events are out of control. Occasionally bored with his job, Ralph Porfilio is angered by events in the world. In 1970, he expressed resentment against the easy capitulation to pressure of companies who hire minority applicants, even when they are incompetent. He stated that aerospace engineers had nobody to blame but themselves for being out of work as their industry collapsed. He said that blacks and Mexican-Americans should spend less time articulating their ethnic consciousnesses and be more concerned with Americanism. He deplored the attitudes of young people, and he was driven to the edge of rage when he thought about the destruction of property during campus riots. He resented the power of labor unions, stating that labor would destroy the economy unless it could find a weapon other than the strike.

If Ralph is estranged from his job, he is hardly aware of it, but many of his political opinions indicate an estrangement from the larger society. His scores on the objective questionnaire placed him at or near the top of scales presumed to measure misanthropy, authoritarianism, and anomie. Such attitudes are detrimental to the proper functioning of democracy. They are not associated with the ideal, allegiant citizen characterized by a sense of his own self-worth and political efficacy.

Can we argue that Ralph's adaptation to the pressures of his work life —or, more accurately, his failure to recognize them—explains his more general estrangement from society, and his failure to develop strong feelings of political efficacy? No; we can only point out that the first trait is associated with the others. A suggestive clue is the fact that Ralph apparently uses his Democratic party registration as a kind of weapon of revenge against his Republican mother. One need not define the "rational integrated personality" with great precision to suggest that the ideal thirty-four-year-old citizen would not base his political party membership on such a need. Ralph and Caroline both treat this as a joke, but it may be a joke that hides a deeper embarrassment.

The third type of personality adaptation to the pressures of work life consists of the ambivalent inability to either accept or finally reject the bureacratic values. Those who adapt in this way are aware of the psychic costs of work in the bureaucracy, particularly resenting decisions made by virtue of position rather than knowledge, but they cannot give up the prestige and power (both related to the pay) that come with rising to higher positions on the bureaucratic ladder. The remainder of Ramona

Heights' affluent technocrats—Barbera, Elliott, Kaub, Pavel, and Weeks—may be described as being, or having been, within this category. Becoming aware of the costs of their organizational life, they have attempted to alter their work circumstances, usually by seeking employment in a different type of firm.

Upon graduation from college, Fletcher Barbera worked for two years as an electronics engineer for a large aircraft company. He then entered the executive training program of IBM. Although IBM's employee benefits were attractive—Fletcher described the company as "paternalistic"—he left it because he felt that his junior position in the gigantic hierarchy was insignificant. He felt he neither contributed much to the firm's goals nor played a part in establishing those goals, and was unlikely to do so for many years. Yet he felt that his training and skills qualified him for participation in such judgments. In such a large bureaucracy, decision-making power tends to accrue to position, rather than to competence. Fletcher had no particular disagreement with IBM policies. He had no feeling that men in the top positions were incompetent, but he did not even have access to information that would permit a careful judgment of their competence.

Fletcher next joined a smaller and newer company, formed, as were so many others, to ride the crest of the wave of demand for the applications of electronic technology. But he soon found himself in an even less comfortable position. Although his position was nearer the top, and he was provided with options to purchase company stock, he soon realized that the firm's policies were aimed at quick profit rather than long-term growth, in an attempt to exploit technological advances quickly, even at the cost of inadequate design. Unable in two and a half years to change this basic approach, he resigned from his position. He said that his ethical sense was offended—and that ethical practices in business eventually turn out to be the most profitable. And this company has since gone out of business.

Fletcher's next company, less than two years old, had twenty-five employees. In an industry dominated by giant IBM, it was little more than an embryo. Headed by a man in his late thirties who was something of an electronic engineering genius, the firm manufactured custom electronic equipment by assembling components manufactured by others. Fletcher was hired as vice president specifically to manage the financial side of the operation. He was able to bring the salesmen-engineers to heel and assure that most of the company's operations were on a profitable basis. But Fletcher could not always make his judgment prevail over that of his two fellow vice presidents, and the company's founder-president sometimes contracted for the fruits of his imagination at a price that did not guarantee the firm a profit.

Fletcher felt that, as creator and head of the company, the president was well within his rights to act as he did. All Fletcher's indoctrination into the teamwork mystique of the large bureaucracy was ineffectual; his conception of ideal business management is the same as that held by his great grandfather Fletcher, the New Bedford ship chandler. A business is in the sole hands of its proprietor; his decisions must rule, and employees either obey or resign. When Fletcher's disagreements with the boss made his position untenable, he resigned.

After four months of unemployment, he became marketing director for a computer software manufacturer in early 1972. But he was not happy in that subordinant position. In the spring of 1973, he became a partner in a small firm that entices executive talent to move from one position to another. He established the firm's Orange County office and traveled two or three times a week to the Los Angeles office. Perhaps he has finally found the independence and authority he always sought. Ironically, his job is to place managers in large, bureaucratic organizations.

Fletcher's attitude toward the role of authority in business organizations may match the conservative content of his political attitudes. But should we expect his job position to be reflected in a sense of political efficacy? Fletcher is well aware of the differences in scale and organization between his company and such an enterprise as the federal government. He is not likely to make a conscious transference of attitudes gained from work to the political realm. He expresses unambiguous trust in the benign purposes of government, but he has not been a political activist, so has had little experience with attempts at exerting political influence. His score on the political efficacy scale, 12 out of 20, places him in the low range of the Ramona Heights microsample. In theory,

> A high trust–low efficacy system describes a subordinate orientation and is characteristic of *traditional* or paternalistic political systems.[18]

Fletcher may indeed feel that paternalistic business organization is best; if so, he prefers to fill the role of father, rather than that of child. Hence his move from large to progressively smaller companies. But he is a complex individual, with a range of political opinions based on broad knowledge of government and its operations. On the job, Fletcher

[18]William A. Gamson, "Political Trust and Its Ramifications," in *Social Psychology and Political Behavior*, ed. G. Abcarian and J. W. Soule (Columbus, Ohio: Merrill, 1971), p. 53.

practices skills that are highly relevant to the functions of a citizen in a democracy. He confers with his partners for what he calls "political reasons," in order to assure that his own judgments are shared. He is well aware of the need to cover the bases of power in the firm before he attempts to initiate a change of policy. In Fletcher Barbera's case, at least, the combination of high trust and low sense of efficacy describes an individual capable of sophisticated political activity who has, so far, not perceived a need for political action in the public realm.

Quentin Elliott also had feelings of ambivalence toward the large rubber company that initially brought him to Ramona Heights. Unhappy with the psychic costs of selling, he was at the same time reluctant to abandon the salary and prestige that came with his position. Only after moving to Ramona Heights, and seeing it as a place where his family could develop the sense of belonging they so badly needed, did his sense of dissatisfaction with the corporation precipitate drastic action. He resigned from the organization to become a schoolteacher, giving up the prestige, income, and promise associated with his corporate position.

If nothing else, Quentin Elliott should have a unique sense of being in control of the progress of his life. And, if our hypothesis is to be supported, he should have a concurrent sense of political efficacy. In fact, he scores 18 out of 20 on the scale presumed to measure that quality. Quentin worked for Senator Charles Percy in Illinois, and he anticipates enlisting in the political battles necessary to preserve the quality of the public schools by persuading the public to support tax increases and bond issues. Although he registered as a Republican in Illinois, he sees the California Republican party as antithetic to his goals and interests. Both Quentin and Deborah became registered Democrats in 1970.

John Wesley Weeks presents quite a different picture. John decided to become an aeronautical engineer when he took his first airplane ride as a small child. He never deviated from that goal, and he is proud of his contribution to the design of the large jet airliners, which fill the sky above Ramona Heights.

But John's work can only be performed in the service of a large organization, and he is aware of the psychic strain of his work situation, where the power to make decisions rests with position rather than competence. He is perpetually irritated by his immediate supervisor.

John: I'm more methodical and operate slowly and generally talk slowly, and since I've known him I've never finished a sentence. He has an amazing capacity for hearing six or eight words, extrapolating to the wrong conclusion, and then reading it back to me. And this just irritates the hell out of me.

But a greater source of strain than the organizational hierarchy is the uncertainty of his employment, which depends upon the company's winning the appropriate contracts. When John's work on the design of commercial airliners was completed, he had no choice but to apply his talents to the design of missile systems, in spite of his doubts about the social utility of such projects as the ABM. He has always had to live with uncertainty.

John: I've been in this business now for around twenty plus years, and I can never remember a time of absolute security. Not one year have I had absolute security where I felt that my job depended merely on how well I did it. . . . It's always been living week to week. . . . Probably one of the reasons I'm heavy is because I worry a lot and I eat. That's my best pastime.

At the time of our initial conversations, John had just had to cancel a planned vacation, because he had to work to meet a contract deadline. But the prospects of a new contract when that was completed were slim. He could lose his job without warning.

He finally decided to prepare himself for alternative employment, and began working toward a certificate in computer technology at UCI. He had been doing this for two years and would complete the course in two more years. Moving from the aerospace industry to the computer industry would mean a salary cut, and he knew he would be less happy if he were no longer involved in aeronautical engineering, his lifelong occupational identity. Yet he could face this with equanimity if he were assured of greater job permanence.

This, then, is John Weeks's mode of adaptation to the pain of ambivalence—to live with uncertainty, to work long hours of overtime, hoping there would be another contract. Work in the aerospace industry, he says, is "either feast or famine." At the same time, John prepares for an alternate job. He keeps on overeating, and Martha Weeks worries about her husband's health.

Kenneth Kaub presents a rather different picture. As a physician, Kenneth is an acknowledged professional, and his professional judgment is normally respected. Nevertheless, employed in a state hospital, he works under bureaucratic rules and feels that an inordinate amount of his time is devoted to the paperwork demanded by the bureaucracy. He occasionally has disagreements with his supervisor, who, he feels, has abandoned the practice of medicine for administration to such an extent that the supervisor's medical judgment is usually inferior to his own. In short, although Kenneth Kaub is a trained professional, he works in a large organization that, within limits, "orders him about." Furthermore, his salary scale is set in Sacramento, and the compensation he gets does not vary according to the amount of energy and devotion he invests in his work. Physicians in established private practices usually earn a great deal more.

Kenneth attempted to establish a private practice in 1961. The first six months, he worked half time at the state hospital, then he devoted full time to the private practice for another nine months. But he found that the overhead expenses were always greater than the income, and he returned to the state hospital staff with a sense of relief. In his own mind, the advantages and disadvantages of working at the state hospital are nicely balanced. He is often irritated by the paperwork and regulations, his income is limited, he dislikes dealing with the guilt-ridden relatives of psychiatric patients, he is frustrated when drugs and supplies run short and the state supplies no further money to buy them. But this is balanced by the regular hours, the security of the employment, and the fact that he may order laboratory tests or other procedures without concern about the patient's ability to pay.

Thus, Kenneth Kaub experienced an initial ambivalent reaction to the bureaucratic work life, attempted but failed to establish a private practice as an alternative, and returned to the bureaucracy in a chastened mood. He now tends to stress the favorable aspects of his job, and seldom expresses envy for his colleagues growing wealthy with fashionable private practices. He supports his family in Ramona Heights in a manner that is comfortable but not ostentatious. More and more he finds his political opinions tending in a liberal direction, simply because he is more aware of social needs than are his wealthy colleagues. His sense of political efficacy measures 14 of a possible 20, in the middle range of the Ramona Heights microsample. He is still a registered Republican, although he is disillusioned with the Reagan Administration. His political attitudes, like his life, present a study in moderation. He is well aware of the world's imperfections, but he is unlikely to initiate a search for political change.

Piotr Pavel is the final example of the ambivalent mode of adjusting to the pressures of bureaucratic life. In 1970, he went on medical leave of absence from his position as research engineer with a major aerospace firm. This status was the equivalent to retirement, for it was unlikely, at age sixty-two, that he would again be employed full time in his chosen profession. He spoke openly of his bitterness and sense of personal defeat caused by the management of his professional life by bureaucratic structures. Like Dr. Kaub, he had tried to escape by establishing his own business. He operated for a time as an independent consulting engineer, and a few years later he established a local radio station in a promising small town in central California. This investment was undertaken specifically to provide a nest egg for retirement. But Piotr was unable to manage it personally, and he finally was forced to sell at a loss. He continued to work for aerospace firms. Typically, they were aircraft manufacturing firms that retained loose organizational structures developed during World War II. In several cases, Piotr's professional decisions were overruled by aircraft men who did not share his expertise in electronics. His attempts to save the taxpayers' money on various projects were thwarted by the administrative and accounting practices of the firms for which he worked. Piotr's investment of energy and time to complete specific projects for specific companies never resulted in building reserves in a pension fund to shelter his old age. Myrna Pavel claimed that her husband's health was destroyed by the aerospace companies' exploitation of engineers; Piotr did not deny it. He felt that he was seldom able to operate with appropriate professional dignity and independence. Piotr had been an electronics engineer for thirty-four years. He summed up that career this way: "I got into the wrong racket, you might say."

Not only does the impact of bureaucracy on his personal life disturb him; he is distressed at the mismanagement of the national pool of technical manpower. The 1969–70 retrenchment of the aerospace industry put many trained engineers out of work. Instead of focusing their skills on such technical problems as pollution or decaying urban transit systems, he said, they were becoming bond salesmen or opening franchised restaurants. Because of a temporary situation—the readjustment of national priorities away from defense spending and weapons development —the supply of technical manpower was being dispersed, and Piotr Pavel pointed out that no new generation was rising to supply future needs. For the prestige of engineering, like the prestige of science and technology itself, had fallen precipitously, and the new college generation was not interested in apprenticing its talents to the engines of technological "progress."[19] Piotr Pavel saw a national tragedy in the making.

[19]The output of American schools of engineering remained constant between 1956 and 1966. In 1956, this was 8.5 percent of baccalaureates awarded; in 1966, it was 6.8 percent. Freshmen entering engineering programs in the fall of 1972 declined 11.5 percent from the previous year. Yet the demand for new engineers will far exceed the supply throughout the 1970s, according to the U.S. Department of Commerce. A 1973 projection saw an

Pavel was not without remedies. He proposed a federal agency to guarantee pension rights for the employees of aerospace firms. Tied as they are to government contracts, these workers are ultimately employed by the government in any case, so they should accumulate the rights of seniority regardless of which firm or contract employs them. He cited the National Aeronautics and Space Administration as an example of an organizational structure designed to achieve technological advance, once national priorities have been determined. A single such agency, dedicated to the preservation of the environment, could organize a concerted technological attack upon the problems created by advancing technology. And it could make rational use of the nation's technically trained personnel.

But Pavel did not have high hopes that this would happen. He wanted to write an article for *Fortune* to bring the problem and possible solutions before the public eye, but he had been ill and was still discouraged. He was very glad that his own sons did not enter engineering, and he said that he had done several young men a service by convincing them not to enter the field. But he feels that there is little that he alone can do to change a system that may lead to the loss of America's technological preeminence, the weakening of her international status, the decline of her economy, and possibly also of her culture.

With a score of 9 out of 20, Pavel was lowest in the sample on the political efficacy scale, congruent with his feeling of defeat and frustration in his professional life.

At any particular time, many of the middle- and upper-middle-management personnel of an organization will feel ambivalent about the psychic pressures of bureaucratic existence. Also, as time passes, many if not most of them will, like the men of Ramona Heights, attempt to exchange their painful situation for a better one. There may be a corollary here to the behavior of American voters. The standard survey research studies, carried out during the time span of a single campaign, are essentially static, emphasizing correlations between party identification, socioeconomic status, and voting behavior. They leave the impression that the individual voter is the fairly passive pawn of large social forces.[20] When changes of mind between campaigns are considered, particularly as they are stimulated by events like the Watergate investigation, one may find that a great deal more of individual reason, deci-

---

annual shortage of 15,000 trained engineers by 1975. See 61 *Engineering Education* 2 (November, 1970), p. 115, and 101 *Intellect* 2348 (March, 1973), p. 350.

[20]See the studies of the University of Michigan Survey Research Center, particularly Campbell, et al., *The Voter Decides*, and *The American Voter*.

sion, and will is involved than the standard studies typically show. Depth interviews with Ramona Heights voters suggest exactly that.

Aerospace Engineers: A Crisis of Individualism

John Weeks and Piotr Pavel are both aerospace engineers, members of a large group in American society, and particularly in Orange County, that was forced in 1969 and 1970 to confront the fact that American society no longer accorded high prestige to their chosen profession. Pavel and Weeks suggest only some of the anguish that members of this group felt as they were forced to adapt their sense of self-esteem to new and limiting circumstances. The impact of such readjustments upon political attitudes is of no small importance.

Early in the 1960s, aerospace engineers rode the crest of a wave of technological advance. President John F. Kennedy established the goal of placing a man on the moon by the end of the decade; NASA organized technical energies for the accomplishment of that goal. Meanwhile, the push of Pentagon planners for the development of ever more sophisticated weapons systems, in an attempt to maintain a lead over the Soviet Union, found only scattered opposition in Congress. Engineers like Piotr Pavel moved effortlessly from one company and project to the next, earning ever-increasing salaries, secure in the knowledge that their well-paid work was contributing to the national defense.

The situation at the end of the decade presented a shattering contrast. Americans had landed on the moon, but the usefulness of further exploration in space was being questioned; the United States was mired in a war in Vietnam which seemed increasingly senseless; tentative steps toward an arms limitation agreement had been made; explosive urban riots indicated pressing domestic needs; and the new attention to ecological issues called into question the further consumption of natural resources through technological development. Defense and space contracts were cut back or canceled; no new contracts took their place. And no clear set of new priorities had emerged for the allocation of technical skills.

The impact of this change upon engineers was increased by their own professional attitudes and by the personnel practices of the aerospace firms which exploited those attitudes. As narrowly trained professionals, engineers were highly likely to accept uncritically the historic American emphasis on personal achievement, which holds that men should reap the rewards of hard work and that poverty results from individual ignorance and sloth.[21] The policies of the aerospace firms encouraged engineers to think of themselves as relatively autonomous master technicians, able to sell their skills to the highest bidder.

What happens to the outlook of such a person when he is laid off and unable to find another job? If he accepts welfare payments or unemployment benefits, does this increase his empathy for other welfare recipients, together with his understanding of American society, and thus create in him a more charitable attitude towards the welfare state? Or does he differentiate his own case by somehow finding himself more deserving of governmental support than the social outcasts?

Fletcher Barbera resigned his job as vice president of a small electronics engineering firm in late 1971. It was a time of reorganization and cutback in the electronics industry; it seemed for a time that he could only find a job that would require the family to move from Ramona Heights. In spite of frantic searching, Fletcher went without a job for four months. He applied for unemployment compensation, but it was denied, on the technical ground that he had resigned, rather than being laid off. He appealed the decision; while it was before the appeals board, he found another job, so he did not press the appeal.

Fletcher described meeting a number of Ph.D.'s in the waiting line at the welfare office. He said that aerospace engineers had grown so specialized in ten or twenty years that they were hardly available for alternative types of work. Some of them, he said, felt all that time that they were more patriotic than their colleagues who worked in commercial industry, but they never rejected the personal benefits of the aerospace boom.

Fletcher: Things were up, you know, and people were getting paid a *lot* of money, and they were getting big annual raises, and nobody complained about it then! Nobody said, "Oh, gee, don't pay us too much, just because you need us now." It's got to be a two-way deal. It can go up, and it can go down, and you have to be willing to go both ways—or not at all.

Question: Well, did the unemployment experience change your attitudes toward the economy, or toward the welfare system?

[21]The historic origins and continued conflict between the values of achievement and equality are treated extensively in Chapter Six.

Maureen: Welfare's a little harder to get than I thought!

Fletcher: I would like to think of it as a character-building experience. [He laughs.] But I'm not sure that's true; I'm just trying.

Piotr Pavel has studied the organization of the engineering profession and proposes changes in that organization that would allow the nation to better utilize its trained technical manpower. Fletcher Barbera, adhering to the values of achievement and free enterprise, does not seek to change the system. But he finds a job for himself outside the bureaucratic tangle of the large corporations.

There is evidence that human beings are not so intent upon making their ideas consistent with each other as some social scientists have presumed them to be.[22] Particularly when a directly felt personal interest is involved, political actions may not be constrained by an ideology which, if logically pursued, would limit such actions. That is, an engineer may continue to believe that welfare recipients are bums, while waiting in line for his welfare check, secure in his feeling that he deserves better from the government than others. Or a Lockheed engineer devoted to minimal government interference in the operations of the free enterprise system may feel the government should nevertheless guarantee a loan to save the Lockheed Company. If he attempts to justify this inconsistency in his own mind, he may argue that Lockheed accomplished marvels in World War II, or on contracts other than the C-5A transport plane, and thus its team of engineers, managers, and technicians particularly deserve government support.

An analysis of letters received from Californians by Wisconsin Senator William Proxmire, who led opposition to the Lockheed loan guarantee, reveals a substantial number who argued, in one way or another, that a government which supports the lazy and contemptible elements of society with welfare payments should certainly come to the aid of the hard-working employees of the Lockheed Company.[23]

Regardless of their attitudes toward hippies or welfare chiselers, the Barberas, Weekses, and Porfilios of Orange County and the nation are

[22]The "cognitive dissonance" literature is summarized and challenged in Daryl J. Bem, *Beliefs, Attitudes, and Human Affairs* (Belmont, Calif.: Brooks/Cole, 1970), pp. 34–39.

[23]This content analysis, as yet unpublished, was performed by Michael Woo upon letters on the Lockheed loan controversy received by Senator Proxmire from California residents. A number of the correspondents threatened to boycott Milwaukee's Schlitz beer in retaliation for Proxmire's opposition to the Lockheed loan.

unlikely to permit abstract ideologies about the role of government to prevent them from calling for governmental action to restore order to a disordered industry and region. And they may withdraw their allegiance from an unresponsive government, or at least from an elected representative, who fails to heed their call.

CHAPTER FIVE

Life Styles and the Social Ladder

Levittowners are not really members of the national society, or for that matter, of a mass society. They are not apathetic conformists ripe for takeover by a totalitarian elite or corporate merchandiser; they are not conspicuous consumers and slaves to sudden whims of cultural and political fashion; they are not even organization men or particularly other-directed personalities.

—Herbert J. Gans[1]

Question: *Would you say that you belong to the upper class, the middle class, or the lower class, or what?*
   Tina Roybal: *With both of us working?*
   Arthur Roybal: *I don't know. If you live in this community here, that puts you in a certain category, and whatever that category happens to be, I would assume it's middle class. I certainly don't think it's lower class, lower class in the sense of economics. Maybe morally or spiritually we're lower class, but not economically.*

Search for a Suburban State of Mind

CONVERSATIONS with twelve families in Ramona Heights reveal a marked diversity of attitude and behavior. The community imposes no common pattern of political party identification, and affluent technocrats dis-

---

[1] Herbert J. Gans, *The Levittowners* (New York: Random House, Vintage Books, 1967), p. 417. It is hardly fair to Gans's richly detailed work to quote only from his conclusion, when over four hundred pages precede it. His study of lower-middle-class Levittown (now Willingboro), New Jersey, has important points of comparison with middle- and upper-middle-class Ramona Heights.

play different modes of adaptation to the pressures of working in bureau-cratic organizations. The mode of adaptation to the work experience is congruent with feelings of political efficacy and, in turn, with actual political participation. However, a sense of efficacy does not reveal the content of political attitudes. Frank McGee, an alumnus of the Birch Society, is a staunch supporter of former Congressman John Schmitz; Quentin Elliott, who worked in Illinois for the reelection of Republican Senator Charles Percy, has registered as a Democrat in California; both score at the top of the efficacy scale.

Thus far, we have not detected common attitudes that transmit a clear message about the American political future. Since World War II, social critics have claimed that a particular state of mind must, of necessity, prevail in suburbia.[2] In the present political climate, it seems that the suburban view of the world can only exacerbate the conflicts that divide Americans and force a confrontation with the core cities.[3] Do the common assumptions about suburbia provide appropriate guides to action? Republicans and Democrats alike assumed that John Schmitz was invincible in 1970, but he was trounced in 1972. Therefore, it seems most fruitful to examine the conceptions of suburbia held by those in a position to influence future political strategy. Frederick Dutton's anal-ysis of *Changing Sources of Power*[4] provides an example of what thoughtful men in high places think about the suburbs. Dutton was secretary to John F. Kennedy's cabinet and an assistant secretary of state. He has been an important strategist in four of the last five Demo-cratic presidential campaigns.

Dutton uses three terms to designate attributes of suburbia: "neo-agrarianism," "homogeneity" (the suburban way of life), and "personal striving." The meaning Dutton attaches to neo-agrarianism is never precise. It seems to consist of a revulsion directed against cities, based on the anti-urban strain in American intellectual and political history,[5] which has accumulated the power of a moral judgment: there is an element of evil in the cities.

[2]For a review of the post–World War II surge of writing about suburbia, and the efforts of sociologists to test the developing mythology in the empirical cauldron, see Scott Donaldson, *The Suburban Myth* (New York: Columbia University Press, 1969).
[3]An exemplar of this conviction is Frederick G. Dutton in *Changing Sources of Power* (New York: McGraw-Hill, 1971), pp. 127–136. Also see Walter Dean Burnham, *Critical Elections and the Mainsprings of American Politics* (New York: Norton, 1970), p. 172.
[4]A key passage from Dutton's book forms the introduction to Part Two.
[5]I have attempted to summarize the anti-urban tradition, from Jefferson to the present, in *The People, Maybe*, 2nd ed. (North Scituate, Mass.: Wadsworth, Duxbury Press, 1974), pp. 413–417.

The charge of homogeneity originated with the discovery of suburbia as a social phenomenon. As streets lined with look-alike, mass-produced, and relatively inexpensive houses filled the landscape on the urban fringes in response to the post–World War II housing shortage, a suspicion arose that the homes' occupants would exhibit a certain mass-produced quality in their social customs and political attitudes.[6] It is now clear that "suburbia" describes a geographical location, rather than a culture, and there are—as Dutton concedes—a great variety of attitudes and patterns of activity to be found there. Yet, at the very least, suburbanites must share some political interest with their neighbors. Dutton agrees with John Peters that "a keen sense of property rights and a sharp concern for tax rates comes with the key to a suburban house."[7] But such interests are likely to come with ownership of any house, regardless of where it is located. Is Dutton implying that the suburban homeowner is most likely to place property rights above human rights? The tone of his description of "suburbanism" as "a way of life and outlook" implies such a conclusion.[8] But Dutton never demonstrates that modern gadgets, personal acquisitiveness, or social climbing are exclusive attributes of suburbia. He never wonders how city residents could have become immune.

A more useful formulation of the "way of life" hypothesis is suggested by Herbert Gans's finding that the residents of Levittown fail to acknowledge the pluralistic nature of society. For a variety of reasons, they do not comprehend the goals and aspirations of other groups. They are intolerant of diversity.[9] Gans found this intolerance to be at the root of conflicts that developed *within* Levittown, as the cosmopolitan upper-middle-class residents fought for their vision of public education or community service organization against the different models in the minds of the lower-middle- and working-class residents. Nevertheless, the cultural predispositions of upper-middle- and lower-middle-class residents in a Levittown are certain to be more like each other than is either likely to resemble the values of impoverished ghetto residents. Attitudes on such matters as the

[6]Such suspicions were the beginning of intellectual concern for the quality of suburban life. Donaldson, *Suburban Myth.*
[7]Dutton, *Changing Sources of Power*, pp. 131–132.
[8]*Ibid.*, p. 135.
[9]Gans, *Levittowners*, pp. 414–416.

sanctity of legitimate birth and the neutrality of law enforcement officers are obvious examples of probable differences—based on experience—between core city and suburban attitudes. A conviction that cities are somehow evil would certainly reinforce an intolerance for the different life styles of urban residents. Suburbia's various ways of life, taken together, offer sharp contrasts with the ways of life of groups trapped in urban poverty. Suburbanites may share with other Americans an inability to empathize with the needs and desires of the less fortunate. Although sharing some ingredients with racism, such an attitude could better be described as a culture-bound myopia.

The notion of personal striving implies that suburban residents scramble frantically upward on the socioeconomic ladder, little caring who they step on or shove from the lower rungs in order to clear a path. An ambitious, socially mobile suburbanite, in this view, will simply not comprehend the outlook of someone who seems content to remain at a lower level of society. Committed to the value of achievement, he will regard that person as having nobody but himself to blame for a failure of ambition.

If suburbanites are so caught up in relentless personal strivings that they are unable to perceive political injustice, this fact has grave implications for controversies over the extension of the welfare state. It also suggests the further growth of political conservatism, for the socially mobile who are entering a higher level of society tend to adopt conservative attitudes in an effort to establish the legitimacy of their membership in that higher level.[10]

Do the voters of Ramona Heights possess the attitudes and attributes described here? Do they hate cities, fail to empathize with lower social groups, and devote their days to restless economic striving and the pursuit of social standing? If such questions can be answered on the basis of what the respondents say (as opposed to what they may think or feel but refuse to articulate), we may find clues in their descriptions of, and reactions to, their ways of life in Orange County.

[10]S. M. Lipset, "The Sources of the 'Radical Right,' " in *The Radical Right*, ed. Daniel Bell (Garden City, N.Y.: Doubleday, 1963), pp. 278–280. See also S. M. Lipset, "Three Decades of the Radical Right: Coughlinites, McCarthyites, and Birchers," in the same volume, p. 363. Lipset recognizes that the small size of his sample (particularly of Birch Society members) limits his assertions about the link between upward mobility and extreme conservatism.

There are substantial differences among the twelve families; none is quite like the others in employment, social activities, recreation, or degree of participation in organizations. Is some common theme hidden behind this superficial diversity? Before plunging into the data we should remind ourselves, in an Aristotlean mood, that vices may only be virtues practiced to excess; what seem evils to the observer may be benefits to the participant. Or, in the words of Robert Lane,

> So much comment and criticism seem to forget that every position on every issue offers some good at the cost of giving up another. Man and society are in a state of tension by the very nature of things.[11]

Suburbia has been castigated for its homogeneity, but the suburbanite may find in his neighborhood only a comforting compatibility, a surcease of tension, and an agreement on values. The mothers of Levittown sought "not homogeneity of occupation and education so much as agreement on the ends and means of caring for child, husband, and home."[12]

The Natural Superiority of Ramona Heights

If "neo-agrarianism" is defined as an intellectual and moral judgment directed against cities as cities, the Ramona Heights microsample must be found not guilty of harboring it. Indeed, Piotr and Myrna Pavel are staunch defenders of urbanity, while Kenneth Kaub has vivid memories of his rural youth and feels no nostalgia whatever for that former style of life.

Mrs. Pavel discussed a visit to New York.

Myrna: Just walking on Fifty-seventh Street was a sheer delight. It took me back many years. I love that, and I love the life, the promise of life. I don't see it as a place of decadence, a place of filth, a place of death; I just see a place of movement, of creation.

Piotr: I always lived in big cities. . . . Of all the cities in the United

[11]Robert E. Lane, *Political Ideology*, paper ed. (New York: Macmillan, Free Press, 1962), p. 476.
[12]Gans, *Levittowners*, p. 167.

States, I like San Francisco best . . . and I think what I really miss is the stimulation which a big city gives you—simply even walking the Boulevard, as in Paris.

The Pavels are such city dwellers at heart that they seem like displaced persons in Ramona Heights. Their emotional attachment to urban existence is firm, and there is nothing in their cultural heritage to support a fondness for country living.[13]

Kenneth Kaub's background is precisely opposite. Raised in the farm country of Kansas, he has experienced the provincial viewpoint and inward-looking gossip of small-town existence, and he prefers to live in a more urban environment.

Kenneth: Most of the people at home are interested in farming, maybe in sports, maybe in local affairs; their views on international affairs were fairly limited, fairly stereotyped—"The whole world is going to wrack and ruin," and that sort of thing. . . . They just prefer to be concerned with their own problems, I think, and I guess would rather talk about each other than the world in general. Because there aren't any secrets in a small town.

Critics charge that suburban life is characterized by a loneliness that is alleviated only by compulsive social contacts.[14] Kenneth Kaub sees the other side of the coin and reacts positively to the chance for privacy. His attitude could well be labeled "anti-agrarian," although, being a gentle and essentially placid man, he hesitates to judge people or their styles of life.

A search of the transcripts reveals two families who could be candidates for the neo-agrarian label—the Rineharts and the McGees. All the other respondents must be placed somewhere between the extremes represented by the pro-urbanism of Dr. Kaub and the Pavels, and the anti-urban sentiments of the Rineharts and the McGees. But are the attitudes of the latter two couples really neo-agrarian, in the sense of rendering an intellectual and moral judgment against the cities?

Asked to define the attractions of Ramona Heights, Richard Rinehart immediately mentioned the urban-rural contrast.

---

[13]Gans notes that "Jews are still more favorably inclined to city living than any other group." See *ibid.*, p. 287, and sources cited on p. 302, n. 77.

[14]One example is cited by Dutton, *Changing Sources of Power*, p. 132.

Richard: Well, we're away from the big city. . . . The heavy traffic, and the problems that come with a central core city, we have fewer of. We're closer to the outdoors here. . . . We find many people who have similar tastes, and it's easier I'd say to make friends here than perhaps it would be in an apartment in Los Angeles. . . . I think in a big city, you kind of lose your identity. You're there and you are a part of it, but you don't feel a part of it.

Alice and Richard explained that they had found life in the Orange County town of Tustin even more rewarding, in some ways, than in Ramona Heights. Tustin (at least when they lived there) offered both a city and a neighborhood of smaller scale. Neither of them has lived in absolutely rural surroundings; because of their remarkable sociability, they would no doubt be made miserable by the physical and social isolation. Therefore, what seems on the surface to be a negative attitude toward cities can as well be described as a positive reaction to the chance for easy association with compatible neighbors.

This leaves the McGees. Frank McGee was raised in a mining town, and his wife lived in an Irish ethnic neighborhood of Chicago before she moved to Pennsylvania as a high school student. But Frank worked summers in New York during his high school and college days, including a job at the 1939 New York World's Fair. Asked his reaction to New York, he says, "It's very interesting. New York is a fascinating town." They have no desire to live there. Frank and Mary are completely happy in Orange County, because of the climate and the friendliness of the people, and they occasionally partake of the cultural life—including professional baseball—of Los Angeles.

Toward the end of our conversations, I asked the McGees to describe the ideal American society. Frank said that the troubles of America were not due to the sheer size of its population (as a devout Catholic, he is opposed to birth control), but rather to the poor distribution of the population.

Frank: It's just that there's a concentration of people in certain areas, and probably less urbanization and more rural life would be the answer there.

Rural America, or their conception of what rural America must be like, symbolizes many of the social virtues that are important in Frank and Mary's political philosophy. While they feel that less urbanization would benefit the nation, Frank does not resist the increasing urbanization of South Orange County. As a real estate salesman specializing in income properties, he knows that the phenomenon of urbanization in large measure supplies his livelihood. The McGees' attitude toward cities is too complex to be called "neo-agrarian."

Along with other Americans, the Ramona Heights voters are dismayed by many attributes of present-day American cities, including air pollution, crime, decay of public services, and poor housing.[15] None is under the illusion that cities are ideal places to live. Quentin Elliott is the most outspoken, when he describes present-day New York. In the late 1930s, he lived on Fifth Avenue, opposite Central Park, and was taken to the Park by a governess. But his memories of that time are vague. As an adult, he lived for a year in Peter Cooper Village, a middle-income apartment complex in lower Manhattan.

Quentin: I think if you can live in New York City you can live anywhere in the world. I never lived in Calcutta, but I'll bet it's true there. I think of New York City as Gotham. I think only Batman and Robin can survive there now. It's pretty bad, but that's New York.

The respondents feel they are fortunate to live in Ramona Heights, although this is tempered by some ambivalence about the sameness of its architecture. They do not feel that by virtue of residence they are somehow superior to city dwellers. The natural superiority of Ramona Heights is acknowleged, but only in the narrowest sense: it is blessed by nature. To many of the couples, the opportunity to enjoy their leisure hours in attractive surroundings was a key attraction of Ramona Heights. The beach is four miles away; swimming pools, tennis courts, and golfing greens are scattered liberally throughout the surrounding area.

As often as they can, the Elliotts pile all four children into the car and drive to the beach for a day in the sun. Marie Kaub was the first in her family to take up golf, and now her husband and son join her on weekends. Arnold Garcia once nearly bought a thirty-six-foot Chris-Craft, but he finally decided against it, feeling that boats make no sense as investments unless one lives on board. Besides, he adds, he can go sailing with his nephew whenever he wants, or else rent a boat. Ralph Porfilio shares with Fletcher Barbera a desire to own a cruising sailboat, although neither wants to squeeze the family budget now in order to afford such leisure toys. Fletcher's feelings on the subject apply as well to the other families with young children—the Elliotts, Barberas, and Roybals.

[15]For survey data on national attitudes toward air pollution, crime, and federal aid for the cities, see *The Harris Survey Yearbook of Public Opinion, 1970* (New York: Louis Harris and Associates, 1971), pp. 49–51, 63, 64.

Fletcher: I think when the boys get a little older I'd like to have a small boat, but primarily I think it would be a great vehicle for family fun, as opposed to something I think I need. And I think if we had lots of money we'd probably have a membership in maybe the Bay Club or something like that. But again, primarily I think, because it would be a vehicle for family recreation, as opposed to something I think I've got to have because my friends have it or something like that.

When asked what might be added to their version of "the good life," a majority of the respondents mentioned extra time and/or money for recreation or travel. They prefer to wait until such time as they can easily afford it to expand their leisure activities. Quentin and Deborah Elliott had seriously considered buying into a mountain condominium but they decided that "it would limit us to one location, and we'd worry about whether we were making ends meet and so on, and so we canceled out." The Johnsons made a similar decision when selling their cabin cruiser; it was taking time and money away from golf.

All those I interviewed used leisure time to relax, to spend time together in the California sunshine, to enjoy the life they can now afford. There is no hint that weekends of golf disguise gratuitous attempts to gather social prestige or conspicuously display to neighbors the instruments of leisure.[16] Neither is leisure time so precious that it cannot in fact be enjoyed, as Lane often found to be the case with his working-class respondents.[17]

Whether they are golfers, swimmers, tennis buffs, or even more distant admirers of the California landscape—as Eldene Markus, who loves the beach she never visits and fervently wants it protected against private development, for the young people she believes it is meant for —they share the same understanding of leisure. As Arthur Roybal said, the "good life" can be simply "enjoying your family and having fun with your family, and having good health and eating well and sleeping well." And, he added, "the weather's good." This is a respectable and rather straightforward perception of the role of leisure.

Home-oriented activities, in fact, are a major source of pleasure for all the Ramona Heights respondents. Alice and Richard Rinehart spent one of their two weeks of vacation last year repainting the many shutters of their home. Myrna Pavel described her favorite form of recreation.

[16]Thorstein Veblen, *Theory of the Leisure Class* (New York: Viking, 1967; first published 1899), pp. 35–67.
[17]Lane, *Political Ideology,* p. 77.

Myrna: When a group of friends get together. We listen to music, have good conversation, good food. That I enjoy tremendously.

More modest pleasures—home gardening, enjoying music on the family stereo, substituting television in the privacy of their homes for downtown concerts or plays, casual gatherings with friends, or simple family roughhousing—are quite acceptable to these families.

Do the members of the microsample recognize how truly fortunate they are? Their comforts result from consuming an above-average share of the national wealth; what about those who are less fortunate? Recognition of the level of economic and social status necessary to realize the leisurely good life they enjoy was largely absent from the interviews. While they would not deliberately deny to others what they themselves enjoy, neither are they fully aware that their pleasure is not so easily available to the great majority of people in any country, or that it might in some way be linked to the unlovely poverty so close to the sunlit hills of Ramona Heights.

The voters of Ramona Heights are well aware of the existence of other neighborhoods that are much higher on the economic and social scale. They need go only a few miles to see homes on Lido Island in Newport Bay valued at several hundred thousand dollars, and others along the Balboa Peninsula with yachts tied up to their private docks. These homes do not represent a kind of goal that the residents of Ramona Heights feel they should strive for. They tend to associate upper-class society with anguish—spoiled children, broken families, and lack of community spirit—which they prefer not to experience. The Rineharts reported that they selected Ramona Heights because some of the other communities in the area would provide a less satisfactory environment for their children. Alice Rinehart said, "Sometimes there is a stronger family tie in a family that doesn't have as much money, or as much affluence." They feel that local schools serve the children of families like their own, families in which parental interest and guidance is firmly felt, so that values developed by the children of the neighborhood will be more predictable.

The Porfilios made a similar point, although it was stated in terms of the ease with which the parents of Ramona Heights are persuaded to participate in activities of the Girl Scout troop.

Caroline: You have higher socioeconomic areas [around here] where you can't get one parent to participate, because they're so involved with their own lives and going their own way that they have no time at all for their children. . . . I don't know what's made it so special in Ramona

Heights, but they're extremely aware of doing things for the family group.

In similar vein, Quentin Elliott mentioned "the yachting set" and immediately outlined the costs of maintaining a yacht, including club membership. He said, without regret, "We aren't in that league."

The general pattern, then, is to enjoy the life Ramona Heights offers. The respondents expressed little desire to "move up" into a more expensive neighborhood or social set. Because of their upper-class Southern California family backgrounds, the Barberas do move in social circles that are a level above those of the other respondents, and they noted with amusement that some of the people they meet look down on the tract.

Maureen: We've been thrown into a couple of parties where we felt we were completely over our heads, mostly with the other guests involved. They'd look at us and say, "Where do you live?" and we'd say, "In Ramona Heights," and they'd say, "Oh, *that* must be *nice.*" And at the nearest opportunity they'd turn off and walk away.

In spite of her wish for live-in help, Maureen appreciates the attractions of Ramona Heights, and there is no hint that she nags Fletcher to somehow find a way to move elsewhere.

Maureen: I think it's a very easy life. The concerns are few. I'm always comparing myself back with what I think I would be feeling in Pasadena if we were there. Such as, I can go to sleep happily at night without thinking that there was someone who was going to be coming in the door, and I don't have to worry about the schools. . . . I think the people are quite congenial. It's healthy, it's happy; so far we have money to afford it.

Although she comes from a strongly contrasting background, Marie Kaub expressed her appreciation for Ramona Heights with similar enthusiasm.

Marie: I think, once in a while, just coming home to this hill, and just knowing you're coming home to a cool sea breeze, is part of the good life. And me, knowing that I have good friends here.

The values which our microsample find in Ramona Heights are widely shared by the American population. They have an economic position which permits them to act out a large part of the American dream. They live a life which they find good, and they can hardly be blamed for expressing enjoyment of it, unless their affluence results from a deliberate exploitation of those less fortunate, or their style of life limits their ability to perceive the ills of the greater society. The first of these possibilities is remote. These families are not members of a *rentier* class (defined as "functionless investors"), which even John Maynard Keynes,[18] not to mention Karl Marx, was interested in suppressing. The second possibility—inability to see the greater ills—is more likely.

To Live the Good Life

The combination of freedoms and constraints operating on the residents of Ramona Heights—a mixture of the motives which brought them there, and the rewards they have found—may indeed create a common set of values with political implications. Their one obvious common bond is that they are all tenants of the Irvine Company, for their land is leased, and all except the Elliotts and the Markuses must make monthly payments to retire the mortgages on their houses. Quentin Elliott resists the idea that residents of the neighborhood are likely to develop a common outlook.

Quentin: Does a sharing of real estate mean a sharing of values? The fact that you've got doctors, lawyers, and Injun chiefs of all walks of life living in Ramona Heights is proof of the fact that there's got to be a tremendous divergence of opinion. So I think that mainly we're sharing real estate.

The respondents had no image of a new life style that Ramona Heights would provide; asked to recall reasons why they came, they think of more limited, precise, and practical considerations than are usually included in some phrase such as "way of life." There are six themes common to the descriptions of motives for moving to Ramona Heights:

1. *Proximity to the place of employment.* The choice of the general area was influenced by shorter commuting time for the breadwinner: mentioned by the Weekses, Markuses, and Roybals.
2. *Investment purposes.* The house in Ramona Heights was seen as likely to appreciate in value at a rate greater than general inflation.

18See John Maynard Keynes, *The General Theory of Employment, Interest, and Money* (London: Macmillan, 1954; first published 1936), pp. 221, 376.

This factor was an afterthought for most couples, but it was part of the original motivation for the Pavels, McGees, and Arnold Garcia; since Piotr's semiretirement, it has become nearly an obsession with the Pavels.

3. *Natural attractions.* The hilltop location, good climate, and proximity to beaches and water sports were mentioned by all respondents. It was of primary importance to the Johnsons, Porfilios, Roybals, Rineharts, and Arnold Garcia.

4. *Price.* All factors considered, this seemed the best home available for the money at the time of purchase: mentioned particularly by the Elliotts, Weekses, Rineharts, and Porfilios.

5. *Floor plan.* The arrangement of their particular house was so superior to others that other considerations became secondary. This factor was mentioned by Marie Kaub and Maureen Barbera. They were both enamored of the four-bedroom model which presents a wall, gate, and garage door to the street; its front yard is an enclosed private patio.

6. *Social attributes of the area.* The Roybals were attracted by the good schools, the Barberas by the apparently "compatible" neighbors, and the Rineharts by the sound, family-oriented values which seemed to characterize the neighborhood.

The residents of Ramona Heights are a few steps above the residents of Levittown (Willingboro), New Jersey, on the social and economic ladder, but their motives for moving are quite similar. They came primarily for the house, rather than because they were seeking an ideal social environment.[19] The house, in its design, and particularly in its location, represented a good value. Herbert Gans's Levittowners were largely moving to the suburb from Philadelphia; our respondents came to Ramona Heights from another suburb, either in Orange County (Rineharts, Johnsons Markuses, McGees) or in Los Angeles County (Pavels, Garcias, Kaubs, Barberas, Weekses, Roybals), or from far away (Elliotts, Pofilios). American cities have increasingly become the homes of the very rich and the very poor; it is not surprising that the householders of Ramona Heights, whose status is middle or upper middle class, were confirmed suburbanites before they came. Unconsciously, they may have been seeking higher status, more prestige, or greater comfort; consciously, they sought only a more satisfactory version of the life they were already experiencing. And that greater satisfaction is stated in practical, not philosophical, terms.

[19] Gans, *Levittowners*, pp. 32–37.

Some of them discovered satisfactions they did not particularly expect. John and Martha Weeks found in Ramona Heights a small-town atmosphere created by friendly neighbors, yet a chance for privacy. Martha says they live on a "warm street," although she has talked to other wives in the tract who feel their own streets are "cold." What is a warm street?

Martha: No matter what you want in any direction, whether it's an emergency or whether it's just friendship or "Who was that kid that threw the rock at my car window?"—everybody knows everybody. But yet you still have your own privacy within your own family.

There could be no thievery in broad daylight on that street—the wives know enough about each other's business, and whether or not they're likely to be home, so that the phony television repairman will not carry household goods away unchallenged.

Quentin and Deborah Elliott provide the most striking example of finding more in Ramona Heights than they sought. The attractions of the community impressed them so that Quentin decided the time had come to leave the unsettled life of corporate management in order to provide his family with a chance to "put down roots." In the literature, the lack of "roots" is linked to conservative extremism; suffering from a surfeit of mobility, the suburbanite seeks refuge in a kind of political fundamentalism.[20] But Quentin's moderate liberalism, expressed in working for Republican Senator Percy in Illinois, led him to register in the Orange County Democratic party.

Is there any common theme in the interviews that expresses values shared by the respondents which make them natural allies in local, state, or national politics? Obviously, none of them wants to see Ramona Heights bisected by a freeway, or the public beaches consumed by private interests, and all of them favored the installation of a traffic light on the busy intersection of Alessandro Boulevard. But these are hardly matters of ideology. Although most of them mention the growing traffic at Orange County Airport as a source of irritation, Martha Weeks welcomes the air traffic. She said that if she no longer heard airplanes overhead, she would call the airport to ask what was wrong. Nobody is happy with the Irvine Company's future plans, but they offer praise for its past accomplishments. In general, they need pay little attention to local politics, and they don't. Yet, when interests are directly threatened (the freeway, the traffic signal) they are as prepared as the next American to become activists.

[20]Lipset, "Three Decades of the Radical Right."

Just as they see no inherent charm in political activism, the voters of Ramona Heights avoid membership and involvement in civic and social organizations until some personal interest is touched. The children of our families have at one time or another joined the Scouts, the Campfire Girls, the YMCA, the Little League; the Kaubs' young son is an avid Sea Scout; both Elliott sons are involved in the Scouts and the YMCA; the young Porfilio and Roybal girls are members of Girls' Club and the Campfire Girls; and Julie Weeks, her mother says, has "awards coming out of her ears" from the Girl Scouts. In many cases, the children have brought their parents into active involvement with these groups.

The families with young children participate to some extent in parent-teacher groups, and the older couples recall doing so when their children were young. The Weekes, Rineharts, and Porfilios are willing to participate in activities affecting the children as an important part of community involvement. To others, it has less meaning; Arthur and Tina Roybal, educational administrator and elementary school teacher, naturally perceive any involvement with the PTA as a paid duty, not a parental privilege. Marie Kaub was quite involved in the parents' group of the parochial school her son attended before he transferred to the public junior high school.

There is another sense in which personal interests are served by involvement in diverse social groups. Moving into a new home in a new location often stimulates social activity, facilitated by more or less formally organized groups. In newly constructed residential developments, families come together in rather contrived situations to meet and make new friends.[21] Ramona Heights gave birth to a number of get-together clubs—from a book exchange club to the Ladies' Thursday Gourmet Luncheon Club—only some of which have survived, because they proved to be of value beyond the initial period of getting acquainted.

There is a positive relationship between the value placed by our individual respondents on the quality of the local community and their propensity to participate in locally oriented groups. The Weekses, who speak so fondly of the "small-town atmosphere" they enjoy in Ramona Heights, are also the most actively involved of the twelve couples (belonging to five local clubs between the two of them). Similarly, Marie Kaub—to whom a sense of belonging is particularly important—was an original member, and after six years remained an officer, of the Ramona Heights Arts and Crafts Club. Mrs. Porfilio has sought a broader role as community actor through her involvement in the Candy Stripers and annual Easter Seal activities.

21 Gans, *Levittowners*, pp. 44–52.

While the women of our sample are, for obvious reasons, more likely than their husbands to be "joiners," they do not seem involved in time-consuming socializing for its own sake. Eldene Markus is a former member of some of the tract's women's clubs; she dropped her memberships after her husband's illness and subsequent retirement.

These families prefer more private forms of leisure to participation in large organizations; but when they do belong, they cite clear motives for membership. The activities of their alumni group attract Alice and Richard Rinehart, who maintain contact with old college friends. Fletcher Barbera is active in the Amherst Club of Southern California; his interest, however, is stimulated by concern over the policies of the Amherst administration, and the recruitment of bright Orange County high school students, rather than the social possibilities of the club.

There is a different kind of group membership that is common to our respondents—perfunctory membership in professional, business, and civic associations, and in the tenants' organization. For example, Piotr Pavel belongs, or has belonged, to half a dozen different professional engineering-oriented associations. With the exception of Kenneth Kaub, for whom the CSEPA (California State Employees Physicians Association) has been a vehicle for collective expression of discontent with the mental health policies of the Reagan Administration, and perhaps of Jan and Eldene Markus, early in their careers as members respectively of the International Brotherhood of Electrical Workers and the International Ladies Garment Workers Union, our respondents found little meaning in these professional organizations. Often they hesitated to add such groups to the list of their organizational memberships; asked if all memberships had been mentioned, Arthur Roybal—after being reminded by his wife—added, ". . . just professional organizations, and there again it's perfunctory because it's expected of me."

Similarly, service or civic clubs, drawing largely on businessmen for their membership, seem to play a small role in the daily lives of the affluent technocrats. Frank McGee derives business and probably political benefits from his service club; the social values, which he also enjoys, are secondary. Harry Johnson was a member of the Rotary Club where they used to live, but felt no need or desire to resume his membership in the Ramona Heights area. He currently belongs to a professional association, which he described as a cooperative "exchange of ideas," dedicated to improving the industry as a whole, and "when it helps the industry it helps each one of us as a competitor." Arthur Roybal explained his former membership in the Optimists Club.

Arthur: Yeah, in my last job I was asked to—hell, I was *told.* Some went to Rotary, some went to Kiwanis, and mine was Optimists, and so I did it. . . . After I switched jobs, why then I dropped it.

By virtue of residence, all our respondents are obligatory, dues-paying members of the Ramona Heights Homeowners' Association. This group holds annual meetings designed to facilitate communication between the Irvine Company-as-landlord and its suburban tenants. While many of the tenants in our small sample at least attend the annual meeting, nearly half do not grant it even that much time. Apparently the organization is not perceived as serving important needs, and they consequently give it little attention.

Sheer membership, or social activism as an end in itself, is not valued by these suburbanites. There seems, in fact, to be a strain of self-righteous aversion to group membership. The Pavels volunteered a self-description that is repeated in nearly identical words by the Elliotts, Roybals, and Markuses: "We're not joiners, really." Harry Johnson said immediately, "I belong to no organizations whatsoever," although moments later he admitted to membership in a few. Particularly to people like the Johnsons, to whom private life seems most important, group membership holds little attraction. Those families who attach most importance to the nature of community life (the Weekses, Rineharts, Porfilios, and Barberas), most closely approximate the "joiners" of the suburban stereotype.

Except for Alice Rinehart and the McGees, these suburbanites do not perceive political needs which could be served by joining partisan organizations that remain active between campaigns. Myrna Pavel is a "fairly active" member of the nonpartisan League of Women Voters. For the others, the relatively low salience of local political issues is reflected in their lack of interest in local political clubs. State and national candidates and issues are perceived as more important, and most members of the microsample (Arnold Garcia, Marie Kaub, and the Johnsons nearly qualify as exceptions) devote significant energy to their study and discussion. Like most Americans, their status in national politics is that of observers. Participation comes only in the polling booth.

The question to be considered at this point is the extent to which suburban voting may be influenced by intolerance of the life styles of outsiders—members of other social classes (and races)—and the adherents of the "counterculture" among the young of their own social class. Such intolerance is unlikely to be directly expressed. The education of our respondents has, in most cases, resulted in the internalization of the

American norm of equality, at least as an abstract principle. They feel that America *ought* to be a classless society, and they are uncomfortable discussing class differences, at least by that label. This reluctance emerges clearly when they are asked to identify their own position in the hierarchy of classes. One way of discounting the significance of the concept is to dismiss it as being strictly an economic measure, with little other meaning. This route is followed by the Markuses, who then launch a discussion of the unpleasant qualities of "social climbers." It is taken as well by the Johnsons, who conspicuously neglect education as an indicator of class status. In the exchange quoted earlier, Arthur and Tina Roybal discussed social class as being largely an economic measure. If class status has moral and spiritual overtones, those connotations of lower-class membership may be superior to the attitudes of higher classes. If the residents of Ramona Heights have aspirations for further social mobility, they don't advertise them. The Rineharts made the admission but quickly hid it with a joke. When they confessed to middle-class membership, I asked them to specify further between upper middle, lower middle, and middle middle.

Alice: Well, I suppose between middle middle and upper middle. [She laughs.]

Richard: Yeah, economically we're lower middle, but socially we're we'd like to be considered upper middle. If you measure success by debt, why we're right up there. [Laughter.]

Alice: We have a lot of nice bills.

Asked what he thought people mean by the term "social class," Quentin Elliott replied that such labels are never more than stereotypes, and thus he never uses them.

Question: People normally speak of an upper class, middle class, working class, and lower class. If you were forced to designate yourself as a member of one of those, which one would you designate?

Quentin: This gives me the uncomfortable feeling that I have been answering personnel applications. "Would you shoot your dog or walk over your grandmother? Please choose one of these answers, even though you feel uncomfortable." Therefore, having carefully prefaced it, I declare myself, uncomfortably, and with total resistance, to be a member of the upper middle class.

Pressed to name the attributes shared by members of the upper middle class, Quentin mentioned income and education—"not saying that a Ph.D. won't talk to a B.A., but higher education and the access to it." He went on to state that class status does not necessarily create a common state of mind, and he claimed (as quoted earlier) that residents of Ramona Heights share real estate, rather than values.

Much later in our 1970 conversations, Quentin mentioned that his brief residence in Orange County had made him more aware of the existing differences within American society.

Quentin: I think I feel more strongly about defending the rights of minority groups, such as the Chicanos and the Indians, living here. Again, I haven't taken positive action, but I'm aware of the needs. I'm more aware of the tremendous extremes of wealth and poverty that exist within a few miles of each other—Balboa Island on one extreme, and then just over in Santa Ana, another extreme. So, one tends to identify with these things, and feel that somehow it should be equalized.

Quentin's perception of economic extremes is, of course, available to other householders of Ramona Heights, if they will only leave the Santa Ana Freeway and look around. Quentin's first teaching position was in a working-class community between his home and Santa Ana, so he was forced to leave the freeway. But he was nearly unique for volunteering a comment about social differences tied to the feeling that something should be done. Although the Roybals and Markuses also favor new government policies to alleviate poverty, Martha Weeks was the only other respondent to mention poverty in Orange County. The comment came in response to a question about President Nixon's proposed Family Assistance Plan for welfare reform.

Martha: I'm not sure I have the knowledge to say. Because I took our daughter when she was six into Santa Ana to show her poverty, and she said, "Well, why don't"—they were in the dirt playing—"we take them home? We've got grass and parks and everything." She couldn't understand it, and I found myself not being able to explain it to her. . . . That's why I'm one of the people that voted him [Nixon] in, thinking that he would have the knowledge to make these decisions for me, because I'm just not capable of making them along that scope, although I've seen enough poverty in the Midwest as I was growing up.

These two comments come the closest to an admission of the failure of the American dream—an awareness by comfortable members of the middle class that there are serious inequities, not only in American society, but even in Orange County, and that something should be done. Martha and Quentin are not intolerant of the less fortunate; there is even a hinted willingness to reach down and do something for them.

Similar suggestions are found in the transcripts of my conversations with the Roybals, Markuses, and Pavels. These five couples are hardly in the vanguard of the revolution, but they are the most likely to support proposals for social change. This judgment, made on the basis of the 1970 interviews, was reinforced in 1973, when their predispositions were activated by the Watergate investigations. But there was a surprising recruit into their numbers—Maureen Barbera.[22]

These five families hardly fit the picture of suburbanites huddled together, preparing to defend their turf against urban invaders. A number of our respondents, in fact, expressed dissatisfaction with Ramona Heights for being homogeneous—not because they particularly hunger for social contact with the working class, but because their children, brought up in a neighborhood of uniformly comfortable families, will be ill prepared for life in the larger society. I asked the Pavels about the attractions of the area for child-rearing.

Myrna: The only thing I have against it is that the children just see one aspect of living. They see one economic class, one happy medium in education, and in likes and dislikes, culturally. That would be my only objection.

This is not a problem of immediate relevance for the Pavels, since their two sons have completed college and have developed social consciences of which their parents very much approve. For the Roybals, whose children are younger, the issue is more pressing. Early in our conversation, they raised it in response to a question about what changes they would make in their style of life, if change were possible.

Tina: I would like to live in a more ethnically represented community. If I had had this choice, say five years ago, and knew what I know now, I don't think I would have selected this area.

Arthur: We both feel that this is a very sterile community. . . . I think our kids are losing one heck of a lot, by the protective environment we have. All life is not a Disneyland. And I think in Ramona Heights all life is a Disneyland.

Quentin Elliott shares this view; like the Roybals, he isn't sure just what to do about it.

Quentin: It's possible to go into the wrong house in this tract, if you're perhaps a little intoxicated, because the houses look quite a lot

[22]See Chapter Ten.

alike. . . . I feel personally that I have to work very hard on my identity, living here, because, starting with the architecture, there is a sameness about the place. I also believe in more of a cross-section of people in a community. I believe in the concept that it's healthy to have old people and young people and to some extent rich and poor—and by "some extent" I mean you just can't create this ideal condition, but I think you need a Mixmaster social situation to have a real community.

This comment certainly modified, if it did not contradict, his earlier discussion of "doctors, lawyers, and Injun chiefs." Quentin knew that there are no Indian chiefs in Ramona Heights.

Caroline Porfilio also agreed that the class homogeneity of Ramona Heights may be disadvantageous to the children.

Caroline: This is very bad, because they don't get any of the extremes. They just live right along in their own little world, and everybody has the advantages they have. . . . Then they want something bigger and better. If they can't have a new bicycle, they just become horrified.

Caroline's reaction is more akin to feeling that "kids need to be taught the value of a buck" than it is to a call for ameliorating social inequalities. When Dr. Kenneth Kaub was asked if it's a good thing that most of the families in the neighborhood belong to the same class, he responded with a typically balanced judgment.

Kenneth: Well, I think it's good in that they're more likely to have common interests, and it may be bad in that they may not learn the viewpoints of the other classes, by segregating themselves.

Kenneth has become aware of the needs of other social classes through his work in the state hospital; his comment applies to both the adults and the children of Ramona Heights, and it suggests that suburban existence may indeed stimulate an intolerance of diversity, but not in Dr. Kaub.

The Barberas reacted somewhat differently to the question of class homogeneity in Ramona Heights.

Maureen: That's part of the reason we bought our house here. We kind of looked around and decided that if the parents looked compatible, the children were probably going to be compatible.

Question: You don't feel then that your children are missing something by not having contact with the children of working-class parents?

Fletcher: Well, they are missing something. The question is, are they missing anything valuable? I have some reservations about that, yeah.

It's not strong enough to make me want to move.

Maureen: I don't have any reservations about it.

Since none of the respondents has initiated positive action designed to ameliorate social inequalities, the political impact of the attitudes expressed by Quentin Elliott, the Pavels, and the Markuses may be no different than that of the Barberas, as long as Orange County political candidates fail to address such problems.

There was, however, a political resonance to the McGees' feelings about social class differences. Initially, they resisted the use of the concept, as if it were an idea introduced by alien thinkers to cause trouble.

Question: How do you think you determine matters of social class in America?

Frank: I don't think it makes much difference in America. Or again, maybe, in Orange County. Maybe we're different out here.

Question: Well, of course the Marxists claim that social class is everything, the working class must be battling against the bourgeoisie, and so on. Do you think political conflict between social classes is significant and important in America?

Frank: No, I just think there are people who are trying to make it so.

Mary: I don't think we think of classes at all. I mean, well, take Julie, that comes to our house to clean. I never think of her as being the cleaning woman, I think of her as being a friend.

Frank: No, this has never bothered us a bit. I've been in business for a living, and pounded nails, and the whole works, and driven a truck. We have had friends of all descriptions, of all walks of life. It just never bothered us a bit.

Frank is only restating an attitude that was common on America's frontier: people are to be judged for what they are here and now; parentage, background, and the normal labels indicating prestige in society don't count. Not only *should* America have a classless society; he'll behave as if it *does*. But frontier society cannot be re-created through wishing. Resisting the concept of social class, the McGees are enabled to overlook unpleasant realities. They can avoid all exits from the Santa Ana Freeway short of their destination.

The common charge of racism leveled against suburbanites can be supported statistically: whites flee the central cities, leaving blacks behind, and the suburbs become a white ring, compressing the inner core.

This is in part due to the sheer expense of the suburban tracts; lower-income groups cannot afford them. National policies which provided federal guarantees for housing loans failed to consider long-range social impacts. This can be cited as a leading example of unthinking institutional racism.

The question to be confronted at the moment, however, is whether the individual residents of suburbia are guided by racist sentiments. When the question was raised with the Kaubs, Marie thought of the one black family that lives in the tract.

Question: Do you think people in Ramona Heights are resistant to members of minority groups moving in here?
Marie: No.
Kenneth: Of course, I don't think we have to worry too much, because of the price range of the homes; the groups that we get will be the better-educated minority groups.
Marie: Well, obviously, like the Negro family, the gentleman is well educated, or else they couldn't afford the prices of the homes here. I think a lot of it has to do with the income of the group.
Kenneth: So we can afford to be more tolerant, perhaps, than the lower-income groups.

The compatibility of prospective neighbors was related to their income and education (their social class), rather than to their race. They did not mention the possibility that an influx of blacks might threaten property values. In 1972, when I proposed building publicly subsidized housing in Ramona Heights, the Kaubs supported it, provided maintenance could be guaranteed to preserve the neighborhood's appearance. As a Chicana, Marie Kaub has known discrimination; she has won a secure place in the social circles of Ramona Heights, at least in part, by demonstrating that her values and life style are as securely anchored in the middle class as those of her neighbors.

This is a question that the Kaubs have thought about. One could not be so sure that the Johnsons had done so.

Question: Do you happen to know if many blacks live in Orange County?
Harry: I've seen quite a few.
Jacqueline: In Santa Ana, I think, they have a settlement.
Harry: Yes, there's quite a colored community there.
Question: What about Chicanos, or Mexican-Americans, in Orange County?

Harry: Yes, there's quite a few of those, too.
Question: But not so many in Ramona Heights.
Harry: No. Of course, vice versa, there's not very many people from Ramona Heights living there! [He laughs.]

Unhappily, this irrelevancy was not followed by any more penetrating discussion of social inequities in America. The Johnsons did not articulate racial or cultural prejudices; the general topic was not one to which they had given much thought, and they were grateful to change the subject.

An exchange between Alice and Richard Rinehart also suggested, not so much the presence of bigoted attitudes, as the absence of sensitivity to the current state of American society. Richard was discussing a television panel he had seen after the Kent State killings.

Richard· It was a real rough time, and they had a young girl on the panel, and then on the other side was this defensive end, this colored fellow. He is a real good end, I know that—
Alice: Not "colored." A Negro, dear, your children would say.

This suggests that Alice, at least, if not also their children, has somehow missed nearly a decade of the awakening consciousness of black Americans. The Johnsons' awareness is even further out of date.

Comments of this kind do not convict the voters of Ramona Heights of blatant racism, nor even of intolerance of diversity. Of course, unless they harbored bigoted attitudes and were proud of them, the respondents were unlikely to articulate them for a visiting professor's tape recorder. The comments do suggest ignorance. The Johnsons know that there is a "colored community" in Santa Ana, but they aren't about to visit, or try to understand it. Conversely, they feel no compulsion to attack minority groups, either verbally or politically. "Live and let live" could be their motto. Ramona Heights is not a lower-middle-class ethnic neighborhood threatened by a bursting black ghetto. In the words of Kenneth Kaub, the resident of Ramona Heights can afford to be more tolerant.

The Measures of Success

Ramona Heights is a safe haven, well away from the social cataclysms that have rocked the nation. But the possibility that some of its residents may be using the tract as no more than a way station on the ladder of success was acknowledged by a few of the respondents, even though they hastened to deny such motivation for themselves. Ralph Porfilio brought up the subject when discussing what he likes least about the neighborhood.

Ralph: Ramona Heights has people who are either the elderly couple who say, "Fine, this is where I'm going to live and retire," or the person who is on his way up to bigger and better things, along with the lawyer who has been in practice for five years and is about ready to make it into his own private estate, or the doctor in the same situation. Although there are doctors and lawyers on this street who are extremely nice people, and this is all they want, basically. They don't care about the social climate, but you have others who do. That, I would say, is what I like least about it.

These particular families are remarkably well settled, in comparison to the notable mobility of California society. Nine had lived in Ramona Heights since their houses were built in 1964, and all twelve first interviewed in 1970 remained there in 1973. If these families are restlessly striving, they are not striving for a more prestigious address. As noted previously, in expressing appreciation for the comforts of their own neighborhood, the respondents are likely to mention unattractive aspects of the wealthier areas, as when the Rineharts cite family instability, and the Porfilios describe the lack of community spirit, in adjoining areas. This may represent no more than a rationalization of their own status, the adoption of an excuse for not achieving what one's limited income prohibits. But this is unlikely. The values and rewards which one seeks in life are rather intimately entwined with one's life experience. If great expectations are frustrated, the most common reaction is probably to lower the expectations, and then to discover reasons why the expectations were of little value. These considerations soon become more important than the experience of frustration. Thomas Hobbes wrote that the struggle for power of men against their neighbors ceases only in death.[23] In the suburban tracts of a materialistic society, it is easy to suppose that the striving for increased income, possessions, and prestige ceases only in death. But the bulk of the Ramona Heights respondents recognize the comforts they enjoy, budget their income so that the enjoyment does not jeopardize their future, and get on with the process of living. The scramble for possessions at least allows inter-

[23]Hobbes, *Leviathan* (London: J. M. Dent & Sons Ltd., 1953; first published 1651), p. 49.

missions when the possessions can be enjoyed.[24]

That Fletcher Barbera does not take a second job in order to buy a bigger house means that he enjoys an achieved social status. It does not mean that he is eager to share his achieved comforts with those who are less fortunate. Indeed, he expresses hostility to the degree of sharing that is suggested by the graduated income tax.

Status Incongruity

Ramona Heights would seem a neighborhood of comparatively contented suburbanites. No members of the microsample expressed the ruthless and narrow motivation summed up in the word "striving," nor do their ambitions for the future merit description by that term. The fact remains that Ramona Heights is a favored place to live; its comforts, its location, and the styles of life it a offers must rank high on the value scale of most middle-class Americans. The residents of Ramona Heights perhaps react to their good fortune in ways that have overtones for the formation of political attitudes. A fruitful source of hypotheses is found in the theoretical and empirical works employing the concept of status incongruity.

Status incongruity results from social mobility, as an individual rises above, or falls below, the status of his parents. This movement results in tastes and attitudes which are out of phase with one's perceived social rank, as the indicators of status change independently. (The executive son of a worker father may drink wine with his meals rather than beer before them, while still attending the Baptist church.) Status incongruence leads to anxiety which is relieved by adopting changed political attitudes. The most common pattern in American suburbia, it is presumed, is for the newly arrived member of a higher class to adopt attitudes that are even more conservative than those of the established members of the class. This is an example of the phenomenon of "anticipatory socialization."[25]

[24]This is in contrast to the working men studied by Lane, *Political Ideology*, p. 77.

[25]See Andrzej Malewski, "The Degree of Status Incongruence and its Effects," in *Class, Status, and Power*, ed. R. Bendix and S. M. Lipset (New York: Macmillan, Free Press, 1966), pp. 303–308. See also S. M. Lipset and H.L. Zetterberg, "A Theory of Social Mobility," in the same volume, pp. 570–573. For a discussion of the concept of "anticipatory socialization," see Robert K. Merton and Alice Kitt Ross, "Reference Group Theory and Social Mobility," also in the same volume, pp. 510–515. James McEvoy III finds studies of status anxiety less than useful for predicting right-wing political attitudes; see

The signs of status discrepancy are not hard to find among our twelve families, and it is not hard to match their situations with hypotheses from the literature. What is more difficult, if not impossible, is to find a single concept in the social mobility literature which helps explain the political attitudes of more than one family.

Quentin Elliott may be considered downwardly mobile. In dropping out of the corporate world, he is accepting a lower income, and entering an occupation which, he confesses, has less prestige in the eyes of his parents. However, he can do this because he has both economic and psychological security. He knows that his education at a private eastern prep school, followed by an Ivy League college, compares very favorably with that of his fellow teachers; this achievement can hardly be denied him. Consciously rejecting the rewards of the corporate world, he feels no compulsion to maintain an upper-class facade in Ramona Heights. This as a pattern defined by sociologist Andrzej Malewski.

> People whose status is very high and stable pay less attention to behavior as the visible symbol of their high status.[26]

In fact, Quentin's moderate liberalism (as expressed in his admiration for Senator Charles Percy) may be somewhat akin to the noblesse oblige of a Roosevelt or a Nelson Rockefeller, although on a more modest scale. One might speculate that Quentin turned to the left politically, on settling in Orange County, in order to differentiate himself from the outlook of his neighbors, who tend to fall a rung or two below him on the social ladder. However, Quentin has found that his neighbors' political views are quite congruent with his own; the notion of Orange County as a stronghold of political reaction, he feels, is a myth. (But Ronald Reagan is no Percy; Quentin and Deborah registered as Democrats.)

Much closer to the pattern of status discrepancy are the Johnsons. As a worker's son who now owns his own manufacturing business, Harry is "intragenerationally mobile." He and Jacqueline are comparatively wealthy, and they enjoy their wealth, but mostly in private. They play golf largely with each other; they do not move in the social circles to which their income might gain them entry. They vote for conservative Republicans, but they remain registered Democrats. Their chief status incongruence is their working-class background and the fact that they are undereducated, compared to others of their present income level. According to Malewski:

---

his *Radicals or Conservatives? The Contemporary American Right* (Chicago: Rand McNally, 1971), pp. 37–41.

[26]Malewski, "Degree of Status Incongruence," p. 307

If an individual has several incongruent status factors, some of which are evaluated as much lower than others, and when this individual cannot raise the lower factors, he will show a tendency to avoid those people who react to them.[27]

It is possible that the Johnsons live a relatively private life because in the past they have indeed been put down ("negatively evaluated") for being only *newly* rich, as well as being undereducated. Perhaps this is why they continue to live in Ramona Heights, when they could afford a wealthier neighborhood, and retain Democratic registration while voting Republican. Their voting for conservative candidates can hardly be explained as some psychological need to prove the legitimacy of their claim to membership in social circles commensurate with their income. They have little communication with those circles. A more likely explanation of their voting decisions lies with Harry Johnson's status as a businessman and his perceptions of self-interest.

Status discrepancy theories have been used to explain, at least partially, the liberal political attachment of American Jews. Piotr and Myrna Pavel fit the pattern. American Jewish liberalism is viewed as a continuation of the tradition that made European Jews active in socialist movements. In Europe, Jews achieved legal emancipation as a result of long struggle, but it did not include their integration into the social hierarchy. According to sociologist Robert Michels:

Even when they are rich, the Jews constitute . . . a category of persons who are excluded from the social advantages which the prevailing political, economic, and intellectual system ensures for the corresponding portion of the Gentile population.[28]

Denied entry into the upper social classes because their ethnic membership is negatively evaluated, Jews would then be led to reject the evaluational system, including political attitudes, of Gentiles who are their equals on other measures of status. Seymour Martin Lipset adds that "in the United State the bulk of the Jewish middle class supports the more liberal or left-wing parties, even though their occupational and economic position would seem to suggest a more conservative outlook."[29] Tit for tat. Lipset's empirical observation is true, but his causal explanation seems entirely too simple. The liberalism of the Pavels is hardly a reaction to exclusion from the society of Ramona Heights, for they have not sought any special entry. Their social life is based on a

[27] *Ibid.*, p. 306.
[28] Quoted in Lipset and Zetterberg, "Theory of Social Mobility," p. 572.
[29] *Ibid.*

web of friendships formed before they moved into the tract. Myrna Pavel says that she has not experienced anti-Semitism in Orange County. Their liberalism is a matter of tradition and conviction.

Status discrepancies may help explain something about the behavior of Ramona Heights voters. The presumed pattern of adopting ultraconservative attitudes to legitimatize one's entry into a higher social milieu does not apply to the Elliotts, the Johnsons, or the Pavels. Kenneth Kaub may be regarded as upwardly mobile, the physician son of a farmer, but his political attitudes have grown much more liberal than would be expected of one with his Kansas origins. John Wesley Weeks is also upwardly mobile, for his father was a member of the working class. But Weeks's father was a Republican, so that Weeks's adherence to moderate Republicanism represents no change from parental party identification.

This leaves an important group for examination. They are the three Mexican-Americans—Arthur Roybal, Arnold Garcia, and Marie Kaub —whose presence in Ramona Heights represents the most impressive social climb. All three were born into poverty and the limiting vistas of the *barrio*.

Mexicans in an Anglo Suburb

If the adjustment of status discrepancies by the upwardly mobile leads to ultraconservatism, as a way of establishing the appropriateness of membership in the new social class, the three Chicanos of our sample deserve special study. They have traveled the furthest, and may have modified their political attitudes the most. However, it would be straining the definition to label any of them as ultraconservative. Marie Kaub remains a registered Democrat, but she is attracted to several Republican candidates, although she opposes the heroes—Schmitz, Reagan, and Rafferty—of Orange County's right wing. Arthur Roybal is registered as a Republican for "defensive" reasons—he votes for liberal Republicans in the primary contests; when they are defeated, he supports Democrats in the general election. Arnold Garcia has internalized the traditional American values of rugged individualism in a context of free enterprise, and he expresses admiration for George Wallace. But political issues are only marginally salient for him. He is not even activist enough to vote regularly in party primaries. His attitudes are conservative, when measured along a number of dimensions, but they are not so important to him as to stimulate more than a nominal degree of political activity.

These attitudinal differences may be explained in part as resulting from status discrepancies, but only in the context of the three life histories.

Marie Kaub's family suffered more than most from the ravages of the depression. Her father was frequently unemployed, and often the only food came from welfare agencies. As a girl, she lived in a series of two-room hovels, which sometimes had electricity but never bathrooms. The family moved to keep ahead of their debts to a series of landlords.

Life was hard, but when she was very small there was little feeling of being disadvantaged, for life was hard for the neighbors as well, and there was a warm sense of belonging and acceptance in the *barrio*. However, family tradition held that adversity was not their normal lot; a not-too-distant ancestor had been a Spanish general. This "myth of a golden past" suggested climbing back up from the economic depths.[30] Spanish was not spoken much in the home, so that Marie spoke English well before she went to school. Attendance at public school brought awareness of other, more affluent, patterns of life, as well as an intellectual awakening. Marie did well in school competing against the children of Anglo parents, and this also suggested the possibility of an upward climb, with education as the means. Her aspirations were not encouraged by the nuns who taught her in the parochial school, but a Mexican-American teacher in the public high school stimulated her academic ambition.

Her education was interrupted by her first brief marriage, which left her a youthful widow with a small child. Fortunately, her extended family was able to care for the baby while she completed training as an X-ray technician. The break out of the *barrio* was symbolized by moving to California. She met Kenneth Kaub in the hospital where she worked and found, in his sensitive personality, an echo of her own life struggles.

The Kaubs were one of the first couples to move into Ramona Heights. They bought their home on the basis of the floor plan before the first model was even constructed. As a result, Marie was a "pioneer settler" who could greet the new wives as they arrived. If she, as a Mexican-American, had come to an established neighborhood, she might not have been welcomed with enthusiasm, but she was doing the welcoming. She helped found two of the women's social clubs that are

[30]The "myth of a golden past" is a recurrent theme in upward-mobile Mexican-American families. It often takes the form of a belief that one's relatives in Mexico were wealthy, but squandered their substance through gambling, bad marriages, or other personal problems. See L. Grebler, J. W. Moore, and R. C. Guzman, *The Mexican-American People* (New York: Macmillan, Free Press, 1970), p. 338.

still active in Ramona Heights. She speaks with simple gratitude of the good friends she has found there.

The crucial question for political attitude formation is: Which group membership most supports the individual's sense of identity? Marie has left the ethnic community and moves with ease in the spatially limited social circles of Ramona Heights. If she were to adopt ultraconservative views as a kind of "anticipatory socialization," this would indicate that she was grasping for identity with the Anglo social class, and rejecting the Chicano culture. But this is not the case. She refers to herself as a Mexican-American. She expresses deep sympathy for the goals of Cesar Chavez in organizing farm laborers—"Listen, if you ever did stoop labor, you're for it"—although she expresses misgivings about some of his methods. She maintains close contact with the families of her brother and two sisters, who live in Los Angeles County suburbs much less prosperous than Ramona Heights. She feels that members of minority groups must have pride in their identity. She was horrified by the 1970 Chicano riots in East Los Angeles, but she was not sure that Mayor Yorty was justified in naming a park after Reuben Salazar, the Chicano journalist killed during the rioting. She discussed the differences between various ethnic groups quite openly.

Marie: If we must use an example, there are the Mexicans who are the "mañana people" who still carry this kind of thought with them, they still don't have that much push sometimes.

More ambivalent than contradictory, this variety of attitudes indicates Marie's wavering adaptation to her situation, assimilating attitudes from first one milieu, then another. And so it is with politics. She retains the Democratic party identification of her parents, but she defers to her husband's education in matters of political judgment, and she is attracted to a number of Republican candidates. She has achieved a middle-class identity, but it is vulnerable. She does not reject her ethnic heritage, but she will never be a militant spokesman for Chicano rights among her Anglo neighbors.

Arnold Garcia's life history presents interesting points of contrast. The dominant factor in his image of himself is that he is alone responsible for overcoming the disadvantages of his origins; he is a self-made man who has prospered in an environment where only the fittest survive. Arnold admired the same qualities of drive and ambition in his father. His parents were born in Mexico, and his mother never did learn to speak English, so that English was spoken little in the home, and learning it was a major hurdle when he went to school. His mother encouraged him in his school work, and he had a good head for numbers, so he zoomed through the arithmetic books. This ability suggested a career in accounting. In 1942 he was failed in the oral interview section of the Los Angeles County civil service examination, after doing very well on the written section, because of discrimination. Arnold's brother, who changed his name, passed the same examination. But Arnold refused to change his own name; he is proud of his ethnic identity even today, and he refers to himself simply as a Mexican.

Arnold Garcia lives in Ramona Heights, but he does not draw an identity from it, in the manner of Marie Kaub. He speaks of his neighbors with contempt, feeling that many of them bought homes when they could not really keep up the payments. He also mentions the one black family living in the neighborhood. They were only able to move in, he claims, with financial aid from a civil rights organization that purchased the home to achieve a toehold of integration in Ramona Heights.[31] Arnold feels this is despicable. He says he would respect and welcome a black family as neighbors if the family was able to afford the home on their own. He would probably become better friends, he says, than he is with his present Anglo neighbors. But the important thing is that the family be able to own a home in Ramona Heights through its own efforts, without external support.

At one point, Arnold Garcia demanded rhetorically if I had ever visited Mexico, and then described the extremes of poverty that can be found there. Nobody would live like that, he said, unless he liked it. This attitude seems an echo of Marie Kaub's discussion of the "mañana people." There is, in fact, a belief prevalent in Mexico that poverty is virtuous.[32] Both Arnold Garcia and Marie Kaub reject that belief, but Marie is more likely to recognize that peasant poverty may not result from a failure of ambition on the part of the peasant.

Arnold Garcia is an individualist. He opposes fair housing laws, for he feels that the rights of property are close to sacrosanct. He opposes the growth of government power, although he favors wage and price controls to stabilize the economy. He admires George Wallace, but he volunteers the opinion that Wallace is not really a racist (and by implication not really a threat to Mexican-Americans). Rather, he feels that

[31] In fact, the one black family in the tract is West Indian. The husband is an electronics engineer employed at one of the aerospace firms clustered around Orange County Airport. The family's presence is an example of the "brain drain" of technologically educated personnel from the British Commonwealth to the greater opportunities available in the United States.

[32] Grebler, Moore, and Guzman, *Mexican-American People*.

Wallace only used racist appeals in Alabama because of political expediency. Arnold Garcia has nothing but contempt for the younger generation and the complaints it voices, and he speaks disparagingly of his two sons. Although he does not say so, one senses his pride that his older son is a student in dental school, determined to serve in a *barrio* clinic after graduation. Garcia waves his hand vaguely at his own spotless home and says that his sons don't understand how tough the world is. Once on their own, they'll have no place to go but down. He doesn't mean, he says, that Ramona Heights is the top; "but it's pretty good for a Mexican."

On any contemporary scale, Arnold Garcia's political attitudes would be labeled conservative. But they are attitudes which result from his own convictions about the nature of life and his experience with the realities of economic competition. They do not reflect his adoption of political attitudes of upper-middle-class Anglos, as a method of proving the legitimacy of his entry into that social class. He doesn't care about the opinions of his neighbors, or of anyone else. He is a relentless materialist; if Anglos of lesser income despise him for his origins, that only demonstrates their stupidity. Garcia ranks at the top of the microsample on the scale designed to measure authoritarianism.

Like Garcia's parents, Arthur Roybal's mother and father were both born in Mexico. However, the children brought English home to their mother and made it the home language. The family was poor, but tightly knit. Both parents encouraged their children to continue with their education; Arthur eventually earned a master's degree in education. Ambition was instilled in all the family; his brothers all have excellent positions, with incomes higher than his own.

Arthur: I hate the term "Mexican-American," and yet that's what I am. . . . And I think that there is a very negative stigma attached to the Mexicans. And I resent it, and that's why I said I'm American, first and last. . . . I'm an American, period. When you've pulled yourself up out of a cesspool, you don't like to smell it again. And I did. And I recognize that I probably should, using the old cliché, be helping my brothers. But I think I can help them in a different way.

A description of the pains of social mobility experienced by Mexican-Americans reports:

Instead of comparing themselves with their parents and congratulating themselves on how far they have come, they compare themselves with others in the Anglo world and depreciate their accomplishments. Instead of looking ahead to a better future, they often look behind in fear of the abyss from which they have climbed.[33]

Arthur Roybal says he is forever barred from the upper circles of society because of his ethnic origin. The elite clubs, he says, are for WASPS only. In a way, Arthur is the most troubled of the three Mexicans in Ramona Heights. Marie Kaub has achieved a warm amalgamation of identity ingredients that includes positive attributes of the Anglo middle class without suppressing the attractive features of Mexican culture. She has achieved fame in the neighborhood for the Mexican specialties she serves at dinner parties. Arnold Garcia surrounds himself with the material symbols of his success, and he sees political issues from the businessman's point of view. He is tough and cynical; whatever psychic wounds he may have suffered during his upward climb are well hidden. But one catches a sudden glimpse when, referring to his 1969 income, he says, "You wouldn't believe that a Mexican could make that much money." Garcia comes the closest of any of the microsample to fitting the stereotype of the suburban striver. His striving is made more poignant by his daily drive (in an air-conditioned Porsche) into East Los Angeles, where he derives a large income from the *barrio*. But he has little further interest in the welfare of its residents. If they are poor, he feels, it is their own fault.

Arthur Roybal has not achieved the kind of firm commitment to his style of life that Marie Kaub and Arnold Garcia exhibit. On the one hand, he views Ramona Heights as a "sterile" community, because of the homogeneity of its class membership. On the other, he specifically rejects the label normally applied to members of his own ethnic group. He acknowledges the miserable quality of the ghetto schools, but he is not eager for large-scale social experimentation to redress the balance, although he would like to "help my brothers."

Arthur: If a little black kid or a Mexican-American wants to come to our school, I think we ought to allow them to come to our school, provided they provide their own transportation.

Arthur's statements seem contradictory, but there is another way of interpreting them. As an official of the county school system, he is more aware than even Quentin Elliott of the extremes of wealth and poverty that exist in Orange County. He is concerned daily with social problems that Garcia, in his Porsche, and Marie Kaub, in her walled patio, need pay little attention to. (The Kaubs were the only couple in the microsam-

[33] *Ibid.*, p. 342.

ple to vote against an antibusing initiative in 1972.) Roybal is aware of social dilemmas which cannot be easily resolved. He recognizes both flaws and benefits in proposed solutions. What seems an uncertain social identity may actually be a reflection of his greater contact with political reality.

In spite of their differences, the three Chicanos have common themes in their life histories. All are upwardly mobile; all early perceived education as the key to mobility and did well in school. All are intelligent and articulate. And all three have married exogamously, which is a frequent behavior pattern of mobile Mexican-Americans.[34] Marriage to someone outside the ethnic group is a clear signal of readiness to leave many of its values behind. Finally, none of the three is likely to become a political activist, to supply leadership for their comrades still struggling out of the *barrio*. By the very nature of their status in an Anglo middle-class suburb, Marie Kaub and Arthur Roybal are unlikely recruits into the ranks of La Raza Unida, a political action movement based on the cultivation of ethnic solidarity. Arnold Garcia is a rugged individualist who would never merge his interests with those of a group.

This does not mean that they refuse to acknowledge the needs of the *barrios* or of American society at large. It does not mean that they will refuse to support, with money and even work, political candidates who promise social reform—although Arnold Garcia will probably not find his way onto the mailing lists of radical organizations. Rather, what has happened is that Arnold, Arthur, and Marie have achieved such a distance, measured both physically and psychologically, from their origins, that their life patterns are based on other motives; having achieved affluence, and needing no recourse to political skills to assure their daily comfort, their motivations are increasingly private.

It is entirely possible that all the residents of Ramona Heights have achieved such a distance from other elements in American society that its problems—even when reported nightly on television—seem increasingly remote. The phenomenon of privatism, therefore, may be the key to the paradox of Orange County. The voters of Ramona Heights demonstrate that a degree of political liberalism exists at the grass roots in Orange County that is little reflected in its elected leaders and is completely foreign to its stereotyped image. Privatism—the failure to participate in public life—may explain the uncertain linkage between voter opinion and the behavior of public officials in Orange County.

[34] *Ibid.*, p. 410.

PART THREE

Elements of a Political Ethos

The whole world here seems a malleable substance that man turns and fashions to his pleasure; an immense field, whose smallest part only has yet been traversed, is here open to industry. Not a man but may reasonably hope to gain the comforts of life; not one who does not know that with love of work his future is certain.

Thus, in this happy country nothing draws the restless human spirit toward political passions; everything, on the contrary, draws it toward an activity that has nothing dangerous for the state.

—*Letter from Alexis de Tocqueville to E. de Chabrol, 1831, translated in George Wilson Pierson*, Tocqueville in America *(Garden City, N.Y.: Doubleday, Anchor Press, 1959), p. 87*

CHAPTER SIX

God, Country, and Enterprise:
A Search for the Sacred

One need not be a secularist to believe that politics in the name of God is of the devil. . . . Almost any kind of struggle can be interpreted as a contest between Christ and Antichrist.

—*Reinhold Niebuhr*[1]

Alienation, anomie, despair of being able to chart one's own course in a complex, cold and bewildering world have become characteristic of a large part of the population of advanced countries. As the world can be neither understood nor influenced, attachment to reassuring abstract symbols rather than to one's own efforts becomes chronic.

—*Murray Edelman*[2]

"[In the ideal society] I see a complete disappearance of the religious differences of humanity."

—*Piotr Pavel*

SERENE ON ITS HILLTOP, Ramona Heights can be imagined as a kind of vantage point for a new departure in American history. Here, at the water's edge, the transcontinental drive of the American business-dominated

[1]Quoted in Harry R. Davis and Robert C. Good, eds., *Reinhold Niebuhr on Politics* (New York: Scribner's, 1960), p. 203.
[2]Murray Edelman, *The Symbolic Uses of Politics* (Urbana: University of Illinois Press, 1964), p. 76.

culture ended; here, awaiting the next great alignment of political forces, rests a segment of the American middle class; here, if the nation will survive, must be born a realization that the vast natural resources which fueled the advance of American capitalism face exhaustion; and the greed which served a lusty, expanding nation can only destroy a mature and morally exhausted one.

The voters of Ramona Heights do not invest their neighborhood with symbolic importance, nor do they see it as the threshold to a different political future. Examining their most deeply held convictions cannot lead to a prediction that some new system of ideas is about to replace old values. The most that can be gained are clues to the manner in which adept political leadership may enlist their dedication to those values in support of change—change for admirable purposes, or the opposite.

The dominant political and social ethos of the American people has been an expression of the values of the middle class; here, as in no other country, the bourgeois ethic held sway, unchallenged by the remnants of any preindustrial structure of classes or the claims of an established aristocracy. Count de Tocqueville perceived this truth of American society during his visit in 1831, and the dominance of middle-class values has only been challenged, with signs that the challenge may be successful, in the past few years.[3]

The last stronghold of the middle-class ethos must be in affluent suburban tracts like Ramona Heights. Its present status and clues to its future development may be discovered in the interviews with our twelve families. However, the Ramona Heights transcripts gain meaning when set in a historical context. Let us leave the tract for the moment to sketch the growth of some bourgeois convictions which animate American history.

Achievement and Equality: Sources of a Faith

The power of the American middle-class value system arises from the circumstances of its origin, the secularization of a compelling religious perception. The New World was first settled when the Reformation was sweeping Europe. The original immigrants were religious radicals, and Protestant clergymen saw the hand of divine providence at work in

[3]See Peter Schrag, *The Decline of the WASP* (New York: Simon & Schuster, 1971).

conquering the new continent. It seemed as if God had delayed its discovery until the fullness of time, so that the new recipients of his grace might settle and multiply here. America was the New Israel; the colonists would here achieve a new heaven and a new earth.[4] The first Americans felt a sense of divine mission, to be performed in this world, not the next. The implications of divine guidance were reinforced by the compulsion of the Puritans to demonstrate the legitimacy of their membership in the congregation of the select. In the words of Max Weber:

> ... it is not the ethical *doctrine* of a religion, but that form of ethical conduct upon which *premiums* are placed that matters. . . . For Puritanism, that conduct was a certain methodical, rational way of life which—given certain conditions—paved the way for the "spirit" of modern capitalism. The premiums were placed upon "proving" oneself before God in the sense of attaining salvation . . . and "proving" oneself before men in the sense of socially holding one's own within the Puritan sects.[5]

The conception of men predestined by God for salvation stimulated an ideal type of behavior (honesty and industry) through which individuals demonstrated on earth their select status. This conduct became the ethical norm, while its divine sanction was first subordinated and then forgotten. When Tocqueville came to America, the process of secularization was well advanced. He found a nation in which a variety of religious sects flourished together; all were tolerant of doctrinal diversity. He found a populace of merchants bent upon the achievement of riches, in the full flush of confidence that riches were attainable.

The settlement of America was part of the Age of the Reformation, but her independence and political institutions were the work of the Enlightenment. This age was convinced that man's power of reason could direct his affairs, if only it were freed from the constraints of hereditary political authority and temporal religious power. Such constraints were not part of the New World climate, and the attempt to establish a theocracy in New England proved futile. The vast land itself

---

[4]Robert N. Bellah, "Civil Religion in America," *Daedalus,* Winter, 1967, pp. 1–21. Also see William Warren Sweet, *The Story of Religion in America* (New York: Harper, 1950), p. 3.

[5]H. H. Gerth and C. Wright Mills, ed. and trans., *From Max Weber: Essays in Sociology* (New York: Oxford University Press, Galaxy Books, 1958), p. 321. Weber's conception is far from being universally accepted. Compare, for example: "Big business—buccaneering capitalism—is descended more nearly from the great banking houses of the Renaissance, and if Calvinism ever said that prosperity is the reward or the proof of God's favor, at that point it had ceased to be Calvinism" (Roland H. Bainton, *The Age of the Reformation* [Princeton, N.J.: Van Nostrand, 1956], p. 90).

suggested that free reason could conquer nature and subsume its resources to the betterment of mankind.[6]Tocqueville noted that the New World seemed a "malleable substance" that man could "turn and fashion to his pleasure."

One fruit of that free reason was the separation of church and state, formalized in the First Amendment to the Constitution. The growth of religious pluralism weakened the authority of particular dogmas, while the separation between sacred and secular, so firm in theory, became obscured in practice. Soon John Locke's political ideas and Adam Smith's economic concepts flourished in the ethical climate prepared by Puritanism.

Almost from the inception of the republic, a realm of the sacred was established around the national symbols—first the Constitution, then the flag, later the union, and eventually the presidential office. Americans developed, in Rousseau's phrase, a "civil religion."[7]

From the Protestant sects came a profound sense of individual responsibility for salvation, soon secularized as the striving for success in Adam Smith's free marketplace. From the Enlightenment came the conviction that all men are created equal, and their equal rights are best assured, as Locke wrote, by minimal government. These are the sources of what Seymour Martin Lipset has called the two enduring values of American society, achievement and equality. Their jointure supports the concurrent glorification of capitalism and democracy. Americans have held the two values simultaneously, emphasizing now one, now the other, without confronting their implied contradiction.[8] For, when a man husbands the fruits of his achievement, founding vast enterprises and endowing prodigal sons, social differences are created which affront the ideal of equality asserted by the Declaration of Independence. A system of national government was established in the Constitution, which some of its framers felt would protect the rewards of achievement against the leveling instincts of the state legislatures. In our own time, progress toward achieving the ideal of equality has depended more on the federal

[6]Sheldon Wolin points out that the original liberal philosophers were neither as naïve nor as arrogant as they are currently pictured. In particular, they had a profound sense of the limitations on nature's bounty. See his *Politics and Vision* (Boston: Little, Brown, 1960), pp. 293 ff.

[7]Bellah, "Civil Religion in America," *passim*. Also see Lewis Lipsitz, "If, as Verba Says, the State Functions as a Religion, What Are We to Do Then to Save Our Souls?" 63 *American Political Science Review* 2 (June, 1968), pp. 528–530.

[8]Seymour Martin Lipset, *The First New Nation* (Garden City, N.Y.: Doubleday, Anchor Press, 1967), pp. 115–118.

government than on the states. But the two values remain, intermingled, threads in the fabric of American history.

The setting of Ramona Heights symbolizes past beliefs, rather than new convictions. The placement of the houses on flat terraces bulldozed into the sloping contours of the land suggests, if not contempt for nature, at least man's ability casually to revise it. From any of the hilltop homes, one may look down upon the spires of one Catholic and two Protestant churches, a reminder of religious pluralism.

If the Ramona Heights respondents are products of the intellectual history of the American middle class, what convictions will they share? These voters are all over thirty years of age; their perceptions of America were well formulated before the campus dissent and racial conflict of the 1960s challenged the casual assumption of democratic success. If they are adherents of a civil religion, and concurrently hold the values of achievement and equality in high esteem, we may conclude that their thinking about politics will be based upon at least the three following convictions, which they may or may not articulate self-consciously:

1. *We are a successful society.* In spite of riot and turmoil, the American democratic experiment has achieved a basic procedural consensus and remarkable material progress. American governmental institutions have an inspired quality. Because the Founding Fathers wrought so well, basic questions need not be reconsidered.

2. *Most citizens are free to achieve.* The political and economic systems are interdependent; a major purpose of government is to assure free economic competition, so that an individual's success will be limited only by the extent of his ambition, imagination, and effort. Equality is defined as "an equal start," and governmental activity may be necessary to assure this equality of opportunity. But no programs of the welfare state should be allowed to threaten the moral order based upon the necessity for individual achievement.

3. *Political action yields limited results.* Since the basic institutional questions have been solved, and the national ideals have been defined (even if they remain to be completely realized), "politics" is identified as a struggle for partisan or group advantage, rather than a quest for the good of all. Just as politics is little more than a search for "unfair" advantage, the offices established by the inspired Constitution are held by incumbents who are mere politicians. As the Watergate scandals emphasized, their integrity is

often mortgaged to special interests, and they practice demagoguery and other immoral techniques. The daily management of affairs is in charge of complex bureaucracies, staffed by civil servants of established habit who are slow to respond to their political superiors, much less to the public will.

Do the voters of Ramona Heights, despite their differing parties, occupations, and life histories, share these beliefs? The answer emerges from following a twisting trail through the interview transcripts. It begins with a description of the rewards which the respondents find (or fail to find) in organized religion.

The Voice of God
(At Best a Whisper)

The main American faiths are normally categorized as Protestant, Catholic, and Jewish. The Ramona Heights microsample consists of nine Protestants (including one former Catholic, and four who have changed Protestant denominations at least once), eleven at least nominal Catholics (including one former Protestant), and three agnostics (the Pavels, of Jewish cultural heritage, and Jan Markus, whose grandparents were Catholics). This complexity of classification, applied to a mere dozen families, suggests what is the case: differences in the form of religious practice abound, but they are not considered important. The relative ease with which individuals change or simply abandon their religious affiliation suggests that differences in faith are no longer considered worth fighting over.

The suburbs have been seen as the home of a religious renaissance, as exemplified by the three handsome new churches near Ramona Heights, but critics raise doubts as to the depth of religious conviction found in suburbia. The choice of a faith may have little spiritual meaning.

> The main mood of many a suburban church on Sundays is that of a fashionable shopping center. . . . On weekdays one shops for food, on Saturdays one shops for recreation, and on Sundays one shops for the Holy Ghost . . . the suburban church is accepted by the mass as no more than a pleasing and fashionable facet of culture . . . the House of the Lord is being reduced to a comfort station.[9]

[9]Stanley Rowland, Jr., "Suburbia Buys Religion," *The Nation*, June 28, 1956, pp. 79–80.

This charge, like others leveled against suburbia, is really a criticism of American middle-class culture, and the phenomenon it decries has persisted for a substantial period of American history. Sects in America have engaged in waves of competition for new members; the denominations (Baptists and Methodists) which proselytized among the common people during the nineteenth century have become respectable, middle class, and increasingly secularized, while newer evangelical faiths have entered the field beneath them. Each faith was a minority; its own privileges could be protected only by defending the freedom of all, so religious pluralism created a marketplace of faiths. The adaptability of dogma to the convictions of the membership was demonstrated by the divisions of several denominations into southern wings favoring slavery and northern wings opposing it.[10] The description of the church as a shopping center is not far from the surprised descriptions of the tolerance of the American sects for each other penned by nineteenth-century visitors.[11]

The Protestants in the microsample are unanimous in feeling that the slightly different details of dogma and ritualistic practice among the established Protestant denominations completely lack importance. Some form of religious practice is considered important for the sake of the children, but it is not forced upon them, once they are old enough to voice objections.

Maureen Barbera, an ex-Catholic, put her children in a Presbyterian Sunday school rather than the one run by her own Episcopal congregation. She confesses that the Episcopalian ritual, being closer to the Catholic, appeals to her; her instincts are "high church." But for her children, she is more concerned with intellectual content; she feels the Presbyterians offer the best Sunday school in the area. Fletcher Barbera's mother was a devoted Presbyterian and Fletcher was confirmed in that faith, but his father regarded church-going as "hypocritical." Following the paternal pattern, Fletcher stays away from church, but he supports Maureen in sending the children.

Even Richard and Alice Rinehart, the most devoted of Protestant churchgoers, confess that their involvement was greater when their children were young. Setting a good example for the children, Richard says, was uppermost in their minds, and they enjoyed knowing the other young parents with similar concerns. But they admit that religion does

[10]Seymour Martin Lipset, *Revolution and Counterrevolution* (Garden City, N.Y.: Doubleday, Anchor Press, 1968), pp. 313–316. Also see Sweet, *Story of Religion*, chaps. 3–19.
[11]Three such descriptions are found in Lipset, *First New Nation*, pp. 174–175.

not play the role it should for the younger generation.

John Wesley and Martha Weeks were regular participants in the Methodist congregation they helped found in Long Beach. It was the center of their social life. John supervised the Sunday school, Martha served as secretary and bookkeeper, and the minister was a close family friend. When the Weekses moved to Ramona Heights, they did not transfer their church membership, remaining on the roster in Long Beach. They felt that returning nearly thirty miles to church would keep them in touch with their old friends there. But they quickly found a new circle of friends in Ramona Heights, and after the first year they returned to their church hardly at all. Church attendance has dropped out of their lives completely.

John: I think religion is probably a state of mind, and you know, I've never been one that believed that God presides in a church. A church is just once again symbolism, and I think it depends upon the individual, and his character. . . . For the vast majority of people, church is a way of salving one's own conscience.

Caroline Porfilio says that religion is not very important in her life or in her husband's. Although she converted to Catholicism upon her marriage to Ralph, they do not attend mass together, even on major holidays, although she occasionally attends when she is "in the mood." Caroline approves of the modernization of the church but feels that it has not progressed far enough; she feels that clerical celibacy and opposition to abortion should both be abandoned. Perhaps she will attend regularly, she says, when the church "shapes up."

Caroline: But we see that the children go. We aren't just leaving them high up in the air with nothing. I think everybody has to have a little religion to fall back on.

The Elliott family's religious activity was also centered around social needs, before the summer of 1972. Quentin Elliott had been interested in religion for most of his life, attending Sunday services alone when he was only ten. Later he attended an Episcopal preparatory school and enjoyed the compulsory chapel attendance. At Princeton he read theology, but never very deeply, and he toyed with the idea of entering the ministry, but never reached a decision. Drafted into the army, he managed to arrange a transfer to the chaplains' corps, but he always suspected that this was less an act of faith than a desire to leave the infantry.

When they moved to Ramona Heights, the Elliotts joined the nearby

Episcopal church. By 1970, Quentin was singing in the choir, while Deborah taught Sunday school. She was only willing to teach the nursery class, however, because of her personal doubts about the value of formal religious instruction.

In the spring of 1972, their oldest son began studying the trombone with a young musician who had recently changed his life style due to the influence of fundamentalist religion. The trombone lessons were filled with religious discussion, and the son asked permission to attend a Sunday morning meeting held in a circus tent in a nearby city. Quentin went along. When summer came the boy asked to go to Bible camp, and Quentin again accompanied him. At first Quentin remained in the background, playing the role of indulgent father. But he became caught up in the activities of the camp, and began to confront issues of faith that he had never settled within himself. Without a dramatic experience of conversion, he found a new faith.

Quentin: I have a sense of peace now, a good part of the time, or any time that I stop, and pray, and listen to the Word and the truth of the Word, which I never had before. . . . I now realize, in our society, and with my upbringing, I thought you have to experience something first, to believe it. And I'm told that's the scientific way. And, in this kind of thing, with the direct reading of the scriptures, and letting what happens, happen, rather than to question, and doubt, and erect barriers, if I just let it happen to me, then I believe first and experience afterwards. . . . Proof comes just by the acceptance.

Quentin and the older boy began attending the Sunday tent meeting, which in 1972 attracted some six thousand people from Orange County every Sunday. In a manner that may seem typical of California, members of the congregation attempted to propagate the faith by attaching bumper stickers to their cars. Quentin's son affixed a bright sign to their station wagon which read, "Get Right With Jesus." Deborah continued taking their daughters to the Episcopal church for a few weeks, but decided that the difference wasn't that important, so the entire family now attends the fundamentalist church (except for the eleven-year-old boy, who isn't interested).

Quentin emphasizes that his newly found faith is intensely personal; it has no implications for his thinking about social or political questions. Deborah says, however, that the kind of religious experience that helped her son could be of widespread benefit, for it challenges materialistic values.

Deborah: Perhaps in the long run, if enough young people just don't accept the adult values, enough young people need to go in this direction, it just may keep the nation on a more honest trail. It just might help to stabilize things.

Deborah was the only Protestant of the microsample to suggest that some form of organized religion may have a beneficial impact upon society. The other Protestant families (and the Catholic Porfilios) participate in church affairs for the good of the children, or for the social activities, but the church is always held at arm's length. Involvement is temporary. This casual treatment of organized religion does not necessarily imply a failure of personal faith. One of the questions asked of all respondents was whether they felt it possible for a person to have a religious outlook on life without attending church. All answered affirmatively. Ralph Porfilio added, "I don't see what a church has to do with religion." The only substantial modification of the affirmative answer came from the McGees.

Mary: For a Catholic, no. For other denominations, I suppose it is possible.

Frank: Yes, I'm sure there are a lot of Protestants who are very religious and never go inside a church.

Some respondents suggest that their personal faith is deeply held and little connected with formal religious rituals. Martha Weeks, the former airline hostess, volunteered her conviction that the Apollo Thirteen space mission, which faced a failure of its life support systems on the way to the moon, was brought safely back to earth through the power of prayer. Eldene Markus said that she believes in God but quickly added that priests and ministers only cause trouble here below. Jan Markus, who must be reckoned an agnostic, agrees vehemently.

Jan: From what I can read, most of the people who founded this country were not very good churchgoers. And, if they had gotten the same church and state in this country, it wouldn't be the great country it is. We'd have troubles like they have in all those countries that are controlled by some organized religion. And a lot of the countries where they had it, that's where most of the Communism is.

Eldene: And poverty.

Jan: And poverty.

Piotr Pavel's feeling was simply stated.

Piotr: My personal feeling is that teaching religion, beyond a certain point, creates a division in a country. . . . My personal impression of this country—as compared to France, which I probably know best—is that there has always been a consciousness of religion and, therefore, a tendency to reject somebody who does not belong to your religion.

He went on to recall his amazement at finding American engineers who take religion seriously; in Europe, professionals regard religion as a matter "for the masses." Toward the end of our 1970 conversations, Pavel answered a question about his vision of the future.

Piotr: Ultimately, the good things will prevail. It will take a long time, but, in the meantime, a lot of things will happen, a lot of youngsters will die in Vietnam, a lot of careers will be broken, lives will be spoiled. . . . I see in the future some substitute of morality for the external vestiges of religion, which will speak about the actual deed, and not the external abasement, the genuflections, and things of that sort. . . . I see a complete disappearance of the religious differences of humanity.

If the first step toward the disappearance of religious differences is a growing belief that the practices of religion are of little importance to everyday life, the Ramona Heights neighbors of Piotr Pavel are well along the road.

Religion is not at the forefront of our respondents' thinking about American society. When asked what the word "freedom" makes him think of, Pavel replied:

Piotr: Basically, I think of the fundamental freedoms: freedom of speech; freedom of religion, or freedom from religion, for that matter.

He could be speaking as well for the Markuses, Weekses, Porfilios, Barberas, Roybals, and Johnsons: religious freedom particularly includes the right to stay away from church. This attitude is in marked contrast to that expressed by the fifteen largely Catholic working men of immigrant stock interviewed by Robert Lane. The conception of freedom mentioned first, and most frequently, was freedom of religion. Not only do Lane's respondents approve of the chance to worship in their own faith; they are pleased that they can—at least in theory—choose which faith to adopt. Comments Lane:

> [Religious freedom] is salient for these men, most of whom are Roman Catholic, partly, I think, because their religion and national origins are, in their own minds, a shadow upon their Americanism, a barrier to complete integration into the American society . . . religion and national origin are so closely connected in any event, that once the idea of choice in one of these traditional aspects of life has been admitted, perhaps the idea that the other

is open to conscious decision follows. . . . Thus there is a special urgency in the emphasis placed upon freedom of religion—not because people actually choose their religion as they might choose an article of dress, but because they are held accountable for having elected to be Catholics, Jews, or Jehovah's Witnesses. The question "Should I be what I am?" is constantly encouraged by this and other aspects of American society.[12]

Perhaps the difference is that Lane's working men belong to "the masses" for whom Piotr Pavel feels religion has meaning. They feel responsible for continuing to adhere to the faith in which they were raised, but they have not changed that faith. The technocrats of Ramona Heights, on the other hand, either have changed from one denomination to another, or have stopped going to church, or have a wider acquaintance among educated people of different faiths, which leads them to discount the validity of religious differences. "Should I be what I am?" is a question as likely to be asked about one's occupation, or one's political party, as about one's religion. Religion has been secularized to such an extent that the rewards of religious practice are almost completely social, and the respondents want to keep it that way. As products of a technological age, they are likely, first, to seek salvation in this world, rather than in the hereafter; second, to pin their hopes for improvement of the world on the natural or social sciences and the dissemination of their findings through education, rather than through obeisance to religious forms.

Of all the respondents, the only ones to express traditional other-worldly beliefs are the McGees. They responded without hesitation to the question, "What seems to be the main point of human life?"

Frank: To get to Heaven when we die.
Mary: Right.
Frank: Live such a life that . . .
Mary: Yes, right. Christ didn't promise us Heaven on Earth! He promised us a lot of hard work and toil and the rewards would be hereafter. I find it would be pretty rough if you thought, at the end of your life here, that was *it!*

Paradoxically, the McGees are the one couple of our microsample who are most actively trying to modify the earthly situation through political activity. In marked contrast to the simply stated faith of the McGees is Ralph Porfilio's answer to the question about the point of life,

[12]Robert E. Lane, *Political Ideology,* paper ed. (New York: Macmillan, Free Press, 1962), pp. 22, 23.

which contained a hint of that existential despair marked by contemporary social critics.

Ralph: I really don't know. I don't think there really is an answer to that question. Because, man, once you're here, you have no choice. I mean, you can't change, you can look at it, but you just have to make the best of a bad situation.

Asked about the implications of his belief, Ralph replied that individuals do indeed possess the moral right to commit suicide; it's up to the individual to decide, he said, and added with a wry grin that there's no way to punish him once the deed is done. This conviction is completely foreign to the traditional Catholic attitudes toward life and death expressed by Frank and Mary McGee. But these are the extremes within the microsample. The more common answer is somewhere between, and it is marked by an absence of emotional fervor. John Weeks's answer to a question about the main point of life is more typical.

John: Some would undoubtedly say that they must test themselves for a position in the beyond. I'm not sure I completely go along with that.

Pressed to be more specific, he retreated into his identity as engineer-technician.

John: That would require me to stop dealing with the facts which I am accustomed to dealing with, and to go into a more ethereal type approach to things, and I'm really not equipped to do that.

Martha Weeks said that her outlook on life was altered when she first became pregnant. Until her responsibility toward her children is completed, she need not seek for further meaning in life.

The voters of Ramona Heights do not find a guide to political decisions in religious faith. They are hostile to any suggestion that a personal faith might have political implications. Ralph Porfilio and Pioti Pavel mentioned—in different contexts—the First Amendment's separation of church and state as preventing the intermingling of religion and politics. The Roybals, Markuses, Porfilios, Weekses, and Rineharts all said that the clergy has no business becoming involved in politics; the McGees feel that priests and nuns should not become overly interested in the affairs of this world, political or not.

These couples (excepting the McGees and Quentin Elliott) find only social rewards in religious practice and disdain the shield against anxieties afforded an earlier generation by religious ritual and dogma. Are their lives thereby impoverished? Their behavior is not constrained by religious sanctions; no churchly hierarchy can wield temporal power over them; their conduct is not guided by fears of damnation; and it is little influenced by hopes defined in religious symbols. Living in a comfortable suburb, secure from both natural disaster and social violence, they seldom contemplate the inevitability of death. Indeed, surrounded by their families, and with a wide variety of distracting entertainment available on command, they need not recognize an absurdity in existence, with or without the shelter of faith. They are citizens and consumers, not philosophers.

But they are also complex human beings, and they are not immune from anxiety, uncertainty, or even despair. If man cannot live by bread alone, neither can he solely base his life on ownership of a single-family residence, two automobiles, and convenient access to the beach.

A Civil Religion

For most of our respondents the sacred quality has vanished from religion, or at least from religion as practiced in churches. When religious values are not attached to political objectives, politics becomes less compelling, less absolute; it may even become trivial. But compromise is possible, and the will of the majority becomes acceptable. Religious tolerance has done much to establish the style of American politics.

When the sacred quality of religion is lost, a psychological void may result. What kind of faith should be expected to fill it? Dedication to her family serves such a need for Martha Weeks; confidence in technological progress seems to function similarly for Harry Johnson; and Piotr Pavel describes as "holy" the principles of the Declaration of Independence. The void may be at least partially filled by attaching a sacred meaning to the symbols of the state. Robert Lane found that belief in the benign purpose and instrumental effectiveness of American government served for his working-class respondents as a psychological substitute for the fading power of their religious faith.

> A positive faith in one's political system, like a positive faith in religion, reassures a person that he is properly connected to the powers that be; he is not alienated, an outcast, a target for punishment.... If one gives up belief in divine rule, he must accept the belief in human rule; and if legitimacy is not conferred by God, it must be found in an only slightly less mystical belief in the sovereignty of the people.[13]

[13] *Ibid.*, pp. 198, 200.

Belief in human rule, as embodied in the United States Constitution, has psychological functions akin to those of conventional religions; this is seen in the national anguish when a president dies in office, followed by the ready acceptance of, and support for, his successor. Public reactions to the assassination of President John F. Kennedy supplied the most recent example of this ritual of grief and rededication.[14]

The national faith, attached to the reassuring abstract symbols, was a source of stability in that particular time of crisis, and must be credited in part with the fact that life—indeed, "business as usual"—resumed soon thereafter. The sudden shock of the event created a sense of personal helplessness; the resulting anxiety was alleviated by invoking the symbols enshrined by the national faith.

If that sense of personal helplessness is chronic, as Murray Edelman suggests, then the stability that means safety in time of crisis implies stagnation in more normal times.[15] A semireligious attachment to the national symbols can be the substitute for the clear perceptions and analysis needed to act effectively in the political world.

American foreign policy in the 1950s and 1960s may offer a national example of such stagnation. The civic religion found a convenient devil: communism, the antithesis of both democracy, or equality, and free enterprise, or achievement. Most voters do not follow the details of foreign policy. They support the candidate who exudes an image of experience and competence in foreign affairs,[16] or the party perceived as having the best record in the area. "Fighting communism," a value reinforced by the civil religion, provided an easy definition of the best foreign policy. John Kennedy's 1960 inaugural address did, in essence, define foreign policy in just this manner, as well as declaring, "here on earth God's work must truly be our own."[17]

The Ramona Heights respondents reported vivid memories of Presi-

[14]Christopher J. Hurn and Mark Messer, "Grief and Rededication," in *The Kennedy Assassination and the American Public*, eds. B. S. Greenberg and E. B. Parker (Stanford, Calif.: Stanford University Press, 1965), pp. 336–347.

[15]Murray Edelman's statement is a headnote to this chapter. For an interpretation of reactions to the assassination, see Sidney Verba, "The Kennedy Assassination and the Nature of Political Commitment," in Greenberg and Parker, eds., *Kennedy Assassination*, pp. 348–360.

[16]The behavioral scientists who performed computer simulations for the Kennedy campaign made precisely this point in a report to Kennedy: "The public . . . asks for foreign policy leadership in which it can have confidence—*not* particular foreign policies." (Ithiel de Sola Pool, Robert P. Abelson, and Samuel L. Popkin, *Candidates, Issues, and Strategies* [Cambridge, Mass.: MIT Press, 1964], p. 88). Also see A. Campbell, et al., *The American Voter*, abr. ed. (New York: Wiley, 1964), pp. 20–21, 113–115.

[17]Bellah, "Civil Religion in America," p. 4.

dent Kennedy's assassination which show that most of them had at least temporary recourse to the symbols of national faith to get through that anguished time. The event has been fairly well intellectualized, so that most do not recall, or at least voluntarily mention, such physiological symptoms as crying, headaches, upset stomach, and inability to sleep at night. The intensity of emotional reactions to the assassination varied inversely with class status. Given the higher status of Ramona Heights voters, one would expect them to have exhibited "cognitive rather than affective" behavior.[18] The most vivid emotional reaction was reported by Quentin Elliott.

Quentin: I was driving down a highway in Wisconsin on the way to Chicago, taking a Canadian chemist back to O'Hare Airport, and the news came over the radio. And it was first, a complete sense of being stunned, and then bowled over, and then I found myself weeping openly in the car, before this Canadian who never said anything. He was very kind and understanding, he just sat there and rode it out. And when I got to the airport, and had taken him to his plane, I couldn't even remember the number of our office, which I called every day. So I was kind of a confused guy.

Deborah Elliott, who is not as involved with either religion or politics as her husband, recalled a sense of shock and surprise, but she did not weep.

Piotr Pavel reported his shock and grief and recalled that the assassination occurred on the anniversary of the day that he first came to the United States.

The sense of being caught up in the event, of being in touch with very real but only half-understood historical forces, simply by spending hours in front of the television set, and feeling an emerging assurance that the national life would go on, was shared by these respondents, as it was by the nation.[19] The respondents, particularly the Kaubs and the Weekses, gave lengthy descriptions of their dependence on television. The Barberas had gone to New York for a football weekend, an expensive holiday they had been saving for. The game was canceled; they visited old college friends, as planned, but spent the time watching television. They

[18]Parker and Greenberg, eds., *Kennedy Assassination*, p. 371. See also, in the same volume, Paul B. Sheatsley and Jacob B. Feldman, "A National Survey on Public Reactions and Behavior," pp. 149–177.

[19]See William A. Mindak and Gerald D. Hursh, "Television's Functions on the Assassination Weekend," in *ibid.*, pp. 130–141.

remarked on the weird sensation of riding in hushed buses and subways in New York and seeing the television equipment gathered outside St. Patrick's Cathedral. Maureen Barbera summarizes the memory by saying that the assassination "spoiled" their holiday, but adding quickly, "I hate to say what it did to Mrs. Kennedy!"

The more cognitive response, which emphasizes abstract support for the presidential office, is typified by John Weeks.

John: We were very shook up by it. And I was mad, mad that one clown [Oswald] comes along and strikes out the vote of the people. We weren't really supporters of John F. Kennedy, but, nevertheless, he was the President, and as such, we supported him. We were very sad . . .

The status of the presidency as a national symbol is suggested by the fact that these respondents remembered what they were doing on the day of the assassination, eight years before. However, the McGees leaped from the immediate memory to a political observation. Frank had been on the roof of a home he was constructing, nailing the roof rafters, when his partner drove up and told him of the shooting. The next night, Frank attended a humorous speaking contest in Palm Springs, sponsored by his service club. This was the regional final, to which he was sent after winning the local and district contests. The affair had been planned for so long that its managers decided not to cancel it, so Frank and Mary attended the banquet in Palm Springs.

Question: It must have been a pretty dreary banquet.
Frank: Well, it started out that way, but it didn't—the dreary atmosphere didn't seem to permeate the hall all evening long. People went ahead and had a good time.
Question: [to Mary] Where were you when Kennedy was assassinated? At home?
Mary: At home. Somebody called and said, "Quick, turn on your television!"
Frank: It was a real shock. That was sixty-three, and of course we very vividly recall the accusations of, I've forgotten who right now, that the right wing was responsible, and it was very interesting to us. Who was it that accused the right wing right away of Kennedy's assassination? I forget whether it was a politician, or . . .
Question: Could you be thinking of someone like Walter Cronkite?
Frank: That's a good guess.
Mary: Was it the chief justice?
Frank: Warren? Sure, it was.

Mary: Chief Justice Warren, yeah.

Frank: He was later to be on the commission. Yeah, that's right, it was Earl Baby.

Frank was mistaken in believing that former Chief Justice Warren hurried to make a public statement blaming right-wing extremists for the assassination. The John Birch Society's campaign to impeach Warren was in full swing at the time of the Kennedy assassination, and it was also the peak period of the McGees' involvement with the Birch Society. As part of their general feeling that ultraconservatism does not get fair treatment by the news media, they were bound to be sensitive to the suggestion (which quickly arose after the event occurred in Dallas) that the act had to be the responsibility of conservative extremists.

This refusal to dwell very long on the death of a president does not make the McGees a deviant case within a microsample that invests the symbols of national government with a degree of sacred meaning. The McGees relate to the flag, to the Constitution as they understand it (the argument for impeaching Earl Warren was that his Court was perverting the document's true meaning), and to patriotism, which they define as a willingness—even an eagerness—to die for one's country.

A number of social scientists, beginning with Emile Durkheim, have written that the designation of the sacred is a function of society and that, conversely, attachment to the state is similar to a religious attachment.[20] In analyzing these writings, Lewis Lipsitz has concluded that signs of the infusion of religious tendencies into American politics may be most apparent along two dimensions: "intense and often intolerant patriotism, and implicit reverence for the President, particularly in times of crisis."[21] Among the Ramona Heights voters, attachment to the presidential office as a national symbol was separate from their opinion of a particular incumbent. In spite of varying intensity in their reactions to the Watergate revelations, none felt that the legitimacy of American institutions was challenged; they simply hoped that the guilty individuals would be designated and punished. This adjustment was made easier by the fact that even those who voted for Nixon in 1972 had not perceived him as possessing extraordinary integrity.

[20]Emile Durkheim, *The Elementary Forms of the Religious Life* (New York: Collier Books, 1961), pp. 479 ff. Also see the literature summarized in Lipsitz, "State Functions as a Religion," pp. 529–530, nn. 7–15.
[21]Lipsitz, "State Functions as a Religion," p. 530.

The Origin of Patriotic Attachments

How far back can these voters trace their patriotic attitudes? They all experienced the time of unquestioned national loyalty and unity in the face of an enemy that characterized the Second World War. Some were impressionable children at the time; others served in the armed forces of the United States. Several mentioned war bond drives, waste paper collecting, and the growing of victory gardens as childhood experiences that helped to form their concepts of the nation and patriotism. Fletcher Barbera's father was absent for two years, serving in the navy. Marie Kaub particularly mentioned the war movies of that era as "pushing patriotism." Kenneth Kaub (who served in the army medical corps in Korea) still feels military experience is important in forming patriotic attitudes, but observes that the nation has become less militaristic because young men now object to aspects of the military experience which he and his friends put up with "because it was the law, and we were supposed to, and it was the patriotic thing to do." Kenneth seems to approve of the change.

The most vivid—and negative—memory of a wartime childhood is that of Ralph Porfilio. He recalls the prayerful recitation of the Pledge of Allegiance in his classroom and the compulsive atmosphere that surrounded the ritual.

Ralph: It was almost like Hitler's youth movement, where everything was built up—the state, and everything was jammed in the back of your mind. Country above all, and then you can't think of anything else but that.

The respondents who served in World War II include John Weeks, Arnold Garcia, Richard Rinehart, Frank McGee, and Arthur Roybal. Most were willing to talk about the war; some told of combat, while others recounted stories of bureaucratic mismanagement behind the lines. They were citizen soldiers who fulfilled a duty; all either were drafted, or volunteered in order to avoid the draft. None found great attractiveness, much less glory, in military life, although Arthur Roybal said that his navy service was a great awakening—it showed him that he could compete with "the blond-haired blue-eyed boys," and win. None attempted to keep military memories fresh by joining veterans' organizations upon their return to civilian status. In sum, the war experiences of the Ramona Heights veterans do not suggest that any of them became so attached to the symbols of a civil religion as to make that faith a source of political stagnation.

Do their more general statements suggest that any members of the microsample adhere to a national faith, out of a permanent sense of personal inadequacy? Ten of the respondents, or nearly half of the microsample, express intense pride in their American citizenship, a status that is never far below the surface of their political consciousness. For the remaining thirteen, being American is more nearly taken for granted.

Ramona Heights' proud Americans may be compared to the immigrant Catholic working men interviewed by Robert Lane, who felt that their religion and national origin "created, in their own minds, a shadow upon their Americanism." Six of the self-conscious Americans of Ramona Heights are immigrants or the children of immigrants. Of the remaining four, two (the McGees) are Catholics of aggressively traditional views and adherents of the John Birch Society, a "super-patriotic" organization. Two (the Barberas) speak somewhat defensively of their New England heritage; they may feel, subconsciously, that their own Americanism is more pure than that of their neighbors.

As a European intellectual, Piotr Pavel is critical of many attributes of American society. Nevertheless, the day he became an American citizen was "the happiest day of [his] life," and his experience in other nations has increased his appreciation of America. His wife shares this appreciation.

Myrna: I think I'm a patriot. In fact, I know I love my country. I have nothing but tremendous thanks for it. My parents came here simply because this was a haven for them. They had lived through pogroms. My father was a, let me say, a not very active socialist. It was either Siberia or here, and he chose to come here. . . . But to say, "My country, right or wrong," that's being a little stupid.

The Markuses expressed deep pride in being citizens of the nation adopted by their parents. Neither has a desire to visit the old country; their ties are to America. And, while they are intensely critical of much in contemporary America, their guiding principle is to "put America first."

Marie Kaub is descended from the Spaniards who settled the Southwest before the Yankees came. There is no doubt about the location of her national loyalty. At the very beginning of the 1970 interview, when asked what she would like to see changed in America, she called for "more respect for the symbols of what we've started for our country.

They've been degraded quite a bit lately." She and Kenneth expanded on her meaning later, when they discussed the attack on demonstrating students by New York construction workers.

Kenneth: In a way, I was cheering on the hard hats because I felt it was about time that somebody showed a little patriotism for the flag.

Marie: I think we were ready, in our own minds—not to say all of us, but some of us were ready—for a certain amount of just retribution, and we were sort of glad to see somebody strike back for a change. They were doing it for us. Even though we knew it wasn't right.

None of the Ramona Heights voters would endorse affronts to the flag; two of the families regularly display it. Although he doesn't make a fetish of it, to the extent of delaying his departure for work in the morning, Frank McGee frequently raises the flag on a modest flagpole installed in his front lawn.

A more regular display is made three blocks away at the Elliott household. In 1970, half of their two-car garage was filled with boxes still unpacked after their 1969 move. Early in 1971, when the unpacking and storing was completed, they came across an American flag. The children expressed interest, so Quentin fastened the mounting brackets for the small flagpole to the front of the garage. A daily ceremony soon developed: the little girls (then aged two and four) placed the flagstaff in its bracket after breakfast, and the oldest boy brought it in before supper, after practicing his music lesson. I asked what flying the flag meant.

Quentin: Well, I think I want the kids to remember that we flew the flag. This is a time of trouble, and the country needs to do something to gain a sense of unity. And it's really important to the little girls, it adds a sense of ceremony to their lives. Becky [the older girl] marches out with that flag just as proud as she can be.

Quentin reported with a laugh that a neighbor whom he had met only briefly, an adherent of the American Civil Liberties Union, came over to demand what cause they felt they had to support by flying the flag. Quentin reassured his questioner that the family impulse was an honorable one; the neighbor later became a good friend.

Three couples displayed flag decals on their cars that were sent them in 1970 by Ron Caspers, as part of his successful campaign for a seat on the county board of supervisors. I asked each of them what it meant.

Fletcher Barbera: I think it means I'm proud to be an American.

John Weeks: In our case, or in my case, it means solidarity, solidarity with the government. It doesn't preclude the right to dissent, you understand.

Caroline Porfilio: Because I knew him, and I liked the flag he sent.

All these respondents are adults; their socialization as Americans is complete; there is nothing tentative in their sense of national identity. They are indeed "allegiant citizens." They recognize a contrast between national ideals and the social reality. But they feel the basic democratic institutions are sound, and progress is being made toward solving the critical problems.

John Weeks: I think our country happens to be better than any place else, but certainly it's got shortcomings and problems. I think a patriot will recognize that fact, and not try to hide—stick their head in the proverbial sand, you know—but try to change those things which aren't right.

To the extent that the microsample adheres to a civil religion, it supports their conviction that American society is successful. But the attribution of some sacred content to the national symbols is not meant to ease feelings of personal despair, for they are not despairing. As citizens, they can contribute to the solution of political problems. This is one reason for feeling that ours is a successful society.

The War in Vietnam

What kind of event challenges the allegiance of citizens like these? If one were to judge by the statements of former Representative John Schmitz, one would conclude that Ramona Heights must have been a nest of hawks on Vietnam. However, if the notion of an American civil religion holds true, at least some of our respondents must have confronted the reality of Vietnam in the manner of a crisis of religious faith.

When they were first interviewed in 1970, President Nixon's program of "Vietnamization" seemed well advanced. I asked each of the couples about their feelings on Vietnam and whether they had always felt that way. If they changed their minds, how did it come about? In every case, there was substantial husband-wife agreement; the issue had been discussed in each family, and the opinion was shared. To summarize the results:

Four couples (the Elliotts, Barberas, Kaubs, and Weekses) originally supported American involvement but changed their minds to favor the withdrawal of American forces.

Two couples (the McGees and Porfilios) originally supported the nature and scope of American involvement, but, as the conflict continued, changed to a more cataclysmic opinion: either sufficient force should be applied to win, or American forces should be withdrawn. Frank McGee wanted Congress to declare war.

Three couples (the Pavels, Markuses, and Rineharts) were opposed to American involvement from the time they really became aware of it—in the late Kennedy or early Johnson administrations.

Harry Johnson and Arthur Roybal expressed strong support for the continued American presence; they generally supported administration policy.

More important than the scorecard of 1970 attitudes were the respondents' descriptions of how those attitudes came to be formulated. Were they yielding to fashion, or did they make their own agonizing reappraisals? And did a change of mind on the war call into question the legitimacy of governmental institutions?

The most complete account of their change of mind was given by the Elliotts. In the beginning, they felt the United States involvement was both necessary and beneficial. Quentin saw the American presence as part of "manifest destiny": we were required by our role in history to aid the people of South Vietnam. However, as time wore on, they saw that countless lives were being destroyed, but with no obvious benefits. They were living in Canada then, and their first doubts were expressed in whispers to each other; they felt it would be unpatriotic to publicly oppose the war while living in a foreign country. "We just didn't have the guts," Deborah said, "to say we were against U.S. policy."

But the futility of the conflict was not the only factor that turned them against the war. They realized that their own sons were growing older; that, even if the Vietnam war were concluded by the time their sons reached draft age, the experience of Vietnam could well lead to the launching of more "police action" wars. By the time they moved to Orange County, Quentin habitually referred to the Pentagon as the "War-a-gon."

Fletcher Barbera described his change of mind less vividly.

Fletcher: I think probably four or five years ago, I would have said, "Yes, we're in Vietnam, we're protecting our allies, we are holding back the advance of international communism," and that whole thing. And now I think that Vietnam was a mistake.

The most important influence on Fletcher's change of mind was a series of conversations with his brother, a Vietnam veteran. These talks reinforced impressions gained from the media about the brutality of the military presence there, and the difficulty of distinguishing between friend and foe. Independently of his brother's experience, Fletcher reached a new understanding of communism; he no longer saw it as a monolithic international movement. "The Communists," he said, "have as many problems as we do."

John and Martha Weeks originally supported American involvement, feeling that a necessary national task was being performed. But the war did not end, their son approached draft age, and a young man they knew died in Vietnam. They began to question the stated goals of the struggle, and they wondered how much difference a particular government made in the lives of the peasants.

John: I can't see putting in the money, or spending the lives of our troops, our boys, on something that the people just don't give a damn about. You know, I can't help but get this feeling that people over there just don't care.

Kenneth and Marie Kaub echoed the feeling of futility and frustration at the continuance of a conflict they found meaningless.

In every case, the change of opinion was stimulated by the realization that the war touched, or could touch, their own families. All but the Elliotts saw Vietnam as an isolated mistake which did not call into question the general efficiency or legitimacy of procedures for making American foreign policy. In 1970, they could feel that Lyndon Johnson had paid the political price for that mistake, and Richard Nixon had been elected to end the conflict—perhaps with honor. To the extent that these four families—the Elliotts, Barberas, Kaubs, and Weekses— are the adherents of a civil religion, their change of mind on Vietnam did not constitute a crisis of faith.

For those supporting government policies, there was a strong sugges- tion of faith in the symbols of government, although combined with a feeling of frustration.

Arthur Roybal: It's just an unfortunate war. I see no end to the tunnel. And I don't have an answer. I think our natural urge is to say, "Let's get in there and blast out, go all the way." Yet I don't know that that would necessarily solve it. . . . I can't visualize that we've had four presidents, starting with Eisenhower, we've had a reason to be there, and we continue to battle. And I don't think that it's just plain stubbornness. I just don't know.

Those who opposed the war from the beginning disagreed with gov- ernment policy on this specific issue; they did not argue that Vietnam proved the inadequacy of government institutions.

Piotr Pavel: In the beginning, there was no strong public opinion, because it was minor, just like an expeditionary force. . . . All of a sudden, we found ourselves in it; just like sinking in the mud, you don't notice until you're up to your knees.

But the Pavels did not argue that the draft should be abolished, that war was intrinsically immoral, or that the American government was imperialist. They are not pacifists. The memories of Hitler and Nazism are still vivid.

The voters of Ramona Heights were not caught up in the moralistic denunciation of the Vietnam venture that characterized student protests. Their opposition to the war was based on their conviction that it served no useful purpose. They would support the right war, at the right time, for the right purpose, as they supported—and some fought in— the Second World War. The war in Vietnam did not create for any of them a crisis of faith or a turning away from their civil religion.

Equality and Achievement

In his study of political attitudes held by fifteen working-class men, Robert Lane considered the adherence of his respondents to two characteristic values of American society, freedom and equality.[22] He was struck by the fact that, while aware of the inequalities that exist in American society, they did not seek reform in the name of achieving equality. They felt that each man must be responsible for what he makes of himself. They constructed psychic defenses to explain their own modest level of material achievement, and they saw justice in a system which provides the highest rewards for those who, achieving a high level of education, come to exercise the greatest responsibility. Lane concluded that the working class had found reasons to accept its low place in the hierarchy of American society.

> . . . it is not to "The People," not to the business class, not to the working class, that we must look for the consistent and relatively unqualified defense of freedom and equality. The professional class, at least in the American culture, serves as the staunchest defender of democracy's two greatest ideals.[23]

Lane may have been thinking of teachers and lawyers, rather than the affluent technocrats we have met in Ramona Heights. Nevertheless, it

[22]Lane, *Political Ideology*, chap. 4, "The Fear of Equality."
[23] *Ibid.*, p. 81.

is significant that these voters express at best a qualified allegiance to the ideal of equality; it is not, for them, a word to be emblazoned on a banner of political activism. One of the reasons, as noted before, was described by Lipset. As dual heirs of the Puritan tradition and the slogans of the American Revolution, Americans value both equality and individualistic achievement, seldom pausing to contemplate the implied contradiction between them. The concept of "equality" receives verbal praise as an ideal, but they are quick to point to realities which prevent its complete accomplishment. In general, they do not propose massive governmental action to alleviate the inequities which they admit exist. They believe, or at least wish they could believe, that America provides ample opportunities; the success of an individual is primarily dependent upon his own strength of character. Government should intervene only to assure individuals an equal chance.

The respondent holding attitudes closest to those defined as liberal since the New Deal era is Piotr Pavel. When asked about the statement "All men are created equal," he replied:

Piotr: I think we're not abiding by this precept any more. I think wealth and vested interests have more bearing on the issue. Let's be realistic about it, to be an ambassador [of] the United States, you have to be a wealthy man . . . in order to undertake campaigns . . . you have to be a wealthy man, or you have to have some interests who intend to support you, in exchange for later favors. So, I don't think we're adhering to this precept. Although I do believe in it as something very holy, as holy as anything I can think of.

Piotr holds the egalitarian ideal in high esteem, but he is also aware of inequalities of native intelligence and achieved wisdom.

Piotr: Something that has always bothered me is, if Einstein has the same vote as does some sharecropper, how do you adjust it? Do you give Einstein three votes and the sharecropper one vote, or do you just set up certain prerequisites for voting? In which case you are not a democracy any more, but you have an oligarchy.

The voters of Ramona Heights admit that even equality defined in a minimal sense as equality of opportunity does not exist, because inequalities of status resulting from their circumstances of birth handicap some individuals in the competition of life.

Martha Weeks: Unless you feed a very young child and develop his mind and body within the first six years, at the very minimum, then his brain will become uneducable, and then it goes right on.

There is a certain tendency to think of these social inequities as existing far away, with little impact upon Orange County. Quentin Elliott thought of the then-current struggle in Biafra, and he said that a child born to a starving Nigerian mother would never have a chance in a society made up of better-nurtured peers. John Weeks mentioned race as an inherited social disadvantage, but he suggested that the disadvantages for blacks are much greater in the South than in California. Indeed, the Anglo respondents immediately thought of blacks in Alabama or Mississippi, rather than Mexicans in California, as examples of citizens whose freedom is unfairly limited.

When equality was defined as "equality before the law," most of the respondents acknowledged that all Americans do not receive equal treatment. The Markuses pointed out that the wealthy can usually "buy their way out" of trouble with the law. When Piotr Pavel mentioned the unjust treatment of blacks by southern policemen, Myrna interjected that he should "look in [his] own back yard," and compared the treatment accorded middle-class adults with that given long-haired teen-agers by California highway patrolmen. At least eight of the couples mentioned race as a factor that prevents citizens from being accorded equality before the law; three mentioned age or the treatment accorded hippies; six mentioned social standing, or wealth, as receiving deference from the legal system.

Only one couple failed to volunteer examples of inequality before the law. Ralph Porfilio charged reverse discrimination; he claimed that, not belonging to an oppressed minority, he would be unable to get free legal advice from the American Civil Liberties Union. Frank and Mary McGee defined equality as "equality in the eyes of God," adding, "That's about the only way we're equal." Asked whether all Americans receive equal treatment from the agents of the law, Frank conceded that there may be some regional variation, and Mary remembered an "old saying" that wealthy men never die in the electric chair. But Frank said that, "generally speaking," treatment by agents of the law "is fairly equal." A moment later, he stated that the average wage earned by Negroes was probably lower than that of whites, and implied that was an injustice.

Unlike Lane's working-class respondents, who developed self-justifying explanations for their own modest standing on the ladder of material comfort, the Ramona Heights voters did not argue that the unfortunate of American society somehow "deserve" their low status. Indeed, several expressed genuine sympathy for the struggles of the poor. Quentin Elliott spoke of the need to modify the "environment" in which poor people live, in order to assure equality of opportunity; John Weeks used practically the same language. Richard Rinehart spoke of the need for breaking out of "the cycle of poverty" in the black ghetto and mentioned the matriarchal structure of the black family as inhibiting the breakout. Jan Markus spoke contemptuously of successful people who turn their backs on the lower classes.

Jan: I have no use for these kind of people. They made it easy, without taxes, but they don't want *you* to live. And these people are going to have to get that out of their system, because everybody has to live.

All but two of the microsample thus expressed a realization that equality of opportunity is an ideal belied by reality. Yet they differed widely in their conceptions of what, if anything, should be done. The Markuses favor stringent tax reforms and other ways of redistributing the wealth; the Rineharts speak favorably, but rather vaguely, of governmental programs to aid the urban ghettos; the McGees admit there are social inequalities, but they want less government activity in every field, particularly including welfare.

The expressed willingness to support reforms for achieving greater equality of opportunity, as well as greater equality before the law, is inversely proportional to the strength of the respondents' attachment to the value of achievement, the conviction that success depends on the strength of individual character. It is roughly independent of party affiliation; while the Republicans tend to cluster at the achievement end of the spectrum, the Democrats are scattered along it. However, these relationships are difficult to quantify, for *all* the respondents express an attachment to the value of achievement. And they express it voluntarily; no question was designed to elicit a response on this particular point. This is an uncommon agreement among the members of the microsample. The three respondents who are most strongly opposed to further government action aimed at achieving equal opportunity stated the achievement value in particularly strong terms. Harry Johnson, a Democrat who frequently votes Republican, drew an image from the biblical story of the expulsion from Eden.

Harry: I believe they're created equal with the right to progress, not the equal right to lay down and have fruit drop off the tree to them.

Arnold Garcia, a registered Republican and most completely the "self-made man" of any of the respondents, said, of his parents' Mexico, "Some people *like* to live like that [in poverty]." He is certain that his sons will never again know their present material comfort; ambition and determination are the keys to success, and they have life too easy to develop those qualities. Having known discrimination himself, he would perhaps favor eliminating ethnic discrimination in education and the administration of justice, but he asks no special favors, either for himself or for his people.

While the McGees acknowledged some inequality before the agents of the law, they were not disturbed by economic inequality.

Frank: There's nothing wrong with the fact that some people just barely exist. . . . The main goal of life is to get to heaven, and a guy who has to work like a dog all his life on this earth, maybe he's gonna get to heaven faster than a lot of us.

The poor may enjoy a positive advantage. Frank seemed to wish they would, as a group, recognize this fact, and stop agitating. Yet Frank and Mary are not without human sympathy; they respond with charitable impulses when they meet individuals who suffer. The fact is that they are not acquainted with many people who "just barely exist." As long as poverty remains an abstraction, they are able to wax impatient with the poor, both for failing in the competition of life and for failing to perceive the possibility of a heavenly reward.

Many of the respondents believe that hard work—including some adversity—builds character, and they worry about their children. This is particularly the case with those who made their way to Ramona Heights from relatively humble origins—the Porfilios, Markuses, Marie Kaub, and Arnold Garcia. All expressed a concern like Arnold Garcia's that the neighborhood children have not earned the comfort that surrounds them. To enjoy Ramona Heights without having struggled to achieve it casts doubt on the children's future. The strongest expression of this feeling came from Arnold Garcia, who said vehemently that his sons have "no place to go but down."

Other references to the achievement value were made in a variety of contexts. Maureen Barbera implied a belief in the power of motivation when she said that some people will always achieve greater success than others. Dr. Kaub happened to think of the Marxist proposal for distributing goods according to need, and he questioned if it would ever work, for some people are bound to strive for more, while others will be content with less. Eldene Markus favored the right of black children to equal educational opportunities, "if they apply themselves." Her conclusion, based on her own experience, was that disadvantaged groups should not expect social and political recognition, much less equality, unless they are willing to work for it. Arthur Roybal praised the value of competition in life, and he was speaking in the broadest terms, rather than as a former athletics coach. Richard Rinehart admitted the inequalities of society, but he would never blame ghetto crime on social forces alone—individuals indeed have the power to rise above unfavorable circumstances; the black race can produce a Sammy Davis, Jr., he points out, as well as a welfare-dependent family.

The voters of Ramona Heights cannot really imagine a society that would provide substantial material equality. Harry Johnson felt that this would abolish competition, with disastrous results.

Harry: It would be like everyone going out for a track race and saying, "Okay, everyone can run this race in the same time," so eventually there would be no more records to be gone after.

In similar vein, when praising competition, Arthur Roybal stated that he did not wish the nation to become "lopsidedly socialistic." He felt that the maintenance of the economy required "the personal incentive that one has right now."

Even Piotr Pavel, who favors the redistribution of income, did not foresee a classless society. He believes that there are innate differences among human beings which will reveal themselves (as in the case of Albert Einstein), and he approves of the concept of a meritorious elite which may enjoy the advantages that it has earned. He says that he has "a lot of respect" for the British, and that their overt class divisions in society function well for them.

Jan and Eldene Markus also support the redistribution of income.

Jan: The poor guy is going to have to get some help from those who have made it. Maybe we should give up some luxuries to help those people in poverty.

But the idea of groups in society receiving something for nothing—that persons should receive substantial assistance simply for creating a disturbance—is not what they have in mind. At one point, Eldene exploded:

Eldene: Send the colored—the niggers—back there, just send them to Russia right now. They'll level them down.

Richard Rinehart reacts as strongly, but in milder language, to the demand of militants for the payment of cash compensation by his church for the historical tragedy of American blacks. He feels no personal responsibility for the importation of slaves by southern planters centuries ago.

Richard: This business of trying to bring the Negroes up to their proper place. It's going to take time, and they have to earn it. It's not going to be handed them on a silver platter.

The attachment of these voters to the value of achievement is also demonstrated by their responses to a question about the nature of an ideal society, their own Utopia. Only Piotr Pavel can imagine an ideal society in which the profit motive no longer has a place. All others feel that the natural competitiveness of man will forever assert itself, and that a properly organized society recognizes this fact and gains advantage from it.[24]

The voters of Ramona Heights display at least ambivalence, and often complete inconsistency, when discussing the notion of equality. While most are eager to endorse the principle verbally, they acknowledge that reality falls short of the ideal, whether defined as equality of opportunity or as equality before the law. Yet they are hesitant to see the equalization of society through governmental action, for the idea of citizens receiving substantial benefits for which they do no work is abhorrent. They are simultaneously attached to the values of equality and achievement, without being concerned with the implicit contradiction between the two.

Concurrent attachment to two contradictory values yields a commitment of a different order, worthy of a new label. Perhaps the best word to encompass both conceptions is "enterprise." It suggests the importance of individual initiative operating against a background of equality. It should be distinguished from "free enterprise," a value-laden phrase redolent of old-fashioned economic analysis. The voters of Ramona Heights (except for the McGees) do not seek a return to laissez-faire policies. They are willing to support government action that will assure the fairness of the start in life's competitive race, particularly through public education, but most would insist that government has no business on the track itself, or at the finish line—the outcome of the race is strictly the business of the competitors. When the athletes have hung up their track shoes, government concern again becomes appropriate: support for pensions and medical care for the elderly are welcomed. Some might say that a lifetime spent in the race, regardless of the order at the finish, earns a modicum of comfort in old age; others would only be relieved because the retired generation need not burden their still-competitive children.

[24]The Ramona Heights microsample finds considerable difficulty in envisioning any Utopia at all—other than Ramona Heights. See below, pp. 236–240.

Adherence to "enterprise," a value which combines an attachment to equality and to achievement by obscuring their inherent contradiction, places the residents of Ramona Heights squarely within the tradition of contemporary political discourse. Enterprise is possible only in a system of competition: the individual's competitive chances are assured only if his abilities are given free rein; equality is defined as equal opportunity. The metaphor of the race is as inevitable for these voters as for practicing politicians. The major parties accept that metaphor; their only disagreement concerns which of its components—equality or achievement—should receive the most emphasis.

> . . . Here is Ronald Reagan on the subject: "We offer equal opportunity at the starting line of life, but no compulsory tie for everyone at the finish." Here is Nixon: "I see a day when every child in this land has . . . an equal chance to go just as high as his talents will take him." Here is Rockefeller: "I see . . . the welfare concept . . . as a floor below which nobody will be allowed to fall, but with no ceiling to prevent anyone from rising as high as he wants to rise." Here is Humphrey: "I'll take my stand, as I always have, on equal opportunity . . . Our goal is an environment within which all types of business rivalry can flourish."[25]

Dedication to enterprise and its postulate of a free marketplace is basic to the American bourgeois ethos. Individualistic competition is perceived as possessing an intrinsic moral value, but the successful competitor should be assured of material rewards as well. Such rewards should be as little influenced as possible by factors such as the circumstances of his birth, or the inevitable process of attaining great age, over which the individual has no control. At the beginning, an equal start; when the individual has reached the end of his particular race, at least a minimum of comfort.

Is this a conviction about the nature of things as they are, or the statement of a goal to be attained? Both. Individuals who feel that America is fundamentally a successful society are likely to feel that equality of opportunity is an appropriately defined goal, and that considerable progress has been made toward achieving it. *Most citizens are free to achieve* follows naturally from the conviction that *we are*, fundamentally, *a successful society.* A large area remains for disagreement about the extent of America's failure to achieve equality of opportunity, and what should be done about it.

[25]Garry Wills, *Nixon Agonistes: The Crisis of the Self-Made Man* (New York: New American Library, 1971), pp. 223–224.

CHAPTER SEVEN

The Constraints of an Ethos:
Ramona Heights and Welfare Reform

> *Our individualism differs from all others because it embraces these great ideals: that while we build our society upon the attainment of the individual, we shall safeguard to every individual an equality of opportunity to take that position in the community to which his intelligence, character, ability, and ambition entitle him . . . that we shall stimulate effort of each individual to achievement . . . while he in turn must stand up to the emery wheel of competition.*
>
> —Herbert Hoover, 1922[1]

> *A guaranteed income would undermine the incentive to work; the family assistance plan increases the incentive to work. There is no reason why one person should be taxed so that another can choose to live idly.*
>
> —President Richard M. Nixon, television address, August 8, 1969

> *"I think that the [Family Assistance] Plan offers some degree of maintaining human dignity at the same time as receiving assistance. So I think it's worth a try."*
>
> —Arthur Roybal, 1970

THE RAMONA HEIGHTS VOTERS' insistence on the moral value of individual achievement identifies them as heirs of an American tradition that was defined by then Secretary of Commerce Herbert Hoover in his little

---

[1]Herbert Hoover, *American Individualism* (New York: Doubleday, 1928; first published 1922), pp. 9–10.

book, *American Individualism*. They would all agree with the principles stated by Hoover more than half a century ago. If they were told that Hoover was the author, the Elliotts, Pavels, and Roybals—and possibly the Weekses—might be led to reexamine their convictions.

A more important question than the source of such convictions is, What specific policies will they support in an attempt to implement their principles? If the attitudes of these twelve families are widely shared by American middle-class suburbanites, who in turn have veto power over political change, how can their assent be won for programs of change—the agenda of domestic needs that includes such matters as the amelioration of racism and poverty and rescue efforts in the decaying cities? How can effective leadership be exercised?

The Family Assistance Plan

The 1970 interviews with the voters of Ramona Heights included questions about the reform of the national welfare system contained in President Nixon's 1969 proposal for a Family Assistance Plan. In 1972, they talked of George McGovern's plans for welfare reform. Their reaction is a microcosmic sample of the success of political leadership —or its failure. The limitations inherent in the bourgeois political ethos, as it operates in Ramona Heights, are revealed. Potentially contradictory, the ethos generates support for policies which would perfect the equality of opportunity, but it includes a basic cynicism about the potential of the political process to achieve fundamental change. It issues no call to passionate involvement in political action.

President Nixon's presentation of the Family Assistance Plan (FAP) was one of the more striking political events of 1969. It grew from a conviction that existing welfare programs, developed to aid poor families, actually destroy them, by driving fathers out of the household. The Family Assistance Plan was designed to break into the "cycle of welfare dependency," restore a semblance of stable family life to the ghetto, and provide support for the "working poor," the forgotten members of postindustrial society. The plan guaranteed a modest annual income for families with children (originally $1,600 for a family of four), provided the head of the family accepted job training or a job, when offered. In contrast to the Aid to Dependent Children Program, first established under Roosevelt's New Deal, parents earning wages in addition to basic welfare support would not have their income reduced by an equivalent amount. A scale was established so that a share of additional income earned above the welfare support level would be retained, until the family earning power had grown to lift the family out of poverty. The plan was a version of the schemes known variously as "negative income tax" and "guaranteed annual income," discussed favorably by as conservative an economist as Milton Friedman. The new plan proposed nothing less than a modest redistribution of the national wealth. Simply being poor was not enough to win support from the federal government, however: one had to be poor and have children; if able-bodied, one had to accept job training or a job.[2]

The plan was announced by President Nixon in a television speech on August 8, 1969. He reminded his audience that he had opposed the concept of a guaranteed annual income during the campaign, stated that he continued to oppose it, and implied that FAP did not include a guaranteed annual income. Daniel P. Moynihan, the principal White House architect of the plan, later justified this deception on the grounds that the proposal did not involve a guaranteed income as that concept was understood by Nixon's audience.[3]

The President did not dwell upon the plan's potential for reforming the distribution of wealth; he did not suggest that a first remedy for poverty is providing more money for the poor, and a second remedy is providing them with greater political power. Instead, he talked about ambition, initiative, and the willingness to work. His focus was not upon the flaws of the socioeconomic system, but on the personal characteristics of its victims. It was a case of what psychologist William Ryan has called "blaming the victim" as a mode of understanding social problems.[4] It locates the stigma of poverty within the poor person, rather than analyzing social forces. It is perfectly in tune with the outlook of middle-class suburbanites who feel some human sympathy toward the unfortunate classes but have not faced the implication that some of their

---

[2]The origins of the Family Assistance Plan, and its disposal in the 91st Congress, have been recounted by Daniel P. Moynihan in *The Politics of a Guaranteed Annual Income* (New York: Random House, 1973). I have written a capsule history of the birth, consideration, and final abandonment of the proposal in *The People, Maybe*, 2nd ed. (North Scituate, Mass.: Wadsworth, Duxbury Press, 1974), pp. 437–450.
[3]Moynihan, *Politics of Guaranteed Income*, p. 11.
[4]William Ryan, *Blaming the Victim* (New York: Random House, 1971).

own comfort should be given up to correct injustices in the distributive system.

President Nixon's speech was not addressed to welfare families, the intended beneficiaries of his plan. It was addressed to Middle Americans, seeking their support for the plan. In the same talk, President Nixon proposed a plan of revenue sharing, through which Washington would pass along a share of the income tax bounty to local governments, with the implied promise of reduced property taxes for the middle class; a reorganization of the much-criticized Office of Economic Opportunity; and the transfer of responsibility for job training centers from the federal to state governments. Thus there was ample sugar coating for the pill of the Family Assistance Plan: an appeal addressed to the achievement value and middle-class pocketbooks, while passing over the humane arguments, based on the value of equality; and a symbolic dismantling of one national bureaucracy in the name of increased local responsibility.

In 1970 the voters of Ramona Heights were asked their opinions of the Family Assistance Plan. Most of the microsample had heard of it and recalled the details with little prompting. The only members of the microsample to oppose the plan were Frank and Mary McGee, who stated flatly that such matters are not an appropriate concern of government, and Arnold Garcia, who waved his hand in a gesture of contempt—he felt that $1,600 for a family of four was so insignificant that it was hardly worth discussing. More interesting than the support for the plan by the remainder of the microsample are the reasons offered for their support. Dissatisfaction with the current method of administering welfare was widespread. A common charge was that the program of Aid to Dependent Children destroys families by encouraging fathers to abandon their responsibilities. The reasons volunteered for supporting the Nixon proposal referred to the values of both equality and achievement and depended upon "blaming the victim" in varying degree. The reasons offered were of three kinds:

1. The work incentive feature of the plan would curtail the number of freeloaders, while stimulating pride and initiative on the part of family breadwinners.
2. The proposal offered a chance to break into the cycle of poverty, restore family ties, and renew individual ambition.

3. The proposal could restore a measure of human dignity to welfare recipients.

WORK INCENTIVES

Discussion of the work or job training feature of the plan drew most heavily on the achievement value. Quentin Elliott pointed out that welfare costs exceeded the sums spent for public education in some states. He feared that persons receiving a guaranteed income would no longer care to work.

Quentin: I think there's a tendency for many of the people on welfare to enjoy it too much. I think if you can really build these [job training] incentives in and make it work, then you've got true welfare.

Similar reasons for supporting the plan were offered by Marie Kaub (who fought her own way out of poverty) and by Ralph and Caroline Porfilio. But a different reaction came from the Barberas, who are staunch Republicans and call themselves conservatives. For Fletcher, the work incentive feature was almost an afterthought.

Fletcher: Yeah, I think that in a society where there is so much abundance, I think that certain minimum things ought to be provided for everybody. And basically I think it should include food, shelter, and education. . . . But it's got to be given to these people in a way that does not—what's the word?
Maureen: Degrade them.
Fletcher: Degrade them. On the other hand—
Maureen: But I don't think it should be *given* to them!
Fletcher: Well, the condition that a man should be willing to take a job or job training, I think is a reasonable condition. Maybe there are some others, I'm not an expert in the field. But that seems like a minimum condition.

Fletcher's instinctive response seemed a simple appeal for social justice, but it was hardly a clarion call. A habitual Republican, he voted for the reelection of John Schmitz to Congress in 1970.

BREAKING THE CYCLE

According to William Ryan, the conception of a "cycle of poverty" is one of the classic methods of blaming the victim for social problems. It permits the denial of innate inferiority; the poor person is not to blame, he has been made what he is by the inadequacies of his environment. He is "trained to be poor by his culture and his family life."[5] The remedy for poverty, therefore, is not increased income for the poor, but training to modify their character. This reason for supporting the Family Assistance Plan draws heavily upon the achievement value. The intent is to restore the children of welfare recipients, if not their parents, to productive roles in the competitive economic system. The value of equality, or at least equality of opportunity, is also invoked. Alice Rinehart expressed it this way:

Alice: I think that you get generations of people on welfare, you know, because they are not self-supporting, and they don't learn to be independent, self-sufficient. So I think [a Family Assistance Plan] kind of breaks the cycle.

John Wesley Weeks was more specific.

John: The idea of redistribution of wealth can't accomplish this in the strictest sense, and still maintain democracy. You have to have some form of encouragement, incentive for people to develop, and right now in the ghettos, that facility does not exist. These people are absolutely without hope. . . . Some of them are chronic unemployed, and why is that? I suspect it's because they were raised that way.

A statement of this kind, which cites "breaking the cycle of poverty" as a primary reason for supporting President Nixon's plan, was also offered by Piotr Pavel and the Markuses. It was offered as a subsidiary reason by Kenneth Kaub, Deborah Elliott, and Arthur Roybal—and, of course, by President Nixon, to obscure the wealth redistribution features of his plan.

RESTORING DIGNITY

Citing the restoration of human dignity as a reason for supporting the president's plan implied a focus on the anguish suffered by current

[5] *Ibid.*, p. 7.

welfare recipients and a desire to help, rather than blame, them. It emphasized the value of equality more than that of achievement, although there was a hint of the latter in the assumption that dignity includes independence, the ability to earn one's own way. This attitude was expressed vigorously by Myrna Pavel, a former social worker, when her son suggested that government should teach the principles of nutrition and household budgeting to welfare families.

Myrna: People are *individuals*, and they do not want to be regimented. They don't want to be dictated to. They want to still maintain a certain amount of human dignity, to be able to choose the dinner they want.

This exchange came early in our conversations; she returned to the concept weeks later, when asked specifically about the Family Assistance Plan.

Myrna: It will lend some dignity to the household, if it is a household that wants this dignity. It will also provide a wedge for him [the breadwinner] to get back into the working community. Theoretically, I think it's an excellent idea.

Piotr Pavel asked about regional variations in the cost of living. When it was explained that individual states would still supplement federal income payments, he expressed approval of the Nixon plan—and surprise that he could agree with the president about anything.

Some version of the argument that the Family Assistance Plan would restore human dignity was also cited as a primary reason for supporting it by Deborah Elliott and Arthur Roybal and as a secondary reason by Fletcher Barbera and John Weeks.

In 1970, all but three of the twenty-three respondents in Ramona Heights favored the Family Assistance Plan. This proportion was not very different from that discovered in a national survey by the Louis Harris organization. Late in 1969, a national sample of 4,047 was asked if they favored "the Nixon welfare plan—which would give every family on welfare $1,600 a year with a provision that anyone able to work either enter a job training program or get a job." The plan was favored by 78 percent, opposed by 13 percent, and only 8 percent of the sample had no opinion.[6] Although the plan was described as part of the question,

[6]Bayard Hooper, "The Real Change Has Just Begun," report of a Lou Harris–Life survey, 68 *Life* 1 (January, 1970), p. 106. Further evidence of overwhelmingly favorable public reaction is cited in Moynihan, *Politics of Guaranteed Income*, pp. 268 ff.

and an overemphasis on the job requirement encouraged approval, the low incidence of "no opinion" suggests that the initial publicity given the plan struck a responsive chord in voters across the nation, as it did in Ramona Heights.

Appealing to the contradictory values of achievement and equality, the core of the bourgeois ethos, President Nixon created a climate of public opinion favorable to his proposal. Conservatives like Maureen Barbera and Richard Rinehart saw it as a way to improve the character of poor people and implement the value of achievement, while liberals like Deborah Elliott and Piotr Pavel saw it as a way to further the search for equality. The affluent voters of Ramona Heights did not see the plan as a threat to their own comfort.

Public opinion polls do not satisfactorily measure the intensity of opinions; although Middle America passively supported the president's plan, there was no outpouring of public pressure on Congress to enact it, and the plan was initially viewed with alarm by the organizations of those benefiting from current welfare programs. The House Ways and Means Committee held hearings on the bill. In the election of 1970, President Nixon campaigned very hard to increase the number of Republicans in Congress. Attempting to stimulate the creation of a new conservative force in the nation, he voiced the resentment of Middle America against the cultural alternatives personified by the antiwar movement. His efforts failed miserably; the partisan balance in Congress remained essentially the same.

In his 1971 State of the Union address, the president called for the enactment of a "New American Revolution," with his Family Assistance Plan leading his list of six legislative proposals. Passed by the House, the bill died in the Senate Finance Committee. The pattern was repeated in the Ninety-second Congress: passed by the House, the bill was again killed by the Senate Finance Committee, without even a vote by the full Senate. President Nixon quietly withdrew the proposal by failing to mention it in his 1973 messages to Congress.

The intervening event was the presidential election of 1972. During his primary campaigns, George McGovern proposed to reform the welfare system. Several plans were offered; the one which won the most public attention provided a guaranteed annual income of $1,000 per person, or $4,000 for a family of four, compared to the Nixon figure of $1,600 for a family of four. In the California primary campaign, Hubert Humphrey attacked McGovern's plan as being too costly and saddling the middle class with new tax burdens.

I returned to the voters of Ramona Heights during the late summer of 1972, after both national conventions, when the presidential campaigns were gathering momentum. I found that the Family Assistance Plan, which the microsample discussed so knowledgeably two years earlier, had been forgotten. Instead, they expressed agitation over the McGovern proposals.

The Markuses' nephew, a marine second lieutenant stationed at nearby Camp Pendleton, came to their home at the time I visited. His principal distress was with McGovern's proposal to cut back the armed forces and offer amnesty to draft dodgers. But he expressed disdain for the welfare reform proposal, stating that it and McGovern's other economic policies would dramatically increase the tax burdens of middle-income families, those who "earn about twelve thousand dollars a year." Jan and Eldene joined in his condemnation. Although they felt that poverty should be attacked massively by government, they could not understand "giving everybody in the country a thousand dollars, whether he needs it or not."

Piotr Pavel expressed confusion over McGovern's welfare proposals. "What," he demanded, "would Howard Hughes need a thousand dollars for?" Pavel felt that McGovern was clearly not of presidential quality; unless McGovern clarified his stand on this and other issues, Piotr threatened not to vote in November. (But he did; his distaste for Nixon overcame all his misgivings about McGovern.)

John Weeks said that he had figured the cost of McGovern's welfare proposal on the electronic calculator at his office and estimated that the national income would not be adequate to finance it. Fletcher Barbera dismissed the plan as "idiotic."

Arnold Garcia expressed contempt for the McGovern proposal, and for the poor, but volunteered support for rent subsidies to finance housing for poor families. "If you want to pay their rent," he said, "pay their rent. But don't give them a thousand dollars. They'd just drink it and piss it away."

Except for Kenneth Kaub, who followed the career of FAP in Congress, the voters of Ramona Heights were not aware that both Nixon and McGovern had proposed plans for a guaranteed minimum income as a way of combating poverty; the main area of disagreement was over the amount guaranteed, with a secondary disagreement over the inclusion of work incentives. Of course, Nixon had denied the applicability of the "guaranteed income" label, and McGovern never pointed out the similarties between his ideas and those of President Nixon. The amount of attention the issue received suggested that, if the 1972 voters were voting against any specific policy, they were against McGovern's proposal for welfare reform.

If the Ramona Heights microsample is suggestive of national reactions, it would seem that President Nixon won public acquiescence for his proposal by couching it in terms that appealed to values held dear by the middle class; and those values include a desire, which may be only vaguely articulated, that the lower strata of American society should be assured an equality of economic opportunity. Senator McGovern's presentation of a guaranteed income proposal stimulated fear, rather than sympathy. To many, he seemed determined to reward the poor for their lack of success.

The Ramona Heights voters are able to feel sympathy for the less fortunate, but they are committed to the American tradition of individualism. They favored the Family Assistance Plan, which promised to reform a welfare system they perceived as wasteful and restore individuals to "dignity" and a new entrance into the competition of life. But their support for FAP was marked by its lack of intensity. Not one of them wrote a letter in support of the plan to a legislator. They did not contribute funds to an organization supporting the plan, nor did they follow any other avenues of political influence in its behalf. These families have attained comfort and even affluence in a mobile, changing society. They are not the source of recruits into movements for social reform.

Private Joys, or the Public Interest?

Although the Family Assistance Plan appealed to two values—belief in America as a successful society, and the dedication to enterprise—which are identified as central to the Ramona Heights ethos, it did not stimulate them to political activism. The contradiction is resolved when we realize that action on this issue was effectively prevented by the third element of that ethos—their low opinion of politicians and low expectations for the outcome of the political process.

In common with other suburbanites, these voters view the pattern of urban politics of a city like Chicago with distaste. They are relieved to report that most local issues are petty and unimportant. Alice Rinehart expresses a common attitude when she says that local elections, being nonpartisan, are not really political.

No political parties, no politics. This narrow definition of the nature of politics conforms to the respondents' feeling that politics is concerned with individual and group advantage, rather than the search for definition of the common good. If politics is a question of group advantage, one does not engage in it unless one's group is affected.

John Weeks: I probably would not get involved in politics under almost any circumstances for countless reasons, most of all being that I just don't have the time. I did it with church work for years, and the Boy Scouts, and there have been things that have come up in the community—not politics, but community affairs that I've gotten involved in. It's possible that some issue would come up that I felt so strongly on that I'd get involved. But in general, I'd say probably not.

The voters of Ramona Heights turn away from public affairs to pursue private pleasures. This "privatism" is certainly not peculiar to Ramona Heights, or to suburbia in general. But if the suburban plurality holds a veto power over political change, it is important to understand the roots of privatism and its relationship, if any, to political attitudes. The supposition that suburbanites will thwart policies aimed at social reform can be made in terms of traditional interest-group analysis: as long as they can travel through the stench and decay of the ghettos in air-conditioned automobiles on elevated freeways, why should they be concerned with ghetto residents? A somewhat different argument, made by Frederick Dutton, holds that conflict between the suburbs and the core cities will be somewhat less intense because of suburban privatism, which he equates with a retreat from political concerns—even concerns of self-interest—into the search for personal and familial gratification.[7]

The voters of Ramona Heights do not provide any single, or simple, pattern of privatism, for this is an aspect of one's total outlook on life. It is compounded of personality, experience, and reactions to the events of the day. For the purposes of analysis, it is useful to consider four different elements: the importance attached to the life of the family unit ("familism"); the importance seen in strictly local affairs ("localism"); the effect on the respondent's outlook of his or her stage in the life cycle; and, finally, the impact of conflict between generations, when experienced by the respondent in his own family and applied to larger issues.

IMPORTANCE OF THE FAMILY

A tract like Ramona Heights, with its single-family dwellings, fenced yards, and other amenities, is above all a shrine to the values of family

[7]Frederick G. Dutton, *Changing Sources of Power* (New York: McGraw–Hill, 1971), p. 135.

living. The houses have at least three bedrooms, and many have four or five. Childless couples are unlikely to settle there, unless, like the Markuses, they can easily afford to do so. Those who buy such homes probably seek to benefit the family unit. The Ramona Heights respondents make no secret of their familial devotion. At the beginning of our interviews, Martha Weeks said that her life is devoted largely to "home and hearth." Ten minutes later, she revealed her conviction that the performance of her role as wife and mother was a discharge of her duties as citizen.

Martha: I think, because I'm a woman and I'm for home and hearth, that you should take all these things and bring it back to the family unit. As long as we get along, we encourage the youngsters to grow up, and be different if they want to be, but we make them feel at home, and they know they can always come back here if they want to. It starts within the family unit, as I see it, and it expands in rippling waves to the country as a whole.

John and Martha later mentioned acquaintances who are very active in civic and political affairs—but whose children are constantly getting into trouble. They feel the price of civic involvement for the parents of young children can be too great.

Fletcher and Maureen Barbera measure most political issues against the welfare of their family. Many of the attributes of contemporary society—the hippie subculture, drug abuse, pornography, the change in sexual mores—are of concern because of a perceived threat to the welfare of their children. Maureen Barbera stated this explicitly.

Maureen: As each issue comes up, you are going to look at that, as it pertains to your job, your income, your family. . . . The way you're going to look at a particular question is, How is this going to affect perhaps my children? And you can take that and expand to the future of the nation.

Kenneth and Marie Kaub may be accused of familism; both are shy people whose activities are centered around the home and her son. Marie's only involvement in civic affairs has come when she's been invited to attend meetings or do telephoning. Kenneth cites his status as a civil servant as preventing electioneering. They follow news events closely on television; Marie is sometimes greatly angered by news items, but she doesn't do anything about it, "because the potatoes would burn."

Kenneth: The problems are so many, it seems like one person really can't do that much, and we're so busy with other things that are more important to us, which we feel we may have a little more control over.

The Kaubs are hardly apathetic toward politics, but stepping into the public spotlight would be so painful for them that neither is likely to initiate public action.

These three families are the most open to the charge of familism, but each couple exhibits a different form of the trait, and in no case can it be regarded as a simple retreat from political realities. All can imagine issues that would lead them to abandon family activities in favor of political participation. The Family Assistance Plan did not raise that kind of issue.

LOCALISM

A concern for the life of the local community that nearly eclipses any attention paid to political questions beyond the community could well be a component of privatism. The most interesting couple to exhibit this trait is the Porfilios. Their political world seems, at first, to be bounded by what affects their family and the local community. They began by stating that local issues are the most interesting, but they are not controversial, for everybody agrees on what should be done, such as preventing the construction of a new freeway. Caroline is very active in local community organizations. All their members avoid partisan politics; the women won't even discuss political matters among themselves. Caroline could imagine giving active support to a candidate for election to the school board, but only if the candidate were a personal friend. Ralph agreed they are interested only in organizations that are concerned with the life of the local community. Later, without meaning to, he suggested a reason.

Ralph: I don't think that local politics can really influence national politics. Because they're two different animals. . . . You have what we are interested in politically, which affects us directly . . . but on a national level they're [politicians are] too minority group minded to expect that anybody on a national level could agree with us.

Although the Porfilios said they seldom talk about politics any more ("we're basically Republicans in a Republican area"), they discussed national issues with an eagerness unusual in the microsample and a vindictiveness unique within it. They feel that racial minorities in America have gained too much attention and power too quickly, damaging their own cause in the process.

Caroline: They are pushing themselves too fast. I think there was a need to have 'em come forward, but I think they're pushing a little too hard. They've brought bad will upon themselves.

Ralph: They have not accomplished what they really want, which is equality, because all of a sudden people are afraid of them. . . . If they would look at themselves as being—rather than a minority group, a Mexican-American, a Negro, an Oriental, an American Indian—if they would look at themselves as being an American, which is what they are, they would be better off.

But it is not only racial minorities who arouse the Porfilios' ire. Today's teen-agers "haven't earned anything, yet they demand everything." College students confuse liberty with license, failing to respect the rights of others. Organized labor has grown too powerful and too enamored of the strike as a weapon of power. The Los Angeles schoolteachers' strike was led by "ignorant, stupid people." Although they began the 1970 conversations by naming unemployment in the aerospace industry as the most important national problem, Ralph said that the unemployed aerospace engineers had nobody to blame but themselves. They should have known better than to plan careers with companies that depend on defense contracts. Here, as in the discussion of racial minorities, the Porfilios displayed a tendency to blame the victim for problems produced by the system. They seemed to feel that the nation would be in fine condition if only uncouth and unreasonable groups (blacks, students, and unions) would stop making unreasonable demands, or politicians would stop yielding to them.

The Porfilios most nearly fit Frederick Dutton's image of suburbanites who retreat from politics into the search for personal gratifications. In this case, the retreat is brought about by feeling that the operations of the national and state political systems are out of control, their proper courses deflected by "pushy" groups. (The Porfilios rank at the top of the scale intended to measure the traits of misanthropy and authoritarianism.) The situation is hopeless, they feel, so it would be insane to attempt to influence it. The result is not a kind of privatism that will lessen conflicts between the suburbs and the core cities. The attitudes leading to privatism are of such bitterness that they can only exacerbate any conflict which may arise when the Porfilios feel that the serenity of Ramona Heights is threatened by the groups they despise.

The localism of the Weekses is of quite a different quality. Martha

Weeks has often looked for, and found, the warmth of human relationships of a small town. She glories in living on "a warm street" in Ramona Heights; she feels that her duties as a citizen are best performed by staying close to home and hearth; good accomplishment there may spread out, like ripples in a pond. She trusts President Nixon, with his superior sources of information, to know what is best in a field like welfare reform. John Weeks plunges his energy into engineering and golf, not politics, but he supports political leaders who will make sound changes to "keep the system updated."

Two other families could be accused of localism, but hardly of privatism. Alice Rinehart is active in civic organizations and does organizational work for the Republican party, supported by Richard, who is similarly active in the lay leadership of their church. These activities are locally oriented, but they can hardly be considered privatistic. Frank and Mary McGee are extraordinarily active in local politics. They feel that the current national scene is hopeless, but that the true American virtues have a chance for renaissance in Orange County. In 1970, Frank McGee referred several times to the conviction of then Congressman Schmitz that conservatism could well branch out from its stronghold in the Southwest and "recapture the country." This is not privatism; it is a crusade.

POLITICS AND THE LIFE CYCLE

American political organizations in the 1970s seemed to be overwhelmingly staffed by the young. The enthusiasm of youth can put up with the drudgery of precinct organization, or writing the flood of press releases which will be largely ignored by the local media. But political activism attracts only a portion of the young. The incidence of voting, a sign of minimal participation in the political process, rises with approaching middle age.[8] When a career is established, a family launched, and perhaps a home purchased, voting becomes important.

There are, of course, many activities to be engaged in between mere voting and full-time dedication to political activity. Does political activity apart from voting increase with the accumulation of family responsibilities? Will families with young children be exceptions to the pattern of privatism?

Within the Ramona Heights microsample, the reverse is the case. Families with young children are more privatistic than those with chil-

[8]A. Campbell et al., *The American Voter*, abr. ed. (New York: Wiley, 1964), p. 262.

dren in high school; having children in school tends to involve parents in youth-related community activities; when the children have gone away to college or their own spouses, such participation declines. The maximum parental participation in child-centered activities seems to come when the children are in junior high school. This was true of the Rineharts and of the Elliotts, whose teen-age boys lead them into a variety of activities, including the fundamentalist church that became very important to Quentin. The families with only young children (Barberas and Porfilios) devote much time to strictly family activities that do not lead them into outside organizations.

GENERATIONAL CONFLICT

Political activism is often perceived as a role tied to the idealism of youth. It is common to predict that today's college radicals will become tomorrow's stodgy bourgeoisie. "The onset of orthodontistry for their children usually coincides with the making of two more deradicalized reformers."[9] Much has been written in the last few years about a political "generation gap" that grows between the new generation and the old, as parental values are examined by the young and—at least temporarily—rejected. Much of this comment is concerned with generations in the abstract and their images in the media—the hairy hippies versus the uptight Rotarians. The Ramona Heights microsample includes families who have confronted the question of generational conflict within their own households. They have resolved such questions in a manner that seems satisfactory, at least to the parents. Intragenerational conflict is remarkably slight for these dozen families.

These parents have the example of their own children before them to prove that the media image does not define the totality. Their own children—even with long hair—remain human beings capable of deep concern and high ambition, who are occasionally even capable of accomplishing hard work. The Pavels—with one son in medical school and the other a college teacher of physiology—designate the coming generation as the hope of America. The McGees are proud of their two older children for paying their own way in college and for becoming involved in the same conservative political circles as their parents. Their younger son is wrapped up in baseball, as was his father before him. The McGees blame troubles within the college generation on outside agitators, particularly communists.

[9]Richard M. Scammon and Ben J. Wattenberg, *The Real Majority*, paper ed., (New York: Coward, 1971), p. 53.

The Johnsons and Rineharts also have grown children. Their daughters have escaped the pitfalls—drugs, the counterculture, conflict with the law—which threaten modern young people. The parents are grateful, and they feel they can now relax a bit. With the stormy period of adolescence safely passed, parental worries and responsibilities are markedly lessened.

Parents of younger children foresee many problems. Ralph Porfilio admitted that his own child-rearing practices are different from those of his parents.

Ralph: I think I'm probably a little more strict than my parents were. I think it's partly because I see the insubordination and the disrespect of the teen-agers today that I tend to go maybe overboard in demanding things.

The most striking example of parents concerned about the dangers facing their children—when the oldest child is only beginning grade school—are the Barberas.

Maureen: I'm disturbed because our seven year old wants to be a hippie when he grows up. But I think that's because he likes long hair.
Question: You mean he regards that as his intended profession?
Maureen: Yeah, that's going to be his life style, at the moment. I think I'd better stop fighting it, and just let it wear out. He knows he gets a reaction out of me every time he says it.
Fletcher: When you have children that are from zero to roughly twenty, they are immature—they are maturing, but they are still not adult, so their judgment is still being formed. And I think you are a little bit afraid that they're going to get out in the world and pick up some, quote, "bad ideas," whatever those are, and I know what some of them are. And I kind of feel a pressure to be conservative because of that.

The theme of protecting the children from false values crops up again and again in the 1970 Barbera interview. But they see the problem as extending far beyond the walls of their home.

Maureen: One of the main problems is the generation gap. But I feel that maybe it's the parents' fault somewhere along the line, that the proper morality, or something, hasn't been instilled in the younger generation that's leaping around taking pot and getting in and out of bed with everyone on the street. I feel that somewhere along the line the parents, as individuals, have failed. And I can't say that I am not going to fail, I just hope to heck I'm not. And I'm at a loss to understand why there is all this freedom of everything going on. It appalls me.

Fletcher said that although he and Maureen were only ten years out of college and just over thirty years of age, they could not comprehend a college generation that seized college administrative offices to protest national policies. The Barberas, the youngest couple of the dozen, describe themselves as staunchly conservative, and they are the most alarmed by generational conflict. In 1970, their oldest child was seven. They had not experienced an adolescent or preadolescent in their own household, so their judgment of children of that age was determined by the media image, and local gossip.

The parents who do have teen-agers in their own family readily modify the media image. This fact is a source of amusement with a tinge of worry to the Roybals. When asked about the alleged generation gap, Arthur said the distance between parents and children is no greater today than it ever was, but the children of today are better able to exploit the conflict.

Arthur: I think we give in to our kids a heck of a lot more than our parents did.

Tina: We tend to let them influence us more than we should. I don't think we communicated with our parents the way that these children communicate with us, you see.

The general theme adopted by Ramona Heights parents of teen-agers is that the concept of a generation gap is exaggerated. They have, in several cases, "given in" to their children in the sense of adopting a rather more tolerant attitude toward the problems and viewpoint of youth. In some cases, contact with their own children has had the effect of broadening their political consciousness. This is particularly true with the Weekses. Their son, now in college, became concerned with ecological issues during his final years in high school, and wrote an essay, illustrated by photographs he took himself, on the status of Upper Newport Bay and the species of waterfowl and marine life endangered by the Irvine Company's plans for development of the area. As a result, John and Martha developed a new interest in, and concern for, ecological problems—as well as a new pride in their son. The parents of Ramona Heights do not see the values of the younger generation, with their countercultural component, as providing an alternative outlook on life that could triumph over their own structure of values. They treat the outward manifestations of generational difference, such as long hair and disreputable clothing, as a fad. Mrs. Pavel says of the current style of collegiate dress, "This too shall pass!" They exhibit a marked ability to appreciate, and even learn from, their own children, and they are pleased that their children have not adopted countercultural values or habits which threaten their own.

The exception to this general pattern is the Elliotts. They have deliberately rejected the materialistic values of the corporate scramble represented by Quentin's former occupation. They have attempted to slow down the pace of their lives, to simplify their social activities, and to spend more time in close contact with their children. They find certain attributes of the countercultural life style very attractive. They particularly admire the emphasis on emotional honesty and openness.

As a result, the Elliotts share with the Pavels a great faith in the coming generation. At least on the surface, there is a contrast in the content of that faith. While the Elliotts admire some values of the counterculture and look forward to at least a modest transformation in American society to be wrought by the new generation, the Pavels see the "radicalism" of their sons as being a continuation of the good political fight waged by their own parents.

Tina Roybal says that "depression babies" like her husband, who have known hunger, will always work for material goals, but the new generation, which has never known involuntary suffering, may be able to view middle-class standards with greater objectivity.

The general pattern in Ramona Heights is for the parents of young children to worry about looming problems of the generation gap; for the parents of adolescents to view the notion of a "generation gap" as an exaggeration; and for all to listen to, and learn from, their children, although only the Elliotts, Pavels, and Tina Roybal recognize a more attractive structure of values in the new generation that is distinct from the prevailing middle-class ethic, and take it seriously. The actual or imagined threat of generational conflict, which may be related to the phenomena of familism and privatism, has the effect of broadening, rather than restricting, the political knowledge and concerns of the Ramona Heights parents.

Slight Expectations

The voters of Ramona Heights seem destined to remain political followers, rather than leaders. They are allegiant citizens who feel voting is important. Yet their expectations of the changes that can be wrought through political action are relatively slight. This, together with their tendencies toward privatism, may explain their political quietude.

The members of the microsample responded to standard items intended to measure their sense of political efficacy—which is roughly the equivalent of their feeling that personal political action will yield results that are worth the effort. Frank McGee received the highest possible score, and his wife, Mary, scored close to the top. Scoring just behind the McGees were the Rineharts, who have been the second most politically active couple, although their activity has consisted of conventional work within the Republican party and civic organizations, in contrast to the McGees' ultraconservative activism. Richard Rinehart's sense of efficacy was found to be correlated with his sense of mastery and belonging in his work experience, although no causal relationship could be demonstrated.

Our present concern is with what might be called the cognitive elements of a low sense of political efficacy—the belief that political action will yield minimal results, if any. Paradoxically, such a feeling may be prevalent among allegiant citizens. For, as Murray Edelman has written, the residents of industrialized nations, confronted by "a complex, cold, and bewildering world," may abandon any attempt to exert personal political influence on that world, and simply form attachments to "reassuring abstract symbols."[10] The status of the members of the microsample as—to an extent—communicants of a civil religion, may indicate the substitution of an essentially irrational faith for the psychic rewards of personal political activity. Their attachment to the flag, to the presidential office in times of crisis, and to other symbols of the state could be signs of this attachment.

No direct relationship of this kind can be established for the dozen families. Frank McGee finds his political activity deeply rewarding, and has a fundamentalist's attachment to the national symbols. Quentin Elliott's score on the political efficacy scale is as high as that of the Rineharts, but his political activity has been more sporadic, because of moving so frequently to new cities during his corporate career. Piotr Pavel ranks lowest on the scale of political efficacy, which may be related to his unhappy work experience. A more fruitful source of explanation for the low level of political expectation among Ramona Heights voters lies in their own words. Their attitudes are made up of definite ideas about the nature of politicians and bureaucrats. The world may be cold and complex, but it is not bewildering; they have ideas that render it explicable.

With the exception of Piotr Pavel, who favors a parliamentary system,

---

[10]Murray Edelman, *The Symbolic Uses of Politics* (Urbana: University of Illinois Press, 1964), p. 76. The cited paragraph is a headnote to Chapter Six.

the members of the microsample are pleased with the basic institutions of American government as outlined in the Constitution. However, they are at least ambivalent about, and often deeply suspicious of, political leadership. It is not only that the word "politics" has some connotations summarized in the word "dirty." They feel that politicians serve specific and limited interests, including their own personal welfare, rather than the interests of the whole.

Piotr and Myrna Pavel returned again and again to their thesis that Governor Ronald Reagan, the actor in politics, is only a "quick study" who mouths the lines supplied him by the leaders of big business in California, such as oilman Henry Salvatori. They feel that Governor Reagan's election campaigns were exercises in electronic fraud, and they particularly resent what they see as the governor's vendetta against the University of California. In 1970, they voiced similar suspicions about President Nixon.

Myrna: I could never have voted for Nixon. I just didn't trust him. I don't think he's lost his "Tricky Dick" title.
Piotr: He's a trickier Dick now.
Myrna: He's smoother.

Yet the Pavels' suspicion of politicians shades into a lack of faith in the electorate, revealed in the discussion of their own particular hero, Adlai Stevenson.

Myrna: I didn't think Stevenson was really presidential material. He was just too, too good, too much the idealist.
Piotr: I think the average voter is afraid of anybody like Stevenson. He's just too educated. . . . I think the average voter—and I may be wrong, but that's my impression—votes just the way he buys toothpaste. The one that hammers the most on the television screen.

Lack of faith in the electorate would logically lead to a lack of faith in their elected spokesmen. At one point in the interview, the respondents were asked whether politicians, as a group, wield too much, or too little, power in America. Only five respondents—the Rineharts, the McGees, and Quentin Elliott—immediately thought of the electoral process as a device for checking the power of political leaders.

Quentin: Politicians don't have too much power today. If they do, it's because we've defaulted in our responsibility to keep them honest.

The Rineharts' outlook was almost complacent.

Alice: I think they're pretty well controlled by whether they get reelected or not.

Richard: The balance there is pretty good. An election every two, four, six years, whatever it is, pretty much controls that.

The respondents who immediately think of the electoral process as a check on the power of politicians are also the ones who rank highest on the scale of political efficacy. They agree with the rest of the microsample in volunteering the word "integrity" as a description of the leading quality of an ideal politician, the quality that makes a person worth voting for. They also agree that integrity is a scarce commodity among politicians.[11]

If a candidate of true integrity is elected, what can he accomplish? He can only attempt to bend the bureaucracy to his will; and that he has small chance of accomplishing. This theme is common to the Ramona Heights microsample. Jan Markus, for example, has a straight-forward idea of the nature of bureaucracies.

Jan: I think the bureaucrats run the country. Say, for instance, the president. He's never been a president; where do you get training for that? Or where do you get training for all of these other jobs? They get in there and they don't know what to do. Who runs it? The bureaucrats. Or in any office. That's like they have somebody who's secretary-treasurer of the United States; he doesn't know the first thing to do. He's just a front. He's just a name. And the same thing in the big corporations. It takes all the bureaucrats to run it. [He laughs.] Well, it has to be run some way, and the bigger it gets, the less control there is over it.

Sharing this essential opinion of bureaucracy, Richard Rinehart half-seriously suggested a remedy: an "automatic self-destruct" for governmental departments. Each bureau would go out of existence after five years, unless Congress passed a specific law to retain it.

A more thoughtful critique of governmental bureaucracy was offered by Piotr Pavel. Recalling his experience in France and England, he lamented the fact that American civil servants rank so low in public esteem. If their social status were higher, a higher quality individual

[11]In both 1968 and 1970, the search for a worthy candidate seemed like a yearning for integrity on the part of the Ramona Heights voters. The search was suspended in 1972, as neither Nixon nor McGovern seemed to possess the trait. See Chapter Nine.

would be attracted to governmental service, as he believes is the case in England. Then the supply of "dead wood" found in governmental departments would be reduced.

Arthur Roybal reacted immediately to a question about bureaucracies.

Arthur: We're getting to the point where you can't go to the bathroom unless you've filed it in triplicate!

Like many of the other respondents, he immediately associated bureaucracies with needless red tape and endless forms. Instead of mentioning the federal government, however, he cited the Los Angeles city school system as a top-heavy bureaucracy. He suggested that the remedy was decentralization. Tina Roybal also mentioned bureaucracies as harboring institutionalized racism: the insistence of officialdom that all persons they deal with behave in a polite, middle-class manner.

The respondent most nearly able to view bureaucracies with equanimity was Fletcher Barbera.

Fletcher: Bureaucrats are sort of a necessary evil. They're an imperfection of the system. . . . Bureaucracy is impersonal, and, left to their own devices, people do tend to build empires, bureaucratic empires. And that occurs in business, you know, not just in government. From time to time the excesses get brought to the attention of the public, and they get cut back, so it's a cycle . . . I have some uneasiness about perhaps there are a few more bureaucratic inefficiencies in government than in business.

Perhaps the median response was that of Quentin Elliott, who summed up his feeling with his customary neatness.

Quentin: Bureaucracy is a danger; it gets expensive, and it can be very inefficient.

Politicians are suspect; bureaucracies are intransigent. Both operate within an established system which (although it is basically the best in the world) has become large, complex, and rigid. Such a combination of beliefs is bound to lead to the conviction that political action will yield minimal results, if any. Little wonder, then, that the Ramona Heights voters did not form a suburban pressure group to fight for welfare reform. They did not consider writing to their Congressman (who in early 1970 was John Schmitz, an unlikely advocate of a guaranteed annual income). Welfare reform was essentially an urban problem. It did not touch Ramona Heights directly. The microsample found the Family Assistance Plan attractive, for it appealed to a mixture of basic motives, drawing on the dual belief in equality and achievement that has been called "enterprise." But these voters left the question to be resolved by the system, far off in Washington, in the conviction that political action on their own part would have little influence on the outcome.

CHAPTER EIGHT

Conservatives, Liberals, and Democratic Practices

American history is based on the resemblance between moderate liberalism and moderate conservatism; the history of continental Europe is based on the difference between extreme liberalism and extreme conservatism.

—*Peter Viereck*[1]

"Sure, Orange County is more conservative than a lot of other places. But if you go down to individual people, and pull them apart, you'd find that there is a wide spectrum, and that even within one person you'll find both conservative and liberal tendencies."

—*Fletcher Barbera*

AS LABELS to differentiate contending political attitudes within a system supported by public consensus, "conservative" and "liberal" have a long history. Their prestige has varied, and their meanings have been altered. In the late 1930s, "conservative" could be a term of condemnation, but the label was restored to an honorable place in Orange County long before Barry Goldwater won his primary election there.

[1]Peter Viereck, *Conservatism Revisited*, rev. ed. (New York: Macmillan, Free Press, 1965), p. 125.

Several voters in Ramona Heights use these terms to differentiate political leaders and proposals. Most are also willing to apply the labels to themselves. The terms have a contemporary vitality that is independent of their historical meaning.

Since the stereotype of Orange County focuses on its conservatism, it is important to determine what that term means to the Ramona Heights voters, and what political actions it suggests to those who claim it as a self-identification.

A Conservative Majority

Except for Eldene Markus and Quentin Elliott, who resist labels, the members of the microsample readily assign "conservative," "liberal," or "middle of the road" to their political attitudes. Thirteen call themselves conservative (the Weekses, Barberas, Rineharts, McGees, Porfilios, Roybals, and Arnold Garcia). The Roybals say they are only a shade to the conservative side of the middle of the road. The Rineharts say they are "somewhat conservative" for they do not, after all, approve of the John Birch Society. Five describe themselves as liberal—the Pavels, the Kaubs, and Deborah Elliott. The Johnsons call themselves "middle of the road." The position of the Markuses is a compound of contradictions —a yearning for the socialist oratory they remember from their youth, a deep attachment to law and order, the casual acceptance of racial stereotypes, fierce patriotism, and a disdain for the rich and their tax advantages. Nevertheless, Jan Markus accepts "middle of the road" as a self-identification, and Eldene finally agrees.

As mentioned in Chapter Three, there is congruence between party registration and ideological self-identification. All the self-labeled conservatives are Republicans, with the exception of Ralph Porfilio, who registered as a Democrat to spite his Republican mother. The self-labeled liberals are all registered as Democrats, with the exception of Dr. Kaub, who grew up as a Kansas Republican and remains one so the household will receive the campaign literature of both parties.

The majority of Californians register as Democrats but have recently voted Republicans into office. In Ramona Heights, all five "middle of the road" voters are registered Democrats, and in 1972 only Quentin Elliott out of their number voted for George McGovern; on the other hand, his wife, a liberal and a Democrat, voted for Richard Nixon. The Markuses were unhappy with the performance of the first Nixon Administration, particularly in the economic sphere, but they did not like what they saw of the Democratic National Convention, and they were appalled by McGovern's position on amnesty for draft evaders. After threatening not to vote at all, Eldene voted for McGovern, but Jan voted for Nixon. Harry and Jacqueline Johnson never even considered voting for McGovern. In fact, of the entire microsample, only the Pavels, Quentin Elliott, Eldene Markus, and Tina Roybal voted for McGovern. Both Arthur and Tina, who are registered as Republicans for "defensive" reasons, decided late in the campaign. Arthur finally decided that Sargent Shriver was unacceptable as a vice president; Tina selected McGovern because of Nixon's handling of Vietnam and his absence from the campaign, coupled with her growing conviction that "we are in a changing social scene . . . and maybe my social awareness or values are not what I thought they were several years back."

Thus, a microcosm of the 1972 presidential election: no general soul-searching, but a few tortured individuals—four Democrats and one Republican voting for George McGovern, five Democrats and eleven Republicans voting for Richard Nixon. Left out of this accounting are the McGees. Frank McGee voted for his admired friend, John Schmitz, presidential candidate of the American Independent party; Mary McGee, uncertain of the value of a Schmitz vote but unwilling to negate her husband's choice, left the presidential ballot blank.

THE MEANING OF "CONSERVATIVE"

What does the word "conservative" mean to the voters of Ramona Heights? Three themes run through the transcripts. The first is the transplantation to the political sphere of a notion about economics: too much spending results in ruin; liberals are spendthrift, while conservatives avoid deficit financing. The technocrats of Ramona Heights are not professional economists. For some, the resistance to government expenditures is simply the projection of family financial convictions.

Kenneth Kaub: I'd say I was more conservative on the fiscal side, the balanced budget and that sort of thing. Make sure you have the money before you spend it. Fiscal responsibility applies to governments, too, as well as to individual families.

Richard Rinehart: Just take the budget. If you take in a dollar of income, and if you balance spending with that income, then you are probably a conservative. If you spend a dollar and a half, you are probably a liberal. Now, each of them wants to do their very best. The liberal perhaps feels that he's doing more by spending the dollar and a half. The

conservative may say, "I'm doing more because I'm balancing the budget, and there are more evils to spending the dollar and a half than there
are to a dollar."

Closely related to the feeling that government spends too much is the
conviction that government *does* too much, or does the wrong things.
This conviction is not so widespread, even among those who call themselves conservatives.

Frank McGee: I'd like to see less government, I guess, and more
individual responsibility. . . . The ideal citizen is basically a man who
wants to work for a living, buy his own insurance, save for his own
retirement, and help out his fellow man who needs help. . . . That to
me kind of defines the conservative philosophy, so he would be conservative politically.

Ralph Porfilio: To me a liberal is the person who would be in favor
of things like socialized medicine. . . . I think this is a bad term to use,
but I think the liberal is leaning closer to a communist type of society
than a conservative. . . . One of our biggest problems is the attitude of
people that Big Brother in Washington should take care of them, rather
than going out and doing for themselves, what they really want to do,
or are capable of doing.

Similarly, the Markuses have little respect for groups which depend
upon government for favors, but they are eager to use public policy ("a
little more socialism would be a good thing") to limit the unfair advantages of the wealthy.

The third theme is nearly universal among the respondents calling
themselves conservative. All admit that policies once considered danger-
ously radical are now accepted by conservatives and liberals alike, but
conservatives resist further change until they are convinced it will be
change for the better.

As noted before, John Weeks suggests that his support for moderate
change is influenced by his work in a field of engineering where the
systems must be constantly updated.

John: I think that the most perverted word in the world is "liberal,"
so you can see which side of the fence I'm on. . . . The so-called liberal
I heartily disapprove of, because in my opinion the liberal tends to make
changes simply for the sake of making changes, and many times to
attract political notoriety to themselves. . . . We must change the
country. We must continually change it, but we must change it only
where a change is for the better.

Fletcher Barbera tied his definition of "conservative" to the fashionable issue of ecology.

Fletcher: The earth was there a long time before man. And it settled itself into balance. And you start fooling around with the balance and you don't know what's going to happen. . . . The conservative is the guy who says, "Until I'm pretty damn sure that the change is positive, I won't make it."

Maureen Barbera feels conservatism is more a mood than a series of policy preferences. Of her husband's conservatism, she said, "Sometimes it seems like Fletcher just doesn't want to get involved."

These, then, are the themes identified by the voters of Ramona Heights as the main components of conservatism: resistance to deficit spending, dislike for governmental programs which inhibit the development of "individual initiative," and suspicion of change for the sake of change.

The modern statement of conservatism as a political philosophy largely originated with Edmund Burke, the eighteenth-century Irish statesman. He supported the American colonies in their struggle for independence, for he perceived that their effort was to recapture the traditional rights of Englishmen which they had long enjoyed but found abrogated by George III. But Burke opposed the French Revolution and was appalled by its excesses. He felt that the faith in human reason expressed by the *philosophes* was erroneous, and that pride in intellect was a source of evil in human affairs. He did not accept the notions of natural right which Locke and Jefferson found so persuasive; he felt that human societies were artificial creations, but they contained the collective wisdom of the human race, and should be regarded with awe and even reverence. "The individual is foolish," wrote Burke "The multitude . . . is foolish, when they act without deliberation; but the species is wise, and when time is given to it, as a species it always acts right."[2]

The great manifesto of American freedom, the Declaration of Independence, is a product of the Enlightenment, which insists upon self-evident natural rights possessed by all men: it asserts the power of the intellect and the right of men to replace a government which becomes

[2]Edmund Burke, *Reform of Representation in the House of Commons* (1782). Quoted in George H. Sabine, *A History of Political Theory*, 3rd ed. (New York: Holt, 1961), p. 609. Sabine's standard work is but one of the sources in which the reader may pursue further the history of "conservatism" and "liberalism." Another is Viereck, *Conservatism Revisited*.

destructive of their rights. The Constitution is an intellectual attempt to construct a new government for a continent that had known only colonial administration and the loose alliance of the Articles of Confederation. While the radicalism of the Declaration was thoroughly tamed in the Constitution, both documents are products of the Age of Reason.

The established order in America, therefore, is founded upon eighteenth-century liberal principles: a belief in the innate goodness of man, and his capacity for self-government; a conviction that men should be free from governmental restraints in order to achieve their full potential. When liberal thought was applied to economic relationships, the principles of laissez-faire were established: an invisible hand operates in the marketplace, to assure the general good through the pursuit of individual self-interest; therefore, government must not interfere with the operation of the free enterprise system.

The belief of Ramona Heights' conservatives that the government must not interfere with the development of "individual initiative" thus has complex historical antecedents: Puritan notions of predestination, secularized as personal striving; Locke's devotion to limited government, articulated by Jefferson; Adam Smith's laissez-faire convictions; and the contention of the social Darwinists that only the economically fit should survive. The lesson of the New Deal—that certain social forces should be contained or regulated by government—was accepted without changing the basic belief. But the praise of private initiative and the conviction that governmental powers should be limited, in spite of their origin as liberal principles, are accepted in modern America, as in Ramona Heights, as tenets of conservatism.

The mixture is strikingly mild: a teaspoonful of Burke's reverence for the established order, a dash of Jefferson, and two cups of nineteenth-century liberal economics. Is this the fanaticism of the right which gave Orange County its reputation? The moderate views of the Rineharts, Barberas, Weekses, and Roybals hardly fit the stereotype. These affluent technocrats are not much different from such persons in other suburbs across the nation. If Orange County is a hotbed of Birchism, the McGees must be the glowing embers in Ramona Heights.

THE McGEES: CONSERVATIVE OR LIBERTARIAN?

In the process of defining the "Orange County spirit" as the motivating force behind Nixon's White House staff, Michael Davie quoted a description of the staff members by an unnamed Southern California congressman:

They still have a kind of Puritan ethic—my father made it, I made it, so if I can do it, why can't others? They have a very tough ideological approach.[3]

Frank and Mary McGee would certainly be found guilty of defending the work ethic, the value of achievement, a major theme in American history still accepted by many Americans. The McGees distrust parties, politicians, and the bureaucracy, and they would reduce the size and scope of government dramatically. Their attitudes toward political issues and current events are more ideologically colored than those of any other respondents. Frank and Mary are allegiant citizens, with a fierce loyalty to the Constitution as they understand it, yet they are the deviant extremists, the Birchers, of the microsample.

One study of contemporary right-wing movements in America concludes that supporters of the presidential candidacies of Barry Goldwater and George Wallace were engaged in symbolic politics: taking a stand for what one believed was important for its own sake, regardless of any results.[4] They see the values they cherish being challenged by new groups and convictions. The threat need not be based on material considerations; it can be entirely psychological. Frank McGee—former professional baseball player (football has largely usurped its place as the national sport); amateur barbershop quartet singer (an anachronistic musical form); traditional Catholic (the Pope approves offering the mass in the vernacular, but not the McGees); devoted husband and father (the American family is under attack); self-employed businessman (rugged individualism is passé); army veteran and patriot—has any number of reasons for feeling that the purposes to which his life has been dedicated were ridiculed by the demonstrators and other long-haired types (Frank wore a crew cut until 1972), who in his opinion commanded entirely too much attention from the media. His political activity was an exercise in "status politics," an effort to reassert the values under siege. Furthermore, if this is symbolic politics, where the act is more important than the result, then Frank's firm sense of political efficacy need not depend on the success of his political ventures. Standing up to be counted provides its own reward.

The McGees' strong religious faith, their belief in original sin, and

[3]Michael Davie, "The 'Orange County' Spirit," *San Francisco Chronicle*, April 28, 1973. Davie, a correspondent for the *London Observer*, claimed in his article that "a generalized explanation of the Watergate conspiracy" may be found in the Orange County roots of the Nixon staff. The article is quoted in the headnote to Part One.
[4]James McEvoy III, *Radicals or Conservatives? The Contemporary American Right* (Chicago: Rand McNally, 1971).

their adherence to the symbols of American government may fulfill Burke's requirements for the basic tenets of conservatism. However, their reverence is directed toward the past. Convinced that the greatest source of potential evil is governmental power, they wish to return to a simpler time, with rudimentary governmental arrangements. They are not anarchists, but they may be libertarians. When asked to describe the ideal form of government, they replied:

Frank: The ideal might be the libertarian philosophy: no government at all.

Mary: But then you're overlooking evil.

Frank: Well, that's true.

Mary: With the fall of Adam and Eve, you're always going to have evil.

Asked about the size of an ideal society—how many people can live together in some kind of political community—they answered:

Frank: The United States is not too big. It's just that there's a concentration of people in certain areas. Probably less urbanization and more rural life would be the answer there. . . . The ideal society would be like America is, or maybe was twenty or thirty years ago, with some people doing the laboring and some people doing the administrative work, and making good salaries, but not being greedy.

Mary: You have to incorporate charity into your ideal society, definitely. Charity meaning love, right, so that the widows and orphans that have to be taken care of, there will always be people who need help. The poor you will always have.

Frank: And the best type of help for these people would be, we feel, through the church, primarily. Certainly not through the government. Through churches and neighborhoods.

Frank and Mary resolve the problem of human evil within an ideal society by proposing strong, strict punishment for offenders; capital punishment, following trial by local jury, should be retained. Frank adds jokingly, "I suppose a little lynching wouldn't hurt once in a while."

Rural, localized, and self-sufficient. The McGees' vision of the ideal society has elements in common with the life styles adopted by those who would hasten "the greening of America."[5] But there are three differences: Frank and Mary want the basic societal unit to be the

---

[5]Charles A. Reich, *The Greening of America* (New York: Random House, 1970), is a celebration of the countercultural values of the "flower children."

patriarchal family, rather than communes of friends. They would insist on a strong armed force, to defeat communism overseas. And men would get more haircuts. Since their ideal society harkens back to an imagined golden age, the McGees may seem reactionaries, not conservatives. Their feeling that, if less government is better, the best would be none at all, places them within the libertarian tradition. However, this was a discussion of the ideal; what they believe and do from day to day is more important.

Their news of the world's daily happenings comes from two newspapers. They subscribe to the *Santa Ana Register*, the famous ultra-conservative flag paper of the Freedom Chain, founded by the late R. C. Hoiles, and to the *Daily Pilot*, an Orange County suburban paper.

Frank: We don't agree with the *Register* wholeheartedly, and we get the *Daily Pilot* to keep track of what the other side is doing.

Question: What aspects of the *Register's* outlook do you disagree with?

Frank: Their extreme libertarian philosophy.

Mary: Yeah, right. They're a little bit more extreme than we are. They believe in doing away with all police forces, and all national highways, and so forth.

Frank: They want every community to establish its own private fire department and police department, but that's just impractical, I'm afraid. I think there is need for a *little* bit of government. [He chuckles.]

Mary: They feel that there shouldn't be any government, actually, that it's a pyramid, an inverted pyramid. It's top-heavy, and if you don't vote, this pyramid will fall. . . . The philosophy being that, as long as you vote, you perpetuate these politicians in office, and if you don't vote, they are going to fall. But you're *not* going to get 'em out by not voting.

Frank: A lot of people that we know have gone for this complete libertarian philosophy, and they no longer take part in politics, or take an interest in political issues. It's been quite a shock, in some cases . . . It's interesting to see some of the people who have gone all the way.

Mary: Oh, absolutely. No police force. Every person take care of his own. And, if you have a gun, stand there, then that other guy isn't going to bother you. . . . So, talk about extremists, I consider the libertarians quite extreme.

The McGees have considered the implications of libertarianism when carried to its logical conclusion and they reject it. It makes more sense to engage in normal politics, supporting the candidates they agree with and taking stands on ballot propositions. Sometimes their side wins, sometimes it doesn't. Their suspicions of the two major parties were heightened by the Watergate scandals and the Ervin Committee investigation.

Mary: I think the outstanding feature of Watergate is the sin of omission—what the committee fails to bring out: the power play behind the scenes in Washington, and the threat of Red-tainted dollars from Cuba, et cetera.

Frank McGee feels the scandals have greatly increased the chances of the Democratic nominee in 1976, and this may be the entering wedge for the institution of "one-world government." Following the general line of the John Birch Society, the McGees believe that there is an international conspiracy working to undermine American liberties by establishing a single, worldwide government; that the United Nations is designed to aid this conspiracy; and that the leaders of both the Republican and Democratic parties are at least duped by the conspiracy, if they are not actually members of it. When world government is established, it will be communistic.

The McGees are thus "cabalists"; they feel there is a secret conspiracy, operating behind the scenes, which influences the direction of public events through private manipulation. There is another couple, Jan and Eldene Markus, who share many characteristics of cabalist thought, but their party registration is, and their voting record tends to be, directly opposite.

CABALISM IN RAMONA HEIGHTS

Ramona Heights, a sunny settled neighborhood, its homes steadily appreciating in value, seems unlikely to harbor persons who feel themselves victimized by hidden, evil forces. In his investigation of the ideologies of fifteen working men, Robert Lane used the word "cabalism" to characterize the style of conspiratorial thought he found in three men. The men to whom Lane applied the term were outwardly cordial and friendly; they exhibited none of the symptoms of psychotics in the grip of paranoia; they did not feel personally threatened; they did not hear secret voices, or even suspect that their telephones might be tapped. They simply had recourse to conspiratorial theories to explain "what really goes on" in government.

So it is with the McGees and the Markuses. Friendly and hospitable, living lives free of frenzy or fear, they believe they have a special understanding of the forces which control politics. For the Markuses, this understanding has come through experience of the world, almost intuitively; there is no need to examine its separate parts for consistency or conduct research to fill in its details; it is simply there, to be used when necessary. The McGees, on the other hand, spend a significant part of their daily lives in the study of political events, seeking further confirmation of their understanding of "what really goes on." And they know this understanding is not widespread—the mass media are controlled by the conspiracy, so the true meaning of events is not to be learned from the evening television news; it must be sought behind the facade.

According to Lane, there are six characteristics of cabalist thought.[6] Some of these apply to both the McGees and the Markuses.

1. *There is some unofficial quasi-conspiratorial group behind the scenes to manipulate and control public affairs.*

Both families are marked by this conviction. There are hints of it in the conversations of a few other couples, notably the Porfilios, but only the McGees and Markuses have regular recourse to "a secret plot" as a causal explanation for the trend of public affairs.

2. *Each cabal group is responsible to no one but itself; its power is checked, if at all, by only the most tenuous and ineffective forces . . . never is there the notion that power is responsible to the people on whom it is exercised.*

The true cabalist sees the democratic process as a fraud. I asked Frank McGee about his feeling that Southern California is a last stronghold of real Americanism. I said this seemed to divide the country into good and bad, and I asked if there could be no middle ground.

Frank: Well, I suppose it all depends on how far down the road one thinks we might be. It's pretty obvious that many people are not as concerned as others. Many people, I think, feel that the Communists have already taken over the country, but they just haven't told us yet. And, with some of the things that have happened, I, even *I* wonder, sometimes, if that person might be right, much as I hate to think it. But it's a matter of degree—of how far gone different people think we are, as I see it.

Question: But what's your own feeling?

Frank: Who knows, really? How do you find out for sure? There's just no way. You can't tell by reading the newspapers or listening to television. All you can do is think it out and come to a decision on your own.

[6]Robert E. Lane, *Political Ideology*, paper ed. (New York: Macmillan, Free Press, 1962), pp. 116–118.

But this uncertainty about the advance of the communist conspiracy on the national level does not vitiate the usefulness of local political activity.

Frank: I think it is vitally important to look right at the old home town and get started on the right foot here. I think if people had taken more interest in the past thirty or forty years, I don't know how long, I think that maybe we'd have better leadership at the top, now, if we had tried harder to get the right people in there locally.

On the local level, power can be made responsive to the people; using the local base, the people can eventually recapture control of the national government.

The Markuses have not given up on the democratic process, either. They feel that George Wallace was a "front man" for Richard Nixon in 1968, fraudulently winning votes away from Humphrey to assure Nixon's election. They believe that the 1972 Democratic National Convention did not truly represent the membership of their party and did not reach wise decisions. However, they are convinced that the Democratic party remains close to the interests of "working people" like themselves. Jan voted for Nixon in 1972 with misgivings; his worst suspicions were realized by the Watergate scandals, and he is eager to join Eldene in supporting their "own" party.

3. *There are two kinds of cabals; on the one hand, there are the high status big-businessmen, international bankers . . . on the other hand there are the low-status racketeers, Jews, union-bosses, "immoral elements," Communists.*
4. *The cabalist argument is protean . . . no one cabal will do for all occasions.*

The cabalist explanation is certainly protean for the Markuses, but they reject the explanation favored by the McGees: they express specific disdain for the Birch line. Very early in our conversations, Jan Markus declared, "Anybody with any common sense knows that you can't blame all of our ills on the Communists." At other times, however, they designate various groups as having undue, and often secret, political influence.

Jan: Why should those senile men be up there all those years? I think they shouldn't be there. How are they able to keep control of that? To get elected every year? The South is full of that.
Eldene: And I don't believe in letting the southern states run the country.
Jan: Which they are doing.

A moment later, Eldene Markus identified "greed" as the cause of war, and her husband elaborated.

Jan: I think capital is international. And we have American capital going into financing these wars. If they'd stop that, we wouldn't have it. It's money that rules the world, anyway. Look at this war in Vietnam. Everybody—all our allies—they're selling stuff to the enemy, to make money. . . . And why should the international bankers rule the world? Which is what they're doing. And some of them are our own American "patriots" here in this country. They're making money off the war; they sell to everybody.

In the hate literature of four decades ago, the power of international banking was usually linked with anti-Semitism. But the Markuses do not make that link. Their anti-Semitic feelings are separate and mentioned with hesitation.

Jan: I think there are some groups of people that are a minority in this country that have too much to say about our government. And I don't have to tell you who they are!
Eldene: It's the colored.
Jan: No, not only the colored. There's others.
Eldene: Well, the majority, too, sometimes is overbearing on their laws, Jan.
Jan: I'm talking about a minority.
Eldene: Well, who is it?
Jan: Well, the *Jews*. For one thing. They have too much to say. Just like they're trying to get us tangled up there in the Middle East. And they're using pressure to get us in there, and I don't think that's right.

The cabal identified by the Markuses as "running the country" varied with the circumstances. At one point or another, they also mentioned big business, the military, and government bureaucrats. Eldene thinks that Russia and China somehow supported the students who rioted at the 1968 Democratic National Convention, and that those two countries will attempt to influence all American elections, if they can.

The cabalist intellectual style of the McGees is more sharply focused. Rather than being intuitive, it is learned—from courses in anticommunism, from Birch Society seminars, and from the continued study of periodicals published in Belmont, Massachusetts. The McGees believe literally in the existence of an international communist conspiracy; they do not know how much progress that conspiracy has made toward its goals, but they are sure that Nixon's visits to Russia and China were part of the pattern. Toward the end of our 1970 conversations, McGee spelled out his convictions.

Frank: This brother of mine who is a priest talks about communism, but he's speaking of communism with a small "c," which is synonymous with socialism. But, when I'm arguing with him, I'm thinking of Communism with a *capital "C,"* the Communist Conspiracy. I've never seen anything about that [distinction in capitalization] in the liberal press, but I swear that it's important. The nuns in a community live their life in communism. They do different things. One works in the kitchen, one teaches school, and she'll get paid more than the other, but they'll all throw the money in the pot. . . . This is a type of communistic life. But it's *voluntary.* But, when you have that capital "C" there, I think of the atheistic Communist Conspiracy that's out to take over the world.

For the McGees, one cabal does serve for all occasions; further study and research are needed to understand its insidious operations.

> 5. *The affairs, meetings, and decisions of the group are secret and not understood by most people who take things at face value; therefore it is a special gift of insight that permits one to penetrate reality. . . . For the cabalist thinker, every event is willed.*

According to Lane, the cabalist thinker is the "master inside-dopester, who really needs no dope at all, but assumes it." This sounds like the Markuses, who tend to introduce various cabals with something like a wink and a nod; conversing with a political science professor, they seemed to think there were some things that could be understood among us initiates; it did not have to be said. However, this was done with a light touch and made into a joke. The McGees take their politics very seriously. They are not devoid of jokes or laughter, but Frank McGee's political humor is pointed and bitter. His intellectual style is one of insinuation, along the lines of "Is it really an accident that both the Kremlin and the Pentagon have walls with five sides?"

Frank and Mary earlier agreed that their most helpful and dependable source of information regarding public affairs is the Birch Society monthly magazine, *American Opinion.* Mary says of it, "You get stories from all over the world, stuff that you would *never* read in the normal media. And it makes sense, that's all there is to it."

> 6. *The method of the cabals—the way they create wars and depressions and revolutions—are obscure, but they involve extraordinary, almost supernatural powers.*

Mystery is very attractive to the mind of the cabalist thinker. It is akin, Lane writes, to the mystery of religion, particularly that dark side of faith where devils and monsters lurk. This hardly describes the cabalism of the Markuses. Their attribution of secret influence to various cabals happens casually, and there is no logical connection between them. The riots at the 1968 Democratic convention *had* to be supported by Russia and China; but it's a mistake to blame all America's ills on the communists. International bankers obviously profit from wars, but this phenomenon is not related to the support given by American Jews to Israel. At one moment, senile southern senators are identified as "running the country"; the next, international bankers rule the world. The Markuses are not hampered by a requirement of logical consistency. Their cabalism is made up of what Daryl J. Bem calls "opinion molecules." Bem holds that the elaborate theories of cognitive consistency developed by psychologists are fine for their purpose, but they do not account for enough real people. The desire to be consistent in one's attitudes and beliefs is an academic hangup which bothers most people not at all, and which academics probably forget when they venture outside their specialties.

> Opinion molecules serve such a simple function that psychologists have usually ignored them. They are conversational units. They give us something coherent to say when a particular topic comes up in conversation. Accordingly, they do not need to have logical interconnections between them, and they are notoriously invulnerable to argument because of their isolated, molecular character.[7]

The opinion molecule concept is useful for interpretation of the Ramona Heights transcripts. When one realizes that people don't always care about being consistent, one stops expecting it. But the McGees make their explanations of public events consistent by fitting them to the notion of an international communist conspiracy. Their inclusion of the epithet "atheistic" suggests that the forces of communism are identified in their minds with the minions of the Antichrist. Since events are willed, and appalling cultural changes have occurred around them, what could be easier than to blame communism for those changes?

Very often in history, conspiracy theories seem to provide the most economical interpretation. Woodrow Wilson's negotiations at Ver-

---

[7]Daryl J. Bem, *Beliefs, Attitudes, and Human Affairs* (Belmont, Calif.: Wadsworth, Brooks/Cole, 1970), p. 39. Bem credits Robert P. Abelson with coining the phrase.

sailles did not produce an "open covenant, openly arrived at." Stalin and FDR did not publish a transcript of their conversations at Yalta. President Nixon fought to avoid releasing the tapes of conversations about Watergate. Robert Lane concludes that "the material is available, if anyone with such an intellectual bent cares to put such a cabalist construction upon it. It is only when he passes beyond reality limits and becomes suffused with projective and mystical thinking that he qualifies as a cabalistic thinker."[8]

What are reality limits? The Markuses approved of President Nixon's visits to Russia and China, although they thought the results were "a big bluff." Nine other couples, and Arnold Garcia, approved those visits and are relieved at the possible passing of the cold war era. Only the McGees feel that those visits represent a further advance of the international communist conspiracy. Have the McGees then passed "beyond reality limits"?

Frank and Mary McGee believe in miracles. They have visited the shrine of Our Lady of Guadalupe and accept its miracle—appearance of an image of the Virgin upon a peasant's cloth. If the Virgin of Guadalupe is the positive side of faith, the negative side may well be the conviction that an international conspiracy threatens America's safety.

But how does Frank McGee's ability to entertain dark suspicions fit his nature as fond father, barbershop quartet singer, jovial conversationalist, and local political activist? He is the copybook picture of the ideal citizen. He initiates political discussions with friends and attends public meetings to provide input for the democratic process. He organizes seminars for the discussion of public issues . He and Mary find hours of togetherness, working in politics. They never fail to vote in an election, they obey the law, they respect the Constitution, and they are delighted that the Supreme Court has come more nearly to share their understanding of the Constitution.

The Birchite ideology of the McGees has far greater status in their

---

[8]Lane, *Political Ideology*, p. 130. Lane identifies both psychological and social causes of cabalist thought. Inadequate ego strength or sense of personal adequacy and the imperfect assimilation of Freudian, instinctual drives are the psychological sources; a confused understanding of the regulatory mechanisms in society (separation of governmental powers; forces of the marketplace) are the social causes (pp. 122–129). These designated psychological sources of cabalism apply to neither the Markuses nor the McGees, and the social causes certainly do not apply to the McGees, who put free-market competition at the center of their ideology and praise the separation of powers. They only fear that the communist conspiracy is secretly supplanting those traditional democratic modes. Lane's cabalists were "undemocrats," their faith in the democratic process crippled, who secretly —even subconsciously—yearned for authoritarian government. Not so the Markuses and McGees.

minds and lives than do the Markuses' cabalist opinion molecules in their lives. But the dark suspicions do not infect their natures, and they live comfortable and fulfilling lives. They gain considerable gratification from working, right there in Orange County, to save America. It's fun, and they make good friends in the process.

Liberals and Conservatives:
A Narrow Spectrum

Barry Goldwater embarked upon his 1964 presidential campaign in the conviction that, while he might not win, he would certainly make a respectable showing. He would be a conservative candidate, and a substantial portion of American voters identified themselves as conservatives. The Republican party, since at least the time of Thomas Dewey, had nominated "me-too" candidates, thus offending conservatives, who stayed home, rather than vote when no real choice was offered.[9]

Using Gallup poll data gathered during the 1964 campaign, Lloyd Free and Hadley Cantril examined electoral opinion. Liberalism was defined as support for the expanded activities of the federal government and conservatism as opposition to those activities. They developed a series of questions to measure voters' conservatism along two dimensions: on the practical, or operational, level (the reaction to specific public policies) and on the ideological, or theoretical, level. They found that a substantial majority of American voters are predominantly liberal on the operational level; they approve of the welfare and regulatory activities of the federal government undertaken in the last four decades, and of many other such activities which are only proposed. At the same time, a substantial majority of the electorate are "rhetorical conservatives"—they agree with conservative statements such as, "The federal government is interfering too much in state and local matters." There was a substantial overlap; even when measured stringently, one of every four persons surveyed was simultaneously a rhetorical conservative and an operational liberal. Such persons agreed that the federal government has assumed too many, and improper, activities; yet they could not name a single activity they would have the federal government abandon.[10]

[9]This "myth of the hidden conservative vote" has been thoroughly examined. See Philip E. Converse, Aage R. Clausen, and Warren E. Miller, "Electoral Myth and Reality: The 1964 Election," 59 *American Political Science Review* 2 (June, 1965), p. 323.

[10]L.A. Free and Hadley Cantril, *The Political Beliefs of Americans* (New Brunswick, N.J.: Rutgers University Press, 1967).

The paradox is explicable if we accept Bem's contention that most people do not seek consistency in their ideas.

Questions like those of Free and Cantril were posed to the voters of Ramona Heights, both in the interviews and in separate questionnaires. The results were not unlike those obtained by Free and Cantril, except that the rhetorical conservatives showed an even greater tendency to be, simultaneously, operational liberals. (The exceptions, of course, were the McGees.) The Rineharts, for example, identify themselves as "somewhat conservative," express agreement with the statements of conservative rhetoric, and yet must be regarded as operational liberals. Indeed, when asked whether they would prefer living in some past period of American history, Alice Rinehart mentioned the social security system as one of the benefits of the modern era.

One way of recognizing the discrepancy between conservative principles and the state of the world is to shrug one's shoulders and make the best of it.

Fletcher Barbera: The company that I work for has zero retirement benefits. The last company I worked for had zero retirement benefits.
Question: Well, you'll be sixty-five in about two thousand and two.
Fletcher: Exactly.
Maureen Barbera: You know, I think we both have this kind of funny attitude. You've asked about stowing money away for college, and things like that. I really figure that, by then, everybody is going to be taken care of, the way things are going.
Question: You don't really approve of that, but you think it's coming?
Maureen: No, I don't approve. I think it's coming, and probably there's less need to sock it away, month by month, and really do without right now. Just because we think it's going to come then.

While the McGees would dismantle the welfare state, the Barberas are prepared to relax and enjoy it. They disapprove of welfare programs rhetorically, but they expect to be taken care of in their old age by social security, and they anticipate public help for the college education of their children. (They need not depend entirely on public largess; Maureen will inherit a substantial sum when her mother dies.)

The main difference between this attitude and the operational liberalism of the Rineharts, Weekses, Roybals, and Porfilios is that the Barberas recognize the contrast between conservative convictions and liberal expectations, and they are amused. The others simply feel that a realistic view of politics is that the scope of the national government is not likely to be diminished, and welfare programs are here to stay, in spite of the danger to individual moral fiber.

If our conservatives are at the same time operational liberals, how do the self-identified liberals rate? Piotr and Myrna Pavel score the lowest on the scale of rhetorical conservatism and the highest on the scale of operational liberalism. They believe in a more active government, equal rights for all, increased controls on the corporate enterprise system, and the policies that would put their principles into practice. Their thought processes are also free of racial stereotyping, as measured by attitude scales and revealed in their transcript. However, the Pavels confess that they will compromise their own liberal principles if a vital personal interest is at stake. I asked if they would favor the construction of subsidized public housing in Ramona Heights. Painfully, they confessed they would oppose it, for the equity in their house is a major source of financial security in their retirement years, and they fear that the housing of poor blacks in the neighborhood would destroy their home's value.

The Kaubs, who also identify themselves as liberal (Kenneth says, "I'm a liberal Republican; I couldn't ever call myself a liberal Democrat"), present a less consistent picture. They both score in the lower third of the microsample on measurements of rhetorical conservatism, but only at the mean on the scale of operational liberalism. Kenneth says that he can think of areas in which government should be doing more, such as controlling pollution, but when his tax bill comes he's convinced that the government is doing enough. He also confesses to a certain distrust of labor unions and their influence through government policy. Marie Kaub admits to conservatism on local issues that would affect her home and neighborhood.

Quentin and Deborah Elliott are not easily categorized. Deborah accepts a liberal tag, but Quentin rejects all labels. Deborah scores nearly as low as the Pavels on the scale of rhetorical conservatism, while Quentin scores just below the mean. However, they both score just below the mean on the scale of operational liberalism. This is related to their lack of faith in government activity, stimulated by Quentin's experience with large corporations and their political influence.

Just after Quentin had resigned from his corporate position, he identified the main problem facing the nation as "moral decay." He saw this as the tendency of corporations to worship at the altar of profit, failing to develop a corporate ethical sensitivity. But he felt that government could do little about this, as it could do little about racial prejudice. These were matters which could only be resolved through a rebirth of conscience and clear-sightedness on the part of corporate managers and the general public. This conviction is consistent with Quentin's 1971 joining of a fundamentalist church that largely ignores social issues.

The voters of Ramona Heights do not disagree that much among themselves. Excepting the McGees (as usual) the conservatism professed by the self-proclaimed conservatives is a mild and rather pale collection of ideas. Those ideas remain curiously abstract. When it comes to specific policies, the conservatives do not disagree that much with the liberals.

Elements of a Consensus

Democracy is possible, according to some commentators, because most citizens accept the procedures followed in reaching political decisions, reconciling themselves to the outcome of issues on which they have supported the losing side. This has been the historic case for presidential elections. The winner is accepted as winner, no matter how narrow—or even questionable—his majority. The outcome of contests over issues and programs is similarly accepted. Maureen Barbera disapproves of social welfare programs, but she looks forward to enjoying them. Richard Rinehart states that no Republican in possession of his senses would attempt to repeal the social gains made under Democratic administrations. Harry Johnson, owner of a small factory, expresses appreciation for the role played by unions, and he accepts collective bargaining as a way of business life.

This acceptance of yesteryear's political outcomes reflects an adherence to the rules of democracy. The respondents were invited to define "democracy"—what the word means to them—and to speculate on its future in America.As good Birchers, Frank and Mary McGee objected to the term as a label for the American system; they insist that ours is actually a representative republic; classic democracy is equivalent to rule by the mob. Alice Rinehart and Ralph Porfilio entered the same objection, but more tentatively, as if they wished merely to clear up a technicality. The other nineteen were not concerned with this detail. The first reaction of five respondents was the circular one of saying that "democracy" is "the American system"; according to one critic, democracy has no further connotations than that for the majority of Americans.[11] Most of the voters of Ramona Heights, above average in education and in-

[11]Geoffrey Gorer, *The American People: A Study in National Character* (New York: Norton, 1948), p. 222. Quoted by Lane in *Political Ideology*, p. 82.

come, should volunteer further meanings, and they do.

Two principles are foremost in the minds of the respondents: majority rule, and individual rights or liberties. All the respondents immediately mentioned one or both of these concepts, but none mentioned the protection of deviant minorities from majority displeasure. Only Harry Johnson immediately equated political and economic systems, saying that democracy means free enterprise: if every person received the same rewards, regardless of effort, democracy would be dead.

John Weeks: It's always difficult to define democracy. It's, it can't be defined as complete freedom. . . . Democracy would almost have to be classified as a, well, almost a state of mind, where you have the rights to do most of the things you want to do as long as they don't violate the rights of somebody else.

Quentin Elliott: The word "democracy" has in it the implication that democratic values prevail. That there is, therefore, a combination of freedom of behavior, and yet, the implication, too, that one must behave in a responsible way. And this means that We the People—in this democracy, as we call it, in the United States—are free to behave as we see fit. Providing that we are fair in our dealing with our fellow man. . . . Democracy has in it—if it's organized properly—an insurance factor. And that insurance factor is the right of the people to change things peacefully.

Richard Rinehart: The advantage of the American system is the responsiveness of the person in the political office to the will of the people. And it's very direct. Should they not fill the bill, there's an election every four years.

The voters of Ramona Heights, therefore, are able to come up with the copybook answers: democracy is equated with individual liberties and the political rule of the majority. However, when one probes more deeply, variations upon those two themes come to the surface.

The Pavels and McGees—poles apart politically—express reservations about the universal applicability of majority rule. They are not sure that every person should have the right to cast an equal vote. Piotr and Myrna have mild reservations about universal suffrage in view of the unequal distribution of educational attainment among voters. Piotr's thought of giving a triple vote to Albert Einstein has been noted. For the McGees, the problem is not one of education, but of experience.

Frank: I wonder sometimes how many people actually deserve to vote at all. I really do . . . I swear there are an awful lot of people that, really,

I wonder if they deserve to vote. Then again, you wonder sometimes how those lines should be drawn. Should he own property, maybe? I don't know. . . . Should everybody vote just because he has been born in the country? Should there be tests that you have to pass?

Later in that 1970 interview, I asked Frank and Mary whether they favored granting the vote to eighteen year olds. The policy was being debated in Congress at the time; I asked about it as one way of testing reactions to the youthful activism of the 1960s.

Frank: I think the age should be raised to twenty-five, as Harry Truman once said. No, I think twenty-one is certainly as young as they should be. . . .

Mary: No, I don't think eighteen year olds should vote. In the first place, most of them are not self-supporting, and they haven't been active members of society, or contributed to it yet. Although some would be knowledgeable enough, I am sure.

Frank: A few.

One or both members of six other couples opposed voting by eighteen year olds. They were Maureen Barbera, Caroline Porfilio, Tina Roybal, Harry Johnson, the Rineharts, and Arnold Garcia.

Caroline: I don't think they have enough experience. They have a lot of talk and a lot of blow-hard, but they don't have enough experience. I think eighteen year olds feel very good because they have been top dog in their high school, and they don't know what's really coming off.

Harry: At eighteen, I don't believe you've been in the world to where you've been out competing for a livelihood. Most candidates and propositions affect the working man who's already been in the world and has a job.

Nevertheless, most of them said a man old enough to be drafted and sent to war should be old enough to vote for the representatives empowered to determine his fate. They wished the draft were not necessary. Then they could keep the voting age at twenty-one with a clear conscience.

However, in 1972, the same couples accepted the eighteen year old vote as a fact, and an influence on the upcoming presidential election. The Markuses felt that the predicted youth vote for McGovern would not materialize, for they knew of young people who would be voting for Nixon. The Rineharts, Johnsons, Barberas, and Roybals accepted the youth vote without resentment. They were perhaps influenced by the extended period of quiet on the campus and the general withdrawal of young people from political confrontations; their lack of resentment also reflected an acceptance of the political process.

Frank McGee viewed the youth vote with overtones of terror when he watched the Democratic National Convention.

Frank: How could anyone stay a Democrat after seeing those crummy people? The youth, the blacks, the long-haired devils. They've really taken it over, haven't they? That's one thing I'll say about the Republican convention; they had a more decent group of people representing them. . . . Nixon may run away with it, but I guess an awful lot of youth, a great percentage, are registering Democrat. If they do get out and vote, there are millions and millions of them!

The Porfilios discoursed at length about young people who have contributed nothing to the state of California but come to the state and qualify for welfare and free college educations. (They had to be reminded of the tuition charge.)

Thus the only couples who continued to express misgivings about the new voting power of young people were the McGees and the Porfilios. The McGees fight back through their local political activities. The Porfilios only complain.

DELAYS OF THE DEMOCRATIC PROCESS

Another attribute of democracy which citizens may find dismaying is the capacity for simple delay. Building a consensus in support of proposed policy takes time, and free speech allows all interested factions to be heard. The resulting confusion often seems all talk and no action. The Ramona Heights voters agree that this is true, but they feel the advantages of the system far outweigh this disadvantage. Kenneth Kaub says that delay in reaching decisions is "one of the prices we have to pay" for democracy.

Quentin Elliott: Democracy is organized chaos. I have the feeling that confusion is necessary, because, if you're going to have a genuinely free society, you are going to have so many different movements. All of these forces, many of them are going to be in conflict. . . . If everybody gets mad enough and stays mad long enough, then I think we're in for real trouble in this country.

Alice Rinehart: It's not inefficiency. They've said that many times. It takes time, I think, to hear the voice of the people.

An important reason for accepting the delay inherent in the political process is the belief that "giving everybody his say" has positive results. Since they recognize the variety of interest groups which operate in the American political process, the respondents may be described as pluralists. And they have a pluralist conception of the outcome of conflict between contending interests. Asked about the power of such groups as big business, organized labor, and even the military hierarchy, they reply that the contest between such groups tends to produce a balance, with the result that no single group exercises inordinate power. As Fletcher Barbera puts it, "The system is self-correcting." Even after the political distress of the 1960s, they remained confident of the ability of the American system of government to ameliorate conflicts and create an arena in which group differences can be compromised. Yet, paradoxically, they have little respect for politicians who act as the negotiators of compromise.

In spite of according the politician such a low measure of esteem, the voters of Ramona Heights accept the "rules of the game" that are part of the American political process. They feel that the majority eventually rules, but they think it entirely proper that the noise and delay generated by the process should prevent it from ruling right away.

THE AMBIVALENCE OF LIBERTY

If one side of the democratic coin is imprinted with "majority rule," the other clearly reads "minority rights." Robert Lane found that the working-class men he interviewed in the 1950s focused on neither of these principles, but rather on a hybrid—majority rights. Lane wrote that "democracy as a popular concept centers in the freedom of the nondeviant individual to do what the majority thinks right."[12]

Such a conception of democracy faced a challenge in the turbulent 1960s, when groups that had hardly been visible in American society found first a consciousness and then a voice. Much of the resentment tapped by the campaigns of George Wallace could be described as resulting from an impoverished idea of democracy like that held by Lane's respondents. How do the voters of Ramona Heights understand minority rights and individual liberty, and how are those attitudes connected with their political responses?

The firm hold of the value of achievement on the minds of the Ramona Heights voters colors their understanding of individual freedom. They immediately think of freedom to work; they cannot conceive

[12]Lane, *Political Ideology*, p. 83.

of freedom to be lazy. When asked to define "democracy," the Markuses were at no loss for words.

Eldene: Equal rights, freedom of speech, freedom of religion. I think of the Constitution.

Jan: Well, I think you have more of an opportunity in a democracy than you have in any of these other forms of government. Everybody isn't as fortunate as somebody else, but I think everybody has a better chance. If you live in some of these other countries, you never have an opportunity. If you're poor, you just stay that way.

The Johnsons responded in a similar manner.

Jacqueline: Your freedom of speech and to live where you want to live.

Harry: Free enterprise. . . . Men are created equal with the equal right to progress, not the equal right to lay down and have fruit drop off the tree to them.

A more complete reaction to the turmoil of the 1960s was expressed by the Roybals, when they were asked if America might be losing democracy. They were the only others to join the Markuses and Pavels in saying a kind word for socialism.

Tina: Socialism is also democratic, I think, in its implications. It would depend on whether you were talking about change where it would benefit the good of the people. And I still feel we have control of that.

Arthur: I would hate to see it get to the extreme where it becomes more socialist-oriented than not. I think that would take away the personal incentive that one has right now, economically. Yet, I think there's many areas in which change is indicated and change should occur. And it should occur by plan and design as opposed to the chaos we're witnessing now. . . . The handwriting was on the wall when World War II ended; when you saw the black man coming home for the first time after having lived in an area where you have three squares a day, clothes on his back and sheets to sleep between, and having to go back to a rat-infested ghetto area; and these were going to be the fathers of many children. . . . The Democratic party saw a real need. Of course, it was politically expedient, but the GI bill was certainly one of the tools. And yet it was very abruptly stopped and there were very few provisions for change after that point. . . . We are in a revolution right now, I think.

Tina: Yet, I think I'm still optimistic enough to believe in the future. That the change will be positive.

Arthur feels that programs which help the disadvantaged minority member help themselves—similar to the benefits of the GI bill—are the answer. His notion of liberty means equality of opportunity; his idea of freedom is the freedom to achieve. Thus there may be a hint, in Arthur's attitude, of a conviction that democracy does equal the right of the "nondeviant individual to do what the majority thinks right," although, having experienced ethnic prejudice, he would like to dismantle the barriers to racial equality.

The Markuses make no bones about their requirement of fealty to country.

Question: Should public school students be required to salute the flag, even when their religion prohibits paying homage to man-made symbols?

Eldene: Yes.

Jan: They should salute the flag, same as everybody else. They've got religious freedom here, and the reason they got it is because of our democracy! They shouldn't be exempted from any of that. We have too many of these religions. To me, they don't make sense. It's just something to hide behind.

The Markuses feel that one's origins should be submerged or forgotten. Eldene remembers that where she went to grade school, the Irish students sat on one side of the classroom, the Poles and the Czechs on the other, as a reflection of the neighborhood segregation of the town. But she overcame the effects of ethnic prejudice through her own efforts.

Eldene: We can't sympathize with some of these people who don't try to do anything for themselves. Because you have to do something about it yourself.

Question: So you don't really have very great sympathy for the Mexican-Americans who say it's important to retain their sense of culture, and sort of stay apart from the rest of America?

Eldene: No, I don't agree with that.

Jan: It's a mistake. Where I worked, they had a lot of them there, and they were rattling off that Mexican right in front of you, and they can speak English. And then they wonder why people resent them. Well, *anybody's* going to resent it. I could speak Czech, but if we were among people, we'd never talk it. Never. That's the last thing we'd do. We'd talk it at home with our parents, but never like that. But the two people who do that the most are the Mexicans and the Japs. They're the worst offenders, from what I've noticed.

Eldene: I think they're the most clannish, really.
Jan: See, our people, they weren't clannish.

The persistence of racist attitudes is usually seen as the most certain threat to the achievement of true equality in America: when citizens insist on using the mental shorthand of racial stereotypes, rather than judging individuals on their merits, their adherence to the principle that "all men are created equal" is an abstraction, rather than a guide to action. The Markuses were the exception, in the 1970 interviews, in openly expressing racist attitudes—or opinion molecules. One would not expect that persons of the educational and social levels prevailing in Ramona Heights would express racist sentiments to a stranger. Therefore, when I returned two years later for additional interviews, I asked the respondents to complete another set of attitudinal questions. Scattered among the questions on other topics was a series designed to measure the degree of acceptance of racial stereotypes.

The distribution of scores on this (admittedly crude) measurement device was a rather flat curve. Most of the respondents were clustered around what was the mean for the Ramona Heights microsample. At the top—indeed, scoring the highest possible—was Jan Markus, followed closely by his wife, Eldene. Tied with Eldene were Harry Johnson and Ralph Porfilio. Next came Arnold Garcia and Jacqueline Johnson. By contrast, at the lowest end of the scale (where persons rejecting the use of racial stereotypes are found) were Quentin Elliott and Marie Kaub. Tied for the next to lowest score were Myrna Pavel, Deborah Elliott, and Fletcher Barbera, with Piotr Pavel and Martha Weeks tied in the place just above them.

Acceptance of racial stereotyping is usually related to the lack of formal education; the Johnsons and Markuses did not go beyond high school. Persons like the Markuses who have themselves known ethnic prejudice may indulge in stereotyping as a kind of self-punishment, or at least demonstrate it as the residue of great psychic trauma.[13] This hypothesis could account for Arnold Garcia's high score, for Arnold sees life as a competitive struggle, in which he's won but many other Chicanos have not. It does not account for Marie Kaub's low score. A gentle person, she has found peace and friendship in Ramona Heights, and her psychic wounds are healed; there is every reason for her to reject racial stereotypes. (Besides, as Kenneth says, they can afford to be tolerant now.)

---

[13]For one example, see the discussion of self-stereotyping in L. Grebler, J. W. Moore, and R. C. Guzman, *The Mexican-American People* (New York: Macmillan, Free Press, 1970), pp. 387–389.

The presence of Fletcher Barbera among the low scorers is a reminder that racism and political conservatism need not march together; remember opinion molecules.

With this distribution of scores on a measure of racial stereotyping, the Ramona Heights microsample makes possible the examination of an hypothesis: that reaction to the 1972 Democratic National Convention and its highly visible minority group delegates set in motion the turn against George McGovern by habitual Democratic voters which became so pronounced in November. Racist feelings could have been a major component in that revulsion.

I revisited Ramona Heights shortly after the 1972 nominating conventions. Myrna and Piotr Pavel had watched the Democratic convention avidly. Running through their reactions was the theme that the nation was not yet ready for George McGovern, or for the 1972 delegate selection process. They typified "old liberals" struggling to adjust themselves to a situation in which the values they had long professed were being realized, faster than they anticipated, and possibly too fast for the country.

Myrna: I think the Democratic party was trying too hard to cater to the minority issues, and by that I mean the women and the blacks. I noticed that the Chicanos were not as well represented as they should have been, if there was going to be equal representation. And, now, having a woman chairman and a black vice chairman, here again, they're trying to please everyone. Did they do it simply because it was a black and a woman? A Ms.? Or, were they *the* people to have?

Piotr: That's a good question.

Myrna: I think it's something we're going to have to evolve, and I don't think it's going to be evolved in these four years.

Piotr: I'm all for equal rights for blacks. But, after all, they're only eleven percent of the population. You can't just put them in every job —or the Chicanos or Jews or Greek Orthodox, or some other minority.

Myrna: What is the word I want? They were serious; but it was a superficial form of being serious. It wasn't a seriousness of depth. It wasn't one of knowledge, or of training, or one of experience.

Question: Do you mean that you think the amateurs have taken over?

Myrna: Exactly. Believe me, I don't want Bella Abzug setting up the rules and regulations for me to follow. She did not speak for me, even though I am a woman. I didn't think abortion was an issue for a political campaign. There were many things which I felt they were very petty about. They just reminded me of a bunch of kids at a "Yipsel" meeting —you know, the Young People's Socialist League—where they don't know what it's all about, and yet they sit there debating . . .

Piotr: Well, to summarize, I feel that the Democratic party is definitely on the decline—and a very steep decline.

Piotr said that unless McGovern could explain his platform, including the welfare reform proposal, so that the people could understand it, he himself might "defect" and vote for Nixon, or not vote at all. Myrna laughed at him. When they reported their vote after the election, Piotr said that he had at no time considered voting for Nixon. So the negative impressions of the Democratic National Convention did not, in the end, cancel their positive Democratic party identification, nor override their dislike of Nixon and the Republicans.

The situation was quite different with the Markuses. I called on them on a sunny Sunday afternoon in late August. They were being visited by their nephew, Jan Kiedrowski, who was named after his uncle. They are proud of the young man, who is not only a college graduate but a lieutenant in the marine corps. Stationed at Camp Pendleton, he frequently visits the Markuses on weekends.

Eldene: Sure, we watched a lot of the convention, especially the last parts of it. They had a real cross-spectrum of people, all walks of life, in there, all ages.

Lieutenant Kiedrowski: I don't feel they were representative; I think McGovern stacked the deck in his favor. Like, I heard that a third of the South Dakota delegation was black, and I don't believe the population is a third black in South Dakota. There were other states the same way, but that was the worst one. I don't think it was representative *at all.*

Eldene: They had all kinds. They had a lot of Chicanos, and the poorer class of people. They had a mixture. They even had a Baptist choir—

Lieutenant Kiedrowski: They weren't delegates, they were strictly lobbyists.

Eldene: They were entertainers, I guess. There were a lot of coloreds there. The coloreds took over a little bit, I think.

The resentment felt by the Markuses against minority groups who seek support from public policy was bound to be activated by the visual image of the Democratic convention delegates. Their adherence to the value of achievement is not necessarily a racist sentiment, and their references to minority representation at the convention are relatively mild. Their strongest reason for opposing the election of George McGovern was the Democratic candidate's stand on amnesty. Although Jan and Eldene favored the immediate withdrawal of American troops from Vietnam, for they felt the war was a mistake, they did not feel that young men should be permitted to decide which wars are a mistake and which are not.

Eldene: That Jane Fonda is in Hanoi right now, and she's there for *no good.* And she's spending money and seeing how they're suffering. Let her see what the American boys are doing, and what treatment they're getting. Now, if we had every boy who refused to go, what kind of country would we have here? We wouldn't have no protection at all, either, if they all felt the same way. I'm not for war. But I don't believe in that amnesty thing, either, McGovern's idea. That'll keep me from voting for him.

Jan: I'm against that, too.

The Markuses' outrage at McGovern's amnesty proposal was directly linked to their insistence upon the achievement value, rather than to racial stereotypes. As allegiant citizens, they are grateful for the freedom of opportunity supplied by America; they regard service to America in time of danger as a debt owed by everybody; and they feel that the government, not the individual citizen, is best equipped to recognize danger.

All the Ramona Heights voters who watched the Democratic National Convention for any substantial period of time expressed a negative opinion of the delegates and the process of their selection. Ralph Porfilio (who is a registered, but only nominal, Democrat) withdrew whatever identification he may have felt with his own party when he described the 1972 convention.

Ralph: If that's the people supporting their party, something's terribly wrong. Because I don't think that's the majority of America today.

Since Ralph habitually votes Republican, we can hardly assert that racist reactions to the image of the convention turned him against the Democratic candidate.

The same could be said of the Johnsons. Lifelong Democrats, they have frequently voted Republican during the last decade. Harry Johnson said he opposed the reforms made in the selection of Democratic delegates because he felt that delegates should earn their way to a convention, rather than being brought in to provide minority representation.

He did not oppose broader representation, he added, but felt there must be a better way of achieving it.

Gentle Kenneth Kaub, who was certain to vote for Nixon in any case, said that the Democrats "went overboard trying to satisfy minorities and youth and some of the women" while turning their backs on the ethnic groups (symbolized by Mayor Daley) that had previously been influential in directing the party's affairs. Marie Kaub agreed, and she eventually voted for Nixon, although she is a registered Democrat.

In no case can we label the racist overtones of such reactions as the basic reason for a vote against George McGovern. McGovern supplied voters with several additional reasons, which they readily articulated. The image of the Democratic convention had an impact upon the voters of Ramona Heights, but not a decisive one.

There is an ambivalence in the adherence of the Ramona Heights voters to the principle of minority rights. When that principle conflicts with their acceptance of the achievement value, achievement tends to win out. Even Myrna Pavel wished that the 1972 Democratic delegates had shown a "seriousness" based on "experience." Having lived through the turmoil of the 1960s, however, Ramona Heights voters are aware of the existence of minority cultural patterns, and, if not enthusiastic, they are at least resigned to coexistence with those cultural patterns. Discussing the turmoil of the 1960s, Fletcher Barbera said, "In the end, it will be broadening for Americans to go through all this." They are a long way from the attitude of Lane's workers of two decades earlier, who equated democracy with majority rights and denigrated the "deviants" who did not pattern their lives on values accepted by the majority. Ramona Heights voters may have resented the presumed over-representation of blacks, youth, and women at the Democratic National Convention; they may have felt the party managers made a tactical error in establishing such rules for the selection of delegates; but none would claim that such groups should not have been represented at all.

Failures of Vision

To the extent that we have sketched a consensus among the microsample, it is a modest and unsurprising one. They are allegiant citizens; they understand the American political process in a relatively sophisticated manner; they endorse the concepts of individual freedom and minority rights, although this acceptance is secondary in some cases to their insistence on the achievement value. The respondents acknowledge imperfections in contemporary American society, but they do not generally accept the curing of those ills as a personal responsibility. Perhaps one should not expect comfortable suburbanites to march in the vanguard of political reform; the more important question is, What may motivate them to at least march in its rear ranks? Or prevent them from joining the opposition?

The linkage between public opinion and public policy is at best indirect; there are many intervening variables, such as the quality of political leadership, the political pitfalls that obstruct the progress of any new policy, and the power of special interests. Nevertheless, public opinion does place constraints upon the process. Some policies (such as the social security system) win such wide acceptance that they become *traditions*. At the other end of the spectrum are policies (state endorsement of polygamy might be an example) which are so unthinkable to the public that to propose them would be *sacrilegious*. Politics takes place in the area between tradition and sacrilege.[14] A policy may move from sacrilege to public acceptance during the career of a single politician. Contrast Richard Nixon's cold war stance when vice president with his presidential visits to Russia and China.

What is the source of new proposals, the standard by which present policies are judged and found wanting? One enduring source of inspiration leading to political change has been Utopian thinking. The ability to imagine a perfect society has laid bare the faults of the current one and suggested values for change.

> From Plato's *Republic* onward, men have concretized their values in visions of a society more noble than any in existence; and though most Utopian thinkers have realized full well that no real society could ever completely match their vision, the imaginative construction of a Utopia implied a constant faith in the possibility of human betterment.[15]

In recent times, despair for the certainty of human betterment has brought forth the anti-Utopias of Huxley and Orwell.[16] One way of testing the political imaginations of the Ramona Heights voters was to ask them to describe the attributes of their ideal society, their own Utopia. Their answers give a clue to the kind of political change they can imagine, and the kind they cannot.

[14]This conception of the constraint placed upon the political process by public opinion is developed by Bernard C. Hennessy, *Public Opinion*, 2nd ed. (Belmont, Calif.: Wadsworth, 1970), pp. 396–400.
[15]Kenneth Keniston, *The Uncommitted* (New York: Harcourt, 1965), p. 451.
[16]See Aldous Huxley, *Brave New World* (any of various editions) and George Orwell, *1984* (any of various editions).

Regardless of how common Utopian thought may have been in past human epochs, it is not a preoccupation in Ramona Heights today. The question took the respondents by surprise; it was obviously not something they had thought much about. In most cases, their answers were formulated by establishing a connection between a better society and some conviction (or opinion molecule) relating to human nature, economics, or the maxims of the American democratic process.

Nobody made the leap required to conceive of an international society, in which people would be freed of national boundaries and jealousies. Since our entire conversations had focused on American society, this was perhaps not surprising. But even Piotr Pavel, the most cosmopolitan of the respondents, could think only of ways in which American society might be better. He suggested, for one thing, that the laws would be more nearly uniform among the fifty states. Thus, while all the microsample but the McGees have a mildly internationalist outlook, support the humanitarian work of the United Nations, and feel that the UN supplies a useful forum for debate, they apparently cannot conceive of surrendering the national identity, nor much of the sovereignty, of the United States.

Also, most of them did not immediately think of personal circumstances much different than they were currently enjoying. Martha Weeks immediately said her notion of Utopia was Ramona Heights. She went on to contrast life in the tract with her life as a child, and the national circumstances of 1970 with those of the depression, and expressed gratification with the change. Utopia is Ramona Heights without the problems of the outside world to worry its residents. As noted in Chapter Five, the respondents volunteered reasons why life in the really rich neighborhoods of Orange County would be less satisfactory than their existence in Ramona Heights.

With the exception of Piotr Pavel, neither the affluent engineers nor any other members of the microsample conjure up a vision in which technology adds touches of perfection to the ideal.[17]Nobody mentioned the elimination of air pollution or transportation snarls, or the growing of food in tanks of water, or the use of atomic energy to supply superabundant power. Piotr Pavel mentioned jet planes and radio as drawing the world closer together, and automation as making a wider distribution

[17]Keniston asserts that "most Americans, if asked to envisage an 'ideal' future, will respond, if at all, with a science fiction fantasy of a technologically improved society" (*The Uncommitted*, p. 344). The ecology issue has blossomed since Keniston wrote, and it is possible that Americans now tend to be more ambivalent about the benefits of technological change.

of wealth possible. But in general the engineers do not see themselves as the agents of societal salvation. This may result from their daily experience with all that can go wrong in the translation of concept to functioning apparatus. It is Quentin Elliott, a dropout from the corporate life, who combines a faith in man's capacity for betterment with a suspicion of technological change.

Quentin: I think a more perfect society will eventually evolve, because I think man was given a brain, and is capable of—in the end—seeing that it is necessary to live shoulder-to-shoulder, and get along with his fellow men, and I see this happening. I also see that this great octopus of technology that we've built up, that has given us so much, will also have to be reduced in importance in order that we can survive.

Accompanying his faith in human reason (which is more tentative than that professed in the eighteenth century) is Quentin's belief that education can help toward achieving a better future. This is an appropriate faith for a teacher. But not even Quentin can imagine a society based on the Marxist principle, "from each according to his ability, to each according to his needs." A structure of incentives is necessary in any human society, and the profit motive provides the most dependable incentive.

Quentin's mention of the profit motive was so striking that I asked the others if they could envisage a society in which it has no role. Only Piotr Pavel could entertain the idea. Most felt that differential achievement was inevitable.

Ralph Porfilio: You're going to have industrious people who are going to go through and accumulate a lot and the unindustrious who are going to accumulate nothing. So, you will wind up with extremes of wealth and poverty, even if everyone started out equal.

John Weeks: I'm afraid if you started out with absolute equality, then an incentive movement would start up, and you would no longer have absolute equality. . . . You would have an unbalanced system, much as we have today.

Marie Kaub: There has to be a motive—whether it's money, or possibly better schools, or better health for people. No matter what, there has to be a motive.

Arthur Roybal: I don't think we *want* to abolish, at least *I* wouldn't want to abolish, the profit motive. Competition is too deeply imbedded within me.

The McGees and the Pavels offered the most coherent visions of a different society. While, as previously noted, the McGees would return to the simpler times of the past, Piotr Pavel's eyes turned toward the future.

Piotr: I think a society a few hundred years from now, and I'm not prepared to say if it's a hundred years or five hundred, will be a society based on morals. . . . I'd see the society void of bigotry and—what's the other word for bigotry?—hypocrisy. I see a complete disappearance of the religious differences of humanity. You could get from one place to another with an SST in just a few hours, and the communiques on the radio will dispense all the information to everybody. Everybody will know about it at the same time, and they will be almost equally educated, to absorb it properly.

How will people live? I think human beings should work. I don't think, however, that their ability to provide for their needs should be tied down to such factors as we have now. . . . The production methods and mechanization of everything would be such that people would work a much shorter week, and their basic needs and some of their other needs would be fulfilled. I don't see how the profit motive could remain, and still have an ideal society. . . .

I think the wealth will be such that a more equal distribution will be more feasible. And I hope that people come to the conclusion that being a billionaire is lousy. You eat only three times a day, and, when the doctor tells you not to eat, you can't do very much about it.

Piotr envisions a more equal distribution of the wealth, but he would not achieve that redistribution by "expropriating the expropriators" through a Marxist revolution. Change will come gradually, and he agrees with his wife that the best hope for America is its coming generation, as exemplified by their own two sons.

The more general reaction was to point out that society is made up of human beings, who are prey to all the flaws of human nature.

John Weeks: Utopia's a physical impossibility, because, unfortunately, you're dealing with people. People have different mental capacities. They also have different driving forces. Some of them are psychotic. I doubt seriously that this ideal society, which all of us would like to see, is at all reasonable, even remotely reasonable.

Kenneth Kaub: I think we'll always have people who tend to be lazy, and people that are going to steal, and ones that are going to murder, and ones that are going to try to get money that others have worked for. The seven deadly sins, anyway, will still be with us.

Eldene Markus: Man's greed won't allow a perfect Utopia. And, if the perfect society were somehow made possible by perfecting human nature, so that conflict and competition no longer occurred, life would become dull.

Ralph Porfilio: As to Utopia, I think, eventually, it probably becomes extremely boring.

Maureen Barbera: Well, I'd rather be down below, burning! Really!

Perhaps because they feel human flaws will always be present, none of the respondents recommends anarchy. Government has a role in the perfect society. For Pavel, it is a positive force; for McGee, it is a necessary evil. For the others, it is a certainty, like death and taxes.

Their comments suggest that Utopian thought has no part in the lives of the microsample (except, perhaps, for the Pavels and, in their inverse way, the McGees). The microsample would be deeply offended by proposals for massive redistribution of wealth, the abolition of economic competition, or the establishment of a federal world government. These are sacrilege. They are also proposals unlikely to be made seriously very soon.

In spite of feeling that speculation about a perfect society is useless because of the intractability of human nature, the respondents do think that the modification of human attitudes is possible. They supported President Nixon's Family Assistance Plan, for example, because it would supply an incentive for families to stay together and increase the opportunities for education and vocational training.

What does this mean in practical terms? If the inevitable conflict in America is between the suburbs and the central cities, what will the political idea systems of Ramona Heights lead these voters to do? One proposal for the amelioration of urban-suburban (and racial) conflict is to build publicly subsidized housing for poor people within middle-class suburban neighborhoods. Such a scheme has the potential advantage of achieving school integration without busing. During the fall of 1972, I asked the members of the microsample how they would react to a proposal to construct such housing in Ramona Heights.

Deborah Elliott: I guess I would feel threatened, because it's something new, but if it's made into a law, that makes it more acceptable, because you know it's going to happen. We have to do something that gives to people that are less fortunate, but I'd like it to happen slowly, to be sure of the safety of my family. If I could see something that wasn't too threatening to my family, I probably could accept it.

Quentin Elliott: It's time for us to share what we have. We have the best land, we have the best schools, we have the beach. We have everything, and it's time for us to share in this. . . . This would be a good answer to the busing question, a good answer because busing is so artificial. We'd be saying, "Okay, we *will* share our community with some of you who live in Santa Ana." If we do this in a way that is not smug or demeaning . . . I think it's terribly exciting.

Quentin said that such a plan would offer new choices to the poor and demonstrate the possibility of achieving better life circumstances without violence. Deborah recalled the restrictions imposed by the Homeowners' Association (such as no unsightly outside television antennas, limited tree heights, and recommended pastel colors for exterior painting) and reflected that the occupants of subsidized housing would be required to abide by similar restrictions; if they were uncomfortable living under such restraints, they would be free to move elsewhere. It was the closest either of the Elliotts came to suggesting that publicly subsidized housing might prove a threat to the value of their own property.

The only other couple to support the proposal were the Kaubs. Marie said, "It would be all right, providing—well, I shouldn't put in any provisions. It would be all right." Then she went on to say that there should be careful screening of applicants and that the city should guarantee the maintenance of the building exteriors, "so it doesn't start looking like a run-down slum in a few years."

Kenneth: It's probably a better way of desegregating than busing— a general distribution of lower-income groups, rather than haul them all over the countryside in buses . . . I don't think property values would be affected much.

Marie: No, they've already reached their peak. It's just a question of maintaining them, so something like that wouldn't affect it.

Being herself a Chicana, with great pride in her home and neighborhood, Marie was unfrightened by the racial integration aspects of the idea. The Kaubs, an ethnically mixed couple, and the Elliotts, because of their wealth, are the families who could be considered to have the least to lose if such a proposal were instituted.

The Pavels could have a great deal to lose. They reacted very painfully to the proposal, for they immediately recognized that their perceived self-interest was contrary to their announced principles. Their equity in the Ramona Heights house, which is constantly appreciating, is one of their major safeguards against the erosion of their small savings. Their home is so important to their financial planning that they would do almost anything to protect its value.

Myrna: Ideologically, all men are created equal. They should have the right to have the same advantages, to live in Ramona Heights, to have the advantage of the ocean, of a smog-free community, but then is it fair to the other person?

Piotr: In many of these questions, you have two answers, more or less. One, motivated by your belief in social justice, and the other one which affects you directly. . . . No matter how much we'd like to have social justice, if it means sacrificing a large part of the equity in this house, which we need desperately, then we'd think about it twice.

Myrna: We're not that wealthy that we can afford to be altruistic . . . I feel like a dirty hypocrite, and it's purely economics, nothing but economics.

Piotr talked about the contradiction of America's claiming to be a classless society when it is not and repeated his admiration for the "clear-cut" class system of England, where the young of the upper class may be taught a sense of noblesse oblige. He finally said that, rather than moving poor people into subsidized housing in Ramona Heights, the national income should be equalized to the extent they were no longer poor, and their alternative housing choices would be broadened accordingly. The Pavels, then, were firmly against public housing in their own neighborhood, and said they would become politically active to fight against it, if it were seriously proposed. But the pain of admitting this was anesthetized by their declarations in favor of "real" reform.

The Barberas treated the idea of poor people being brought into their neighborhood as something of a joke.

Maureen: That would do it! I mean, I think it's an effective way of combating the busing issue. I might try to find out where they were *not* building one of these developments, and start looking at homes there!

Fletcher pointed out that there is indeed a class-related difference in the achievement of students in public schools. But he felt the only way to assure absolutely equal opportunity in the schools would be to establish a classless society, which would mean socialism, and they are both against that.

Not all the respondents answer so clearly. The Pavels are joined only by the Rineharts and the Markuses in straightforwardly mentioning the presumed threat to property values if subsidized housing were built in the neighborhood. The Weekses, Johnsons, and Porfilios expanded on a theme raised by Myrna Pavel. The plan would not be fair to the poor people, they said, for the poor would only feel greater discontent if they lived in the midst of so much affluence. They either would be unemployed or would face lengthy commutes to work; and their manners might be out of place in Ramona Heights, causing discomfort or shame. Other reactions included:

> *Other public housing projects have turned into slums, or have failed completely.* (The Pavels, Rineharts, McGees, and Porfilios. Said Mary McGee, "From what I've seen of subsidized housing, and what I've read in Dan Smoot's *Reports,* they've been pretty bad. Crime rates always go up.")
> *Such construction must always be done by private enterprise, never by the government.* (Arnold Garcia, the McGees, and the Porfilios.)
> *The races will never be reconciled as a result of government pressure; it must happen naturally.* (The Barberas and McGees.)
> *A little segregation never hurt anybody.* (The Markuses.)

Public housing for Ramona Heights was defeated in the microsample by a vote of 19 to 4, counting Maureen Barbera as being opposed. The question was somewhat artificial, since all usable land within the boundaries of the neighborhood has been built upon, as three respondents pointed out. Many of them thought of the massive, high-rise public housing projects which were built in large cities after World War II and which have been recognized as failures by their tenants as well as by city planners.[18] If they were presented with an attractively designed, well-landscaped plan for low-density townhouses, in which some tenants would pay an economic rent, while the rent of others would be subsidized, to be constructed on the border of their neighborhood, the voters of Ramona Heights might accept it with enthusiasm.

In fact, in 1972, an area not far from Ramona Heights voted to incorporate as the City of Irvine. Concurrent with granting that approval, the voters elected city councilmen for the new city. The more "conservative" slate, allegedly backed by the Irvine Company, was defeated by a slate of candidates advocating curbs on the more flamboyant development plans of the Irvine Company and proposing some neighborhoods in which the tenants would be a mixture of low- and middle-income families. How much the appeal of the winning candidates was based on their interest in social justice and how much on their promise to protect the ecological balance would be hard to determine. But the mere espousal of an economically mixed population in part of the new city did not cause their defeat.

The voters of Ramona Heights, like voters anywhere, hold political

[18]See Oscar Newman, *Defensible Space: Crime Prevention through Urban Design* (New York: Macmillan, 1972).

convictions that are somewhat confused and often contradictory. They profess to a range of emotions and values that are noble, and they admit to several that are crass. Their involvement with political issues is a sometime thing. Political questions will draw them away from private pursuits when their perceived interests are at stake, when they are horrified by a turn of events, or want to gloat over their partisan enemies (as was the case with the Watergate hearings for the Pavels). They go to the polls and register a choice, even when they feel that they can only choose the lesser of evils. But it is also possible for them to work for political leaders they find inspiring (as the McGees were captivated by John Schmitz, the Pavels were entranced by Adlai Stevenson, and the Weekses trusted Richard Nixon for the first five years of his presidency).

This relationship between the members of the microsample and political leaders requires attention, particularly since the Watergate scandals and their aftermath may have challenged the allegiance of allegiant citizens.

PART FOUR

From Attitude
to Action

From early on, liberty was largely interpreted as private liberty, and equality soon came to mean equal opportunity to compete for the prizes of wealth and power. There was little teaching of liberty as public liberty—the power of acting with others to shape the conditions of the common life . . . . The activity of politics was seen as but another of the instrumentalities by which self-interested individuals advanced toward private goals.

—John H. Schaar, in "The Case for
Patriotism," American Review 17
(May, 1973), p. 73

Neither of the two principal parties is of one mind with itself . . . . They are like armies without officers, engaged upon a campaign which has no great cause at its back. Their names and traditions, not their hopes and policy, keep them together.

—Woodrow Wilson, in Congressional
Government (1885) (New York:
World, Meridian Books, 1956), p.
210

CHAPTER NINE

Watergate and the Yearning for Integrity

Generally, "politics" has been regarded as something in which a "gentleman" will not engage. It has been a domain reserved for the very crass or the very young whose elders assume that they will get over their fling of youthful idealism and engage in more acceptable pursuits.

—George E. Reedy[1]

"My criteria are integrity, which I've up to now called, 'character,' and the ability to get the job done. . . . Nixon, I don't have much respect for. His inner integrity is lacking. I think he's just too bloody calculating. . . . The qualities I seek in a candidate are honesty and integrity, which are closely related, if not one and the same. An honest approach to oneself as a man, and, therefore, the lens that he looks through as he looks at American politics. . . . It becomes difficult because politics equals compromise, and we can't have too much compromise."

—Quentin Elliot, 1970

"I don't think any good president has ever been popular."

—Ralph Porfilio, 1970

The Dirty Business of Politics

THE ATTACHMENT of the Ramona Heights voters to the value of achievement is fundamental to their political ethos. The achievement value draws upon a metaphor that compares society to the free marketplace of classical

[1]George E. Reedy, *The Twilight of the Presidency* (New York: World, 1970), p. 120.

economics. The principle of laissez-faire, applied to political questions, means that the only function of government is to maintain the order which makes it possible for each individual, family, corporation, or pressure group to play out its own drama of competitive achievement.

But this is not the activity called "politics" which the voters of Ramona Heights see going on in the world. Rather than operating to assure neutrality, political decisions give an unfair advantage, temporary or permanent, to one group after another. Politics is concerned with power, and, in forging alliances with the organizations of the state, individuals and groups can garner power which they did not "earn" through competitive effort. Politicians operate as brokers between groups seeking power, rather than the guardians of some entity vaguely defined as "the good of all." If the respondents were classical economists, they would argue that the interference of politicians prevents the invisible hand of the marketplace from operating to assure mutual benefit for the entire society.

But they are not classical economists. Instead of talking about invisible hands, they articulate their feeling, often somewhat vaguely formulated, that politics is dirty. The simplest kind of political act can be cursed by this image. When the Barberas were asked if they knew a city councilman they could approach to win installation of a traffic light on a dangerous corner, Maureen replied, "Gee, that sounds kind of dirty."

The dirtiest kind of politics is partisan politics. Secure in their planned community, they regard local problems as hardly political in nature. Local elections are nonpartisan, and local questions are essentially administrative. They can be resolved by the application of common sense, or perhaps scientific knowledge, rather than depending on the outcome of a clash of interests. This attitude toward local problems is being modified as environmental issues stimulate local political activism, but the members of the microsample retain a paradoxical attitude toward government. As allegiant citizens, they respect the institutions of American government. They have an emotional attachment to symbols like the flag and offices like the pre-Watergate presidency. But they do not respect the incumbents who staff those institutions and fill those offices. They regard the governmental bureaucracy as intransigent and self-interested; they regard elected officials at least with ambivalence, if not disdain. They are uncomfortable with the phenomenon of power. Politics is a dirty business, and politicians are tainted by it.

John Weeks: I think surely, somewhere along the line, the politician has done something to get where he is. Perhaps he's made a deal, thinking that perhaps he can achieve more by getting to where he wants to be, and he made this deal even though it's a deal he's ashamed of.

Fletcher Barbera: I like to think of our politicians as being pure, Abe Lincoln type of men. But I don't think they got where they are, in many cases, by being that way.

Politicians must pander to special interests to get elected. Only rarely do they put the good of all above payoffs for supporting groups. These two ideas were held, in one form or another, by every member of the microsample. In considering the attributes of a candidate that make him worthy of support, their first consideration is not his party's program, or his experience, or his ability to communicate. (They do not, by and large, consider women as potential candidates.) These qualities are all important, but they are secondary. The most important requirement is personal integrity. They wish it were possible for political leaders to act in the interest of the "good of the whole" without pausing to consider personal or group advantage. This is the dominant theme in their definition of the word "integrity."

Before the Watergate scandals, the respondents could despise politicians while expressing confidence in the system. All significant groups had political spokesmen, and the contest between them resulted in some kind of equilibrium; the forces of politics, in the long run at least, were likely to balance. Within this framework, political corruption is evil because it mates the authority of the state with a particular group or groups and thus upsets the balance of power. Proof of President Nixon's direct involvement would not only destroy his remaining claim on the image of integrity; it could also call into question the legitimacy of the system.

The Search for Integrity

Before asking about their reactions to the 1970 campaigners, I asked the respondents to define the qualities they sought in an ideal candidate and then to name persons who came close to that ideal. Quentin Elliott's definition of the ideal emphasized personal integrity. This seemed a natural outgrowth of Quentin's concern for religion and ethics and the disillusionment with corporate life which caused him to withdraw from it. Yet every other member of the microsample either volunteered words like "honesty" or "integrity," or otherwise described the ability to serve the good of the whole without regard for personal or group gain.

What is there about a man that makes him worth voting for?

Maureen Barbera: His strength, and his honesty. The fact that you can believe that man, that no matter how many people object to what he's saying, that's what he believes, and that's what he's going to do. And I think Truman was good at this, and Agnew's great at this, and Goldwater. . . . Although he should represent the wishes of his constituency, I'd still like to feel that my congressman had integrity and was voting the way he really felt.

Kenneth Kaub: A certain amount of charisma, a certain amount of honesty plus a feeling that he knows what he's talking about, and has experience in dealing with the problems you know he's going to have to face.

Alice Rinehart: Integrity, I think, would be prime. And concern for the welfare of the country above political feelings.

Eldene Markus: What he stands for, and what he's upholding, and his integrity.

Frank McGee: If I were in public office, I hope I'd have the guts enough, or the integrity, to vote for what would be best for my country, even though the constituents back home don't think so.

The respondents were asked if any actual political leaders come close to realizing their ideal. Invited to range through history and around the world, they thought almost exclusively of American presidents, although Winston Churchill received three mentions, Mahatma Gandhi, Golda Meir, and Pierre Trudeau a mention each.

Harry Truman inspired much bipartisan admiration, being mentioned by ten respondents. They admired him for saying what he believed, regardless of the consequences. As Republican Fletcher Barbera said, "He didn't pussyfoot around." Kenneth Kaub said he opposed Truman while in office, but had since come to admire the man. Arnold Garcia declared his admiration for political leaders who speak out for what they believe in; matching Maureen Barbera, his examples of politicians with this quality were Truman, Barry Goldwater, and Spiro Agnew.

Unlike national samples, the microsample did not exhibit a fixation for Franklin D. Roosevelt.[2] Roosevelt was mentioned favorably by Quentin Elliott and the Markuses; Piotr Pavel says he admired FDR greatly until he learned more about what went on at Yalta. However, FDR was not mentioned spitefully by anybody but the McGees. The McGees must go back half a century to find an admirable national politician; they mention Herbert Hoover and Al Smith as men who had the best interests of the country at heart. Their contemporary example is their personal friend, former Congressman John Schmitz.

John F. Kennedy was mentioned favorably by four couples: the Pavels, Kaubs, Barberas, and Roybals—again, a bipartisan admiration. Said Myrna Pavel, "He brought dignity to the White House; and he had great sympathy for mankind." The theme of selflessness, of dedication to the good of all, was mentioned again and again by all the respondents. This may have been a kind of "halo effect" surrounding the presidential office as a national symbol. When they learned, via Watergate, that the office's incumbent was only another politician, contempt for Nixon was stimulated without destroying the symbolic authority of the office.

When conversation turned to politicians of less than presidential stature, the yearning for integrity became clear. Richard Rinehart mentioned the late James B. Utt, predecessor of Schmitz as the district's congressman, as being a liability. "He was mainly a nest-featherer," Richard said. Both the Porfilios and Roybals mentioned former Senator George Murphy, defeated for reelection in 1970, after it was revealed that some of his expenses in Washington had been paid by his appointment as a consultant to the Technicolor Corporation. They saw this relationship as corrupt, the antithesis of the behavior one hopes for from politicians.

During these 1970 interviews, three couples (the Elliotts, McGees, and Markuses) mentioned Lyndon B. Johnson rather disdainfully as lacking the desirable qualities. John Weeks said LBJ was "a great legislative leader, but a mediocre president," while Richard Rinehart said that

---

[2]In the Gallup polls, FDR remained the most admired political leader, even fifteen years after his death. See John E. Mueller, *War, Presidents, and Public Opinion* (New York: Wiley, 1973), pp. 191–192.

Johnson's record was not too bad, considering that "he had a tough act to follow," and that he sensed a peculiar kind of integrity in LBJ.

Alice Rinehart: Johnson was quite a politician, and he certainly had his good contacts with the Senate, having been a part of it. He knew how to manipulate, and I think one thing that made you just a little dubious about him was that he was *such* a politician, and worked so hard at it. He was inclined somewhat to play party politics, and to reward those that went along with him and helped him. This is where I would question the integrity part, where politics is more important than—

Richard Rinehart: With his background, a long career in politics, the way he saw the best thing for the country would be different than someone who didn't have those long years. He had integrity. For example, if you were from the wrong end of town, it would be possible to have integrity in there, and still be among a bunch of thieves. I'm not saying that that's an exact corollary, but I'm saying that, with his background, he had pretty good integrity.

Richard's comment says it all: politics is a dirty business, politicians are tarred by it, and a president is lucky if some inner strength permits him to rise above his political experience. Richard's own favorite was Dwight Eisenhower, who seemed truly above the petty, partisan aspects of politicking. We never discussed the possible corroding influence of his long political career upon Richard Nixon. The Rineharts were pleased with Nixon's performance in 1970, and they voted for his reelection in 1972. When the Watergate investigation filled the television screens in 1973, Richard Rinehart felt something like a sense of personal betrayal, and he refused to watch.

When it comes to lesser officials, ideology is mentioned: they are "too liberal," or "too conservative." But with presidents, the search is clear: the voters seek a political leader who is above politics, a man who will devote his efforts to the good of the whole. They do not outline a content for that "good of the whole"; they hope that the president will understand the needs of the country, in a way they themselves cannot. Martha Weeks assigned the complex question of welfare reform to President Nixon; she voted for him in the conviction that he would understand such matters. The president is presumed to know more than any voter about what the national security requires, particularly in foreign affairs, and he probably has better ideas about the solution to domestic problems as well. The respondents want to trust a president, to be convinced of his dedication to the good of the entire nation, and to delegate (in the same sense used in the Constitution) a range of matters to him for decision and resolution. The only respondents who made a point of saying that a candidate should agree with their own vision of the good of the country were the McGees. They supported Barry Goldwater in the conviction that his election would indeed have slowed, if not halted, "creeping socialism."

In the aftermath of Watergate, I asked the respondents if they felt that officials of the federal government are ever justified in committing illegal acts, such as wiretapping or burglary, for reasons of national security, when the nation is not fighting a declared war. The majority responded with a resounding "No," although Arnold Garcia was undecided, and six replied in the affirmative, with qualifications. The Roybals, Quentin Elliott, and Maureen Barbera were willing to condone such activities by established national security agencies, provided there were adequate safeguards to assure that national safety, not party advantage, was the goal. Ralph and Caroline Porfilio both answered "Yes."

Caroline: I don't know all the undercover activities that may occur.

Ralph: There is certain information the general public has no need to know and unauthorized release of this information should *be stopped.*

It is clear, from their conversation and from their responses to test items measuring personality attributes and political attitudes, that the Porfilios are the members of the microsample closest to expressing support for truly repressive governmental actions. Any president who is popular, Ralph feels, is pandering to public opinion; he can't be fulfilling his responsibilities. Ralph and Caroline exhibit several traits of the "authoritarian personality," defined in a classic study as that type of person exhibiting the greatest potential for following fascist leadership.[3] Yet, as noted before, they were not attracted to George Wallace as a third-party candidate in 1968. Ralph voted for Wallace in the 1972 Democratic presidential primary, but he was neither surprised nor overly distressed when Wallace lost. There is a large, and largely unknown, distance between personality and attitude traits, and overt political action.[4] Ralph's negative memories of wartime classroom patriotism, his disdain for organized religion, and his clear perception of life's absurdi-

[3] T. W. Adorno et al., *The Authoritarian Personality* (New York: Norton, 1969; first published 1950). This seminal and massive work should be read in conjunction with the leading collection of critical studies, R. Christie and M. Jahoda, eds., *Studies in the Scope and Method of "The Authoritarian Personality"* (Glencoe, Ill.: Free Press, 1954).
[4] This distance is acknowledged by Adorno et al., in *Authoritarian Personality*, p. 972.

ties suggest a psychological autonomy that would make him resist recruitment into any harshly disciplined organization, regardless of its political purposes.

In common with other members of the microsample, the Porfilios express cynicism about the actions of politicians but something like reverence for the symbols of the nation. They are allegiant citizens, and some of that allegiance is attached to such concepts as freedom of speech and freedom of religion.

The Porfilios' belief that the president ought to know best, and that there are certain facts which the public has no right to know, is but the most extreme form of the microsample's general desire to place a man in the presidency to whom they can delegate both knowledge and decisional power. For the others, this is a feeling expressed indirectly and with gentleness. The motivation is not a desire for fascism, but for privatism—when the right leaders are in office, one can pay more attention to private pursuits and be less worried by public affairs.

Integrity and the Electoral Decision

The yearning for integrity in their ideal political candidate is a backward-looking conviction; asked to name those who came close to achieving the ideal, the respondents think of men whose policies can no longer threaten their interests. Most, like Churchill, Eisenhower, and John Kennedy, are safely dead. How that feeling influences their actual decision between candidates is a question of more practical significance. Is the yearning for integrity only an opinion molecule that fades into the background during an election campaign, or does it weigh in the scale of their electoral choice?

The year 1968 was rich politically, and integrity was a frequent theme in the respondents' comments on it. I asked the Republican Barberas whom they would have voted for, if they could have voted in the Democratic presidential primary of 1968.

Maureen: I think at that point I was on McCarthy's side.

Fletcher: Yeah, much as I think McCarthy's a raving liberal, I liked him. Even though I don't like his politics, I liked the fact that he was honest.

Maureen: He came through it honestly.

Fletcher: You know, he said, "This is where I stand. And I'm going to make an issue out of it." I might have even voted for McCarthy if

I could have. I sure as hell wouldn't have voted for Kennedy.

Maureen: As a matter of fact, I remember we had some friends that reregistered.

Fletcher: There was a lot of that going on, yeah. People were crossing over just so they could either vote against Kennedy or for or against McCarthy.

Maureen: I toyed with the idea, maybe for one moment. Because I thought McCarthy was kind of great. I liked him.

Next to the Rineharts, the Barberas are the staunchest Republicans of the microsample. For Maureen to contemplate changing her party registration to support Eugene McCarthy suggests the strength of her reaction to McCarthy, and the importance of the integrity theme in their search for the right candidate.

The Markuses were strong supporters of John F. Kennedy in 1960, and their judgment against Richard M. Nixon, taken then, carried over to 1968.

Jan: I don't think Nixon's going to do all he said he was going to do. I think he's only interested in himself, and not in the masses of the poeple. . . . Like I read one time, usually the men who were already born with wealth, that they were more liberal, and they tried to do more for the masses of the people, to sort of cover up that bad reputation that their fathers had. Like the Rockefellers, they're trying to make good. I think, really, they try to do a better job than somebody who had nothing and gets into power, because *they* forget about the poor man. And I think that's true of a case like Nixon. Or even Hoover. And Coolidge.

With McGovern as the alternative, however, Jan voted for Nixon in 1972. This approval of noblesse oblige is a milder form of the attitude cynically expressed by the Porfilios: rich men make the best candidates because they are already well off and won't be tempted to steal public funds.

Alice Rinehart gave a thoroughly partisan twist to the search for integrity.

Alice: Someone said that they felt the Republicans were very poor politicians, because they went down the line, and they had a strong, moralistic feeling about most things, and they didn't connive a little this way and that in order to achieve their own advantage. This was in a mixed group of women talking, Republicans and Democrats. The Democrats have a reputation of being close to, you know, Tammany Hall. . . . Somehow, they accept that the Democrats can do something that's a little bit off center morally, and, well, that's just the Democrats for you. [She laughs.] But somehow it's accepted, whereas perhaps the Republicans who have built this up for themselves, that they have strong, moralistic ideas, and honesty and truth, and if they stray a little bit they're really bad guys.

In 1970, Ronald Reagan was the Republican candidate for reelection as governor. After a divisive Democratic primary, the speaker of the California Assembly, Jess Unruh, was nominated as his opponent. Unruh, then at the summit of his career, was recognized as the most powerful Democrat in the state. Shrewdly accumulating debts from his fellow legislators by channeling "fat cat" support into their campaigns, Unruh came as close to being a party boss as is possible in the antipartisan atmosphere of California politics. A large man, Unruh was, by the middle 1960s, widely known as "Big Daddy." When his ambitions expanded beyond the legislature, Unruh dieted and dropped the final "e" from his first name. At the 1968 Democratic National Convention, he won credit from the amateur liberal Democrats for his leadership of the California delegation. But the voters of Ramona Heights remembered his earlier image. If any candidate in California was tarred by the brush of long association with partisan politics, it was Jess Unruh.

Ronald Reagan offered a marked contrast. He presented himself as a political amateur during his primary election campaign of 1966. Republican leaders in more liberal Northern California opposed his candidacy and supported the then mayor of San Francisco, dairyman George Christopher. Reagan was able to pose as the good citizen called to civic duty by the press of public events—Cincinnatus returning, not from the plow, but from the TV studio. Reagan won a reputation as a more effective spokesman for the cause of Barry Goldwater than Goldwater himself, and he was a familiar household figure as a television host, huckster, and actor in old movies on the late show.

In the eyes of Ramona Heights, Ronald Reagan retained his amateur image through his first term as governor. During the election of 1970, the Ramona Heights Republicans particularly disdained Unruh's campaign, which linked Reagan with major corporation managers. Arnold Garcia made a special point of labeling Unruh's campaign "cynical." He stated that Unruh had for years been in the business of selling political favors to the moneyed interests of California. John Weeks was more eloquent.

John: Unruh to me is one of the most negative people I have ever seen. He touches off a dissident chord. I don't know the man, [but] I've heard what he says, and he is a man who speaks with a forked tongue. He speaks out of both sides of his mouth at the same time.

Feelings of this kind affected most of the microsample. All the loyal Republicans, as well as the Johnsons and Jan Markus among the Democrats, voted for the reelection of Ronald Reagan. Fletcher Barbera summarized the reasons.

Fletcher: I think Reagan is not really very political. He's pretty straightforward and says what he believes in, you know, and either you like it or you don't like it. "This is where I am, and that's it." I like that, and that's one of the reasons I voted for Reagan, and I still feel the same way about him. And I guess I have a feeling that America needs a little more honesty and a little less manipulation. And I think that Reagan's kind of straightforward.

A perception of Ronald Reagan as being above politics was hardly universal among the microsample; Myrna Pavel, for example, stated that Reagan was a puppet, and business leaders like oilman Henry Salvatori were the puppeteers. Nevertheless, for most of the microsample, the choice of 1970 was between Reagan, the successful political amateur, and Unruh, the tainted professional politician.

The Markuses are a special case; they voted for Reagan in 1966 for a specific reason. When the Watts riot broke out the year before, Democratic Governor Edmund G. Brown was out of the state, and the Democratic lieutenant governor delayed calling out the national guard. Feeling that the first business of government is to maintain law and order, the Markuses voted for Reagan as an expression of their distaste for the Democratic state administration. In 1970, they split their ballots. Jan voted for Reagan, feeling that, as he put it, there was so little difference between the two candidates that a change was not called for. Eldene voted for Unruh, convinced that selfish big business interests were backing Reagan.

There is a limit to the feeling that the candidate of integrity deserves support regardless of other considerations. That line was drawn at the boundary of their own interest. This is illustrated by the three Republicans who voted for Unruh in 1970. The Roybals, both professional educators, were distressed by the Reagan-backed cuts in budgetary support for education; they were sure that Unruh was more likely to improve the environment of their profession. Kenneth Kaub, physician at a state mental hospital, was upset by Reagan's plan to close as many state hospitals as possible, forcing local governments to bear the cost of treating the mentally ill. Kenneth said that Reagan approached such matters with the mind of an accountant, rather than human sympathy, and he was sure that Unruh's election would assure a more promising future for the state mental health program. Marie Kaub saw the wisdom of her husband's position, but she did not like Jess Unruh, remembering the "Big Daddy" image; she finally left the gubernatorial position on her ballot blank.

This yearning for a candidate of integrity, which is bipartisan, reflects the "decomposition" of American political parties.[5] Both the Republican and Democratic parties are losing their hold on the American electorate; increasingly, voters choose candidates on the basis of their personal appeal, as communicated by television.

When the talk turns to less prominent electoral contests, the search for integrity becomes less marked, for the voters generally have less knowledge of both the position to be filled and the personalities of the candidates. The microsample claim they vote for the man rather than the party, from top to bottom of the ballot. In fact, however, their party identification becomes increasingly important as a guide to decision as they move down the ballot.

To the McGees, their friend John Schmitz, the district's former congressman and a declared member of the John Birch Society, personifies the ideal, un-self-interested political leader. They point out that Schmitz resigned from his teaching position to run for the legislature and from the legislature to run for Congress, in contrast to another conservative, Max Rafferty, who retained his position as state superintendent of public instruction while running in the 1968 Republican senatorial primary. The only other couple to express admiration for John Schmitz was the Rineharts, who emphasized his courage and integrity, and felt acquainted with him personally, since they had attended an adult education course he taught on international communism. The rest of the microsample, except for Arnold Garcia and the Barberas, knew of Schmitz's Birch membership, thought it despicable, and voted against him in 1970.

The contest between Max Rafferty and Wilson Riles was seen as unusually important in Ramona Heights. The state school superintendent is the elected executive who administers policies set by an appointed board of education. Max Rafferty, a flamboyant advocate of a return to

[5]Walter Dean Burnham, *Critical Elections and the Mainsprings of American Politics* (New York: Norton, 1970), chap. 4–7. Also see the discussion of Burnham's work in Chapter Three.

the basics in education, raised the position from obscurity by attempting to use it as a springboard for higher office. This transparent ambition triggered the respondents' concern for integrity. They knew little of Riles except that he was black and was Rafferty's deputy. A few felt his race influenced their decision; supporting Riles seemed a kind of compensatory gesture. Generally, the microsample turned against Rafferty for being too much of a politician. They felt that his record as an educational administrator was mediocre, at best; some scored him an absolute failure.·

1972: Suspension of a Search

The 1972 election presented the voters of Ramona Heights with a choice between Richard Nixon, familiar in California and national politics since the end of World War II, and George McGovern, largely unknown to them until his meteoric climb toward the nomination. The microsample was reinterviewed during the early stages of the campaign, shortly after the conclusion of both nominating conventions.

The comments made about the character and performance of President Nixon largely focused on the accomplishments of his first term. Only the Pavels called up the image of "Tricky Dick," formulated during the campaign against Helen Gahagan Douglas so many years before. The others apparently resolved any doubts about Nixon's integrity on the basis of his performance in office. However, they did not say as much: the theme of integrity was absent from their comments. The issue for those who eventually voted for Nixon was simple: proven competence on the part of Nixon, opposed to evidence of incompetence on the part of McGovern. McGovern's incompetence was shown by his handling of the Eagleton resignation, his "idiotic" welfare proposal, and the encouragement offered to his "radical"—young and black—supporters. But there was another theme in their reactions to the Democratic candidate; this was their feeling that George McGovern, in spite of the "new look" of his drive toward the nomination, really offered nothing new. Richard Rinehart said, "McGovern's just about where Humphrey was when he ran four years ago," and Kenneth Kaub complained, "McGovern is sounding more like Nixon every day." In other words, more of the same old politics, with all its connotations of dirt. As long as both candidates were mere politicians, it seemed best to have Nixon, who had at least proven his competence as a politician.

This reaction was obviously not shared by those who selected George

McGovern. The strongest endorsement of McGovern's personality, and a major renewal of the integrity theme, came from Quentin Elliott.

Quentin: There is a kind of honesty about McGovern that people sense, maybe related to his religious roots. A lot of people are basing a lot of hopes on him; you can tell that from the fervor of his supporters. He stands for a lot, and he showed it at the convention by ousting Daley and the machine politicians. So I'm excited by him, because he represents hope, although I still have an admiration for Humphrey. I voted for McGovern in the primary, but I kind of felt guilty, since I've liked Humphrey for a long time. But I wanted to bet on the horse that I thought could beat Nixon.

Deborah: Well, I voted for Humphrey in the primary. I haven't really followed the campaign since then, and I feel guilty about that. I get concerned with my own interests, and I find it easy not to look at those other problems. Maybe the time will come, when the kids are back in school, that I can give it some more time. I don't really *mind* Nixon, but don't ask me why, I haven't made a study of it . . . I think maybe Nixon is the best one for the country in terms of our safety in foreign affairs, and I might vote for him because of that. . . .

Quentin: McGovern owes less to his backers than anybody has owed for a long time. He'll have more freedom, and that's a fantastic advantage. He doesn't owe anything to oil, or to Detroit; he's published his financial contributions.

In November, Quentin voted for George McGovern, but Deborah voted for Richard Nixon.

The Pavels were disturbed by what they had seen of the Democratic National Convention, as noted in Chapter Eight. Piotr was concerned about McGovern's welfare reform proposal, and said he was thinking about "defecting" if McGovern were unable to explain it. Myrna was distressed by her perception of "bitterness and pettiness behind the scenes of the McGovern organization." Above all, Piotr said, somewhat sadly, the election of McGovern would not change the power wielded by special interests: more of the same old politics. "I'm getting to be very cynical," said Piotr. By November, these misgivings had faded. In reporting his vote, Piotr wrote that his reason for choosing McGovern was the need for "political honesty and plain honesty." Myrna was more eloquent, but she said nothing about George McGovern in giving her reasons for supporting him. She wrote:

My pathological distrust of RMN—his hypocrisy and ruthlessness; his corny pose of self-righteousness and concern for "Mr. and Mrs. USA"; his not so subtle undermining of "life, liberty, and the pursuit of happiness." All intellectual and scientific progress has been killed.

Thus, for Myrna, a vote for McGovern was most importantly a vote against Nixon. She did not perceive George McGovern as a paragon of integrity, but he was her only weapon against the incumbent.

The Markuses were also offended by aspects of the Democratic National Convention and the McGovern campaign. At one point, Eldene said that McGovern's position on amnesty was enough to lead her to vote against him. Later, however, she said that she could never vote for Nixon. She saw only one way of resolving the dilemma.

Eldene: I just may not vote; it'll be the first time in my life. My conscience is my guide, really, and I'm not going to have anyone convince me. 'Cause I've lived for fifty-six years, and my mind is made up. 'Cause I don't see any difference between either one of 'em.

Question [to Jan]: But you may go for Nixon?

Jan: I think so. Unless they get somebody *else* up there besides McGovern. [He chuckles.] But I'm going to vote. Like I say, it's part of your duty. . . . But I think, no matter who gets in there, they aren't going to change it much.

In November, Jan and Eldene performed their duty by going to the polls. However, in the presidential contest, they negated each other's choices. Jan voted for Nixon/Agnew; for every other office, he voted Democratic. Eldene voted for McGovern/Shriver and for the Democratic ticket.

These, then, are the McGovern voters of Ramona Heights: Quentin Elliott, captivated by McGovern's integrity and promise; Piotr Pavel, feeling that the choice would make little difference; Myrna Pavel, citing her "pathological distrust" of Nixon; Eldene Markus, who considered not voting at all; and Tina Roybal, who realized that her values were changing and felt somewhat isolated, with her husband and her neighbors supporting Nixon.

The self-described motives of the Nixon voters were just as varied. However, there were several themes—both pro-Nixon and anti-McGovern—that were repeated in several conversations, and one theme—integrity—was conspicuous by its absence. Only one Nixon voter, Harry Johnson, mentioned honesty as a Nixon quality, and he surrounded his statement with qualifications, hinting that, unlike McGovern, Nixon did not let integrity get in the way of his politics.

Harry: I think if McGovern had not been so bold with some of his remarks he made, he would have saved himself a lot of votes, including mine. . . . I'm a great believer that you have to know when to keep your mouth shut and when to open it to get the most done. . . . If [McGovern] can't do it in an election, I'd hate to have him running the government.

The Johnsons both voted for McGovern in the California presidential primary, feeling that he was the best candidate, and particularly that he was superior to Hubert Humphrey, whom they think they voted for in 1968.[6] By that point in the preconvention campaign, however, they had all but decided to vote for Nixon in the general election. Any attractions they felt for McGovern were erased by his handling of the Eagleton resignation.

Harry Johnson joined the other Nixon voters of the microsample in stating that the president had earned a second term. This feeling was best summed up by Martha Weeks.

Martha: I believe that unless a president is really bad, he should be given a chance to carry out his plans through a second term.

Neither of the Weekses entertained the notion that Nixon could be "really bad." They confessed that they had planned to vote for his reelection since the beginning of 1972, certain that he would be renominated, and not caring very much whom the Democrats might nominate. John Weeks saw the nomination of McGovern as the clincher. He wrote that "Nixon was the only qualified candidate."

The anti-McGovern comments volunteered by the Nixon voters considerably outweighed the pro-Nixon statements. If the microsample were representative, the support for the president was not terribly deep, and the magnitude of his victory was misleading. Those who primarily voted against McGovern were not granting an open-ended mandate to President Nixon.

The role of "issues" in any electoral decision is hard to measure. The respondents volunteered their reactions to the personalities of the candidates; they had to be asked about issues. Theories of cognitive dissonance suggest that voters adapt their attitudes on issues to conform with those of the candidate they have chosen, or else perceive their candidate as agreeing with their own stand on issues, thus making whatever mental

[6]Memories of voting behavior are notoriously undependable. In 1970, the Johnsons told me they voted for Nixon in 1968. In 1972, they remembered voting for Hubert Humphrey in 1968. Comparing the context of the two interviews—the quality of the recollections they dredged up—it seems probable they voted for Humphrey in 1968. They wrote me in December, 1972, to say they had been out of the country in November and had not voted in the 1972 election. The analysis here is based on the assumption that they would have voted in November the way they planned to vote in August.

adjustments are necessary to match their beliefs with their voting behavior.[7] This was generally the case for the Ramona Heights microsample. However, there was a balance in favor of President Nixon, after allowing for such psychological adjustments, and it included both Nixon and McGovern voters.

Attitudes on inflation and "law and order" varied according to partisanship and the candidate selected. Voters felt that their man would do the best job of handling inflation; Nixon voters felt that crime probably decreased under the Nixon Administration, while McGovern voters suspected that it had not. Nixon voters approved of Nixon's appointees to the Supreme Court and had a positive image of the trend of their decisions. McGovern voters (particularly the Pavels) were appalled by the decisions of the Nixon-appointed justices. On three emotional issues, however, the microsample sided with President Nixon, with few exceptions. McGovern's confused welfare reform proposal activated their concern for the value of achievement; they opposed awarding a thousand dollars a year to every American with no strings attached. All but the McGees were relieved at the withdrawal of ground forces from Vietnam and with the thaw in the cold war signaled by Nixon's trips to Russia and China. Convinced of the value of neighborhood schools, all but the Kaubs agreed with the Nixon position which would permit the continuation of de facto racial segregation and prevent busing to integrate schools like those in Ramona Heights. Does this give a clue to the reason why several members of the microsample—Harry and Jacqueline Johnson (probably), Jan Markus, and Arthur Roybal— switched their votes from Democrat Hubert Humphrey in 1968 to Republican Richard Nixon in 1972?

Tina Roybal, who voted for Humphrey in 1968, voted for McGovern in 1972, but Arthur Roybal switched to Nixon. Tina said her standpat position resulted from her changing attitudes. She suggested that her husband was led to switch to the Republican candidate because his political outlook in 1968 was much the same as in 1972. Extrapolated to the national electorate, which is far from a scientific procedure, the Roybals suggest a neat explanation for the 1972 outcome. Nixon's cool courtship of "Middle America" touched upon those values, challenged during the 1960s by demonstrators and at the 1972 Democratic conven-

---

[7]The most influential theory linking attitudes and behavior is Leon Festinger, *A Theory of Cognitive Dissonance* (Evanston, Ill.: Row, Peterson, 1957). However, at least in periods of relative electoral calm, the role of "issues" in voter perceptions of their electoral choice is relatively slight. See A. Campbell et al. *The American Voter*, abr. ed. (New York: Wiley, 1964), chaps. 7, 8, and 9. The notion that people naturally seek consistency among attitudes is belied by the phenomenon of opinion molecules, as noted on p. 219.

tion by delegates, which many Americans want to preserve. A Democrat voting for Humphrey in 1968 would vote for McGovern in 1972 only if his values had evolved in the same direction as the party's rules for delegate selection: the voter would need the strength of new convictions about the need for women, racial minorities, and youth to play a more active role in American politics. Such an explanation is congruent with V. O. Key's thesis that voters choose, stay with, or switch to parties nearest their attitudes or convictions.[8] McGovern's Democratic party seemed to have gone "too far" for several traditionally Democratic voting groups, who switched. Key concluded that "voters are not fools."

The pattern is not so clear for the other switchers of Ramona Heights. We are not absolutely certain that the Democratic Johnsons voted for Hubert Humphrey in 1968, as they gave conflicting reports. They did not vote at all in November of 1972, being out of the country. However, their August determination to vote for Nixon was expressed in the strongest possible terms. Harry Johnson was dismayed by the 1972 Democratic convention; he felt that many of the delegates did not "earn their way." He was satisfied with Nixon's handling of the economy, and he was unhappy with McGovern as the nominee, although he voted for McGovern in the California Democratic primary. That they did not bother to vote by absentee ballot in November suggests that they did not feel the outcome was very important, or that they did not feel it was enough in doubt to require their vote, or both. The Johnsons' political feelings are not marked by intensity.

Jan Markus is the final switcher. His decision was hedged with cynical comments to the effect that the choice would not make much difference; the same interests would be running things. But he was pleased by Nixon's handling of foreign policy and appalled by McGovern's proposal of amnesty for draft dodgers and deserters. Although he could have supported some other Democratic candidate, he felt that McGovern was unacceptable, and he voted to reelect Nixon.

Within our microsample, then, the outline of Key's model holds true, but the voting decision for both switchers and standpatters was rather less positive than that portrayed by Key. Except for such strong partisans as the Weekses and Rineharts, the 1972 choice was made rather unenthusiastically between relatively unappealing alternatives.

---

[8]V. O. Key, Jr., with the assistance of Milton C. Cummings, Jr., *The Responsible Electorate* (Cambridge, Mass.: Harvard University Press, Belknap Press, 1966). Also see the discussion of Key's work in Chapter Three.

"The World Outside, and the Pictures in Our Heads"[9]

The Ramona Heights voters feel that they receive adequate information on which to base electoral judgments. Whether they seek clues to the candidate's integrity, or wish to determine his positions, they do not complain of any lack of knowledge about the candidates at the top of the ticket. As noted in Chapter One, they have little knowledge of the actions and attitudes of their own congressman. The source of their information—discounting, as they do, ephemeral party brochures—is the mass media, as distributed in the Los Angeles metropolitan area.

Information is important. The voters of Ramona Heights recognize the vital role it must play in a democratic government. When asked to list the attributes of an ideal citizen, they universally replied, "To be informed," or some variant of that phrase. Most went on to say that, once informed, the ideal citizen becomes active and attempts to influence the outcome of political decisions—certainly by voting (which, most would agree with Jan Markus, is an important duty) and by other activities. But the members of the microsample themselves fulfilled only the first requirement. While their information level was high, their activity level was low. Except for Alice Rinehart and the activist McGees, they treated politics as a spectator sport, until they felt that their direct interests might be threatened. When they were out of the country at election time, neither the Pavels (in 1970) nor the Johnsons (in 1972) bothered to vote by absentee ballot.

The microsample members are sophisticated media consumers. Except for Arnold Garcia and the Johnsons, who only glance at newspapers, never read magazines, and depend almost entirely on television for their knowledge of the world, the Ramona Heights voters read a great deal, watch television news commentaries, and discuss politics with friends and family. More than half agreed with the criticisms of television networks voiced by former Vice President Agnew, but none viewed themselves as the victims of manipulation by television news managers. They would say, "Sure, a lot of that goes on, but it doesn't fool *us.*"

The dominant newspaper in the metropolitan area is the *Los Angeles Times.* If conscientious coverage of national and international affairs

---

[9]This title is from the first chapter of Walter Lippmann's classic *Public Opinion* (New York: Macmillan, 1922), reprinted in Wilbur L. Schramm, ed., *Mass Communications,* 2nd ed. (Urbana: University of Illinois Press, 1960), pp. 468–486.

and a variety of interpretative comment upon them is necessary to the definition, the *Times* is the only newspaper in the area. All the respondents except the McGees subscribe to the morning *Times* and to the evening *Daily Pilot*, a suburban paper which covers local politics, society, and PTA meetings, in addition to wire-service coverage of matters outside Orange County. In refusing to read the *Times*, Frank and Mary McGee provide the most striking example of selective perception—recognizing only that information which will reinforce their convictions. They insure this by subscribing to the *Santa Ana Register* and to a group of periodicals published in association with the John Birch Society. But selective perception is not lacking in other members of the microsample, where it is found as a tendency to doubt the message when the messenger is mistrusted.

Alice and Richard Rinehart confessed to being "addicts" of the *Los Angeles Times*. Richard said he was particularly attached to the sports section, so he tolerated the rest of the paper. Alice read the paper thoroughly, and she noted that its editorial page offers a variety (or "balance") of columnists. But they both felt that the *Times* was becoming increasingly slanted, and to the left. The paper's policies were much less congenial than they were even a few years ago. Alice commented that a large number of the stories had by-lines. Recalling her own college studies in journalism, she suggested that this is a way for the paper to evade editorial responsibility for the judgments of its reporters. "Personalized" reporting is less likely to be objective, which she believed should be the goal of good journalism. Alice didn't really approve of the *Times*, but she couldn't keep herself from reading it.

In common with other respondents, the Rineharts discerned biases in certain television commentators. Their particular bête noire was Walter Cronkite.

Alice: I'm very sensitive. For example, on Cronkite's program when he starts talking about the president, particularly this last election, and I see obviously that he's been derogatory toward the Republican party, and the Democrats seem to be, you know, clean livers. . . . I haven't heard any Democrats complaining.

They felt that there were no conservative commentators on network television. Richard recalled hearing a straightforward conservative spokesman on the radio, but forgot the man's name.

The champion followers of the news were the Pavels. In addition to the two newspapers, they subscribed to twenty-two periodicals, including eight technical engineering journals. (Piotr worked as a consulting engineer, so the technical journals were important to him.) Their general-circulation magazines included *Time, Newsweek, Harper's, Atlantic, Commentary, New Yorker, New York, American Scholar, Business Week, Fortune, U.S. News & World Report, Forbes, Aviation Week, Travel,* and *Esquire* (borrowed from their son). When I chided Myrna for not reading William Buckley's *National Review,* she replied that she would be happy to, but felt it necessary to draw the line somewhere on expense. They had been subscribing to the *New York Times,* but dropped it because of the cost.

The Pavels watched television, sometimes as much as three hours in an evening, but they were appalled by the networks' assumption of a low intelligence level on the part of the audience. As for politics, they felt that the coverage offered by newspapers and newsmagazines was too sketchy and needed to be supplemented by the in-depth analysis of *Harper's* or *Commentary.*

At the opposite end of the spectrum were the Porfilios. Ralph reads his newspapers hurriedly, scanning the headlines, reading the lead paragraph of the main stories, and ignoring the editorial page. He reads no magazines. Caroline subscribed to *American Home, Sunset,* and *Better Homes and Gardens.* When I asked if she received any newsmagazines, she said, "No, I look at those at the beauty shop."

In spite of the rather slight attention he paid to the media, Ralph was eager to criticize their coverage of radical activities, which he said got "ninety-five percent" of the news space:

Ralph: This I object to. I don't think it is fair journalism. It is news, to a degree. Maybe it is placating of these people to put them in the news, but I wonder, if they got less notoriety, if there would be less problems.

As for reliable information on which to base political judgments, Ralph said that the media are "all tools. You kinda use your intuition. It's the only way." Discrediting the news source probably allows the Porfilios to ignore or discount reports of social problems.

Quentin Elliott adopted a conscious strategy for coping with the news during the turbulent 1960s. He subscribed to the *Christian Science Monitor.* When the *Monitor* arrived each week, he knew that the sensational material that made daily headlines would be sifted for its true relevance.

Quentin: I have insulated myself against this emotional involvement, or at least against the anger factor, by subscribing to the *Monitor,* which never seems to make you mad. And yet, I feel I'm getting the big picture.

Quentin castigated the media for their "accentuation of the negative," and he felt that the greatest fault of news commentators was their pose of omniscience.

Quentin: What Walter Cronkite says, when he says, "And that's the news today, this Tuesday the whatever-it-is of July," I think there's a tendency to *believe* that that really is all the news that there is, when of course it isn't at all the case.

Such an awareness of the complexity of political issues, and the compulsion to become "informed citizens," may be related to these voters' relative inactivity as citizens. A quarter of a century ago, Lazarsfeld and Merton hypothesized the "narcotizing dysfunction" of the mass media.[10] They wrote that fascinated attention to the mass media tends to produce apathy, for it creates an intellectualized, remote knowledge of organized social action, stimulating in the individual a self-congratulation for being so well informed, at the expense of blindness to his own inactivity. Knowledge substitutes for action.

This perception applies to a number of the couples in Ramona Heights. John and Martha Weeks follow the news faithfully in the newspapers, and they normally watch the evening television news on a set in their bedroom before sleeping. Yet John feels he has no time for active politics, nor does Martha—her duties toward home and hearth are too consuming. Richard Rinehart supports Alice in her Republican party activities, but does not spend the energy himself. Knowing that she is active, and why, is sufficient. Kenneth and Marie Kaub follow the news in the papers and on television but are not moved to take political action beyond voting. The Pavels have a compulsion to be informed, as evidenced by the torrent of periodicals they receive, yet they had not been active beyond voting since they campaigned for Adlai Stevenson. They have the excuse of aging, the congratulatory effect of being well informed, and the satisfaction of knowing that the torch of political activism is being passed on to their sons. Quentin Elliott shields himself from emotional reactions to daily sensationalism, but he seeks out "the big picture."

Columnist Jack Anderson serves as something akin to a narcotic for these respondents, serving their central concern for integrity. During the 1972 interviews, five respondents volunteered Anderson's name. They read his column avidly, cheered on his efforts to expose corruption

---

[10]P. F. Lazarsfeld and R. K. Merton, "Mass Communication, Popular Taste, and Organized Social Action," in Schramm, ed., *Mass Communications*, pp. 501–502.

in high places, and confessed to feeling more confidence in the future of the republic, knowing that Anderson was available to fill his role. In that pre-Watergate time, they were confident that merely exposing corruption was enough to control or eliminate it, and they felt that the mere presence of Anderson would do much to keep politics honest.

Frank and Mary McGee, the political activists, limit their consumption of the mass media, convinced that the same conspiracy which would betray American sovereignty into the hands of a world government also controls the popular press and television. The journals they trust are those with an editorial policy that supports this premise.[11]

Although the other members of the microsample would not subscribe to the cabalist explanation of media management offered by the McGees and Ralph Porfilio, they are critical, in various ways, of the sources through which they learn about the world. They do not accept what they read in the papers, or see on television, as being the full truth. Their understanding of the political world is influenced by their life experiences, partisanship, idea systems, opinion molecules, and degree of belief in the responsiveness of the system. These have established pictures in their heads of the world outside. As a result of media exposure, those pictures may be confirmed, or modified; they are not easily replaced. The Ramona Heights voters are not passive victims of the interpretations they read, or see on television. Their involvement with the media is an active one, as they agree or disagree with commentators, and discuss public issues with friends and family. Except for the McGees, who are politically active on a continuing basis, the voters of Ramona Heights can only be shocked into political activism by an event of such dimensions that it leads them to modify the pattern of their daily lives.

Did the Watergate investigations supply such an event?

---

[11]Elihu Katz and P. F. Lazarsfeld formulated and investigated the theory that the impact of mass communications is indirect, a "two-step flow" from the media, via attentive opinion leaders, to the less attentive citizens. See their *Personal Influence* (Glencoe, Ill.: Free Press, 1955). Frank McGee is the only member of the microsample who may qualify as an opinion leader, for others regularly seek his advice on political questions. While I was in their home, Frank received telephone calls asking how to vote on incumbent judges; Frank said to vote against them, they were appointed by former Governor "Pat" Brown. McGee does not fit the model very well, as his perception of the mass media is highly selective.

In Ramona Heights the "two-step flow" is effectively short-circuited. For example, the Barberas were watching a television commercial for senatorial candidate John Tunney. Fletcher commented, "Boy, isn't he a phony?" Maureen replied, "He sure is!"

Watergate: A Betrayal and a Confirmation

The break-in at Democratic National Committee headquarters in the Watergate apartment complex, which occurred during the 1972 election campaign, received little notice at the time. In interviews with the Ramona Heights voters in the late summer of 1972, the specific incident was never mentioned. Richard Rinehart did comment that the Democrats were trying to make an issue out of the methods used to secure Republican campaign contributions, but he didn't think they would succeed. When the pace of Watergate revelations began to quicken, and the Ervin Committee hearings began in the spring of 1973, only the Rineharts were psychologically prepared: they anticipated some effort by the opposition to discredit their own party.

Alice and Richard developed contrasting methods of dealing with the Ervin Committee revelations. Richard refused to watch the hearings or to pay much attention to news stories. He managed the challenge to the security of his belief in the rectitude of President Nixon and the Republican party by failing to perceive the full scope of that challenge. When I asked in November, 1973, about his reactions to the resignation of Special Prosecutor Archibald Cox, Richard said, "I've kind of been sticking my head in the sand over this whole business," and he chuckled. Alice did watch the hearings, and she compared her own impression of what transpired with the reports in the *Los Angeles Times*. She found the *Times* to be slanted against the Republicans. An active clubwoman, she regularly attended meetings at which Watergate was discussed. Few meetings were partisan, but the membership tended to be heavily Republican, and her friends reinforced her own perception that, regardless of the truth of the matter, the investigation was being pursued by the Democrats for partisan advantage. Activating her previous convictions about the leftward slant of the press, she was able to avoid full consideration of the deeper issues Watergate may have raised.

This reaction can be characterized as a feeling of confirmation. The Watergate revelations confirmed preexisting attitudes, Watergate was easily accommodated within the consciousness of the individual, and life went on. In one way or another, this kind of initial reaction was shared by thirteen of the twenty-three respondents: the McGees, Johnsons, Porfilios, Rineharts, Kaubs, Fletcher Barbera, Arnold Garcia, and Martha Weeks. The events of the fall—Attorney General Elliot Richardson's resignation, the "nonexistent tapes" episode, and others—led them to reexamine their opinions.

For the McGees, Watergate was just another episode in the degradation of America. They knew that "the real truth" was being hidden, rather than revealed, by the Ervin Committee investigations. Frank wrote that he hadn't taken the investigation too seriously, for "it all appears a bit phony." In assessing the eventual outcome, he felt that the Democratic presidential candidate would have an excellent chance in 1976, and this "might be the perfect setup for the beginning of one-world government." Mary agreed.

Mary: I think the outstanding feature of Watergate is the sin of omission—what the committee fails to bring out: the power play behind the scenes in Washington, and the threat of Red-tainted dollars from Cuba, et cetera.

Mary felt that the actual incidents investigated by the Ervin Committee were "just politics," the normal operations of the major parties. She pointed out that she was already a member of the American Independent party; if that were not the case, Watergate's revelations of the practices of the traditional parties would certainly have persuaded her to switch.

The Johnsons have never paid much attention to national politics, and Watergate did not force them over the brink of attentiveness. Jacqueline reported that she spent about an hour a week following Watergate developments, while Harry spent half an hour a week. Harry dismissed the incident as "just politics."

Jacqueline: I believe it is a serious matter, but I also believe that it has always been going on.

Both felt that President Nixon should cooperate with the Ervin Committee's investigation, but they felt that Watergate "will soon be forgotten." Registered Democrats, they had supported Nixon in 1972, because they found McGovern's candidacy unattractive, but they had not felt strongly enough to cast absentee ballots. With no great emotional investment in Nixon's reelection, they did not feel betrayed by the revelations. They did express support for the reform of laws governing campaign finance.

In their previous interviews, the Porfilios expressed cynicism about the political process, a low opinion of the electorate, and disdain for the media. Watergate initially confirmed, rather than modifying, these convictions. Both felt the incident was "just politics"; Caroline said it was "blown out of all proportion by the press coverage," while Ralph wrote that "Watergate should be put in its correct perspective—BREAKING and ENTERING." Following the pattern of Richard Rinehart, Ralph ignored the news reports of Watergate, except for what he heard on the car radio. Uniquely among the microsample, Ralph did not, in August of 1973, call for any gesture of cooperation by President Nixon with the investigation. Ralph stated only that the president should explain his actions after completing his term of office. Caroline felt that the investigation should be shifted from the legislative to the judicial branch, where it could be handled "quietly." She did not ignore the Ervin hearings, however. She reported watching them about six hours per week. She also discussed the matter "at great length" with relatives of one of the minor witnesses in the investigation, an Orange County resident who held a subordinate position in the Committee for the Re-election of the President during 1972. Perhaps these talks contributed to her opinion of the group of men who rose to positions of power in the White House.

Caroline: I think that they were bright young men. Power happy maybe, and didn't go out for any popularity contests.

Events of the fall forced Ralph Porfilio over the threshold of attentiveness. By November, both Ralph and Caroline feared the national agony that would result from impeachment proceedings, and they felt that the evidence against Nixon was inadequate to sustain impeachment. Neither favored resignation by the president, but Ralph predicted that he would resign.

In a manner similar to the Johnsons' reaction, several other respondents did not allow the Watergate investigations to overshadow primary concerns with business affairs or local issues. Arnold Garcia slighted the Watergate reports and regarded the matter as "serious, but just politics." He had no opinion concerning the president's involvement in the original break-in, nor in the subsequent cover-up, nor of what actions should be taken by either the president or Congress. Further implication of President Nixon in the scandals surrounding Watergate only confirmed his cynical attitude toward politicians.

Fletcher Barbera had recently changed jobs at the time of the first round of Ervin hearings. Required to drive to Los Angeles three times a week, he avidly followed the hearings on his car radio, and felt that "the president did not get full disclosure from his staff; how much he got is hard to tell."

Fletcher: This group lacked sufficient experience and broad judgment to have been placed in such positions. Nixon is at fault for having put them where they were. Their motivations were fairly selfless, but their judgment and personal character was not as strong as is required.

Fletcher felt that the president should cooperate fully with the special prosecutor (then Archibald Cox), and he hoped that political leaders would, in the future, pay more attention to following fair campaign practices, and that Congress would enact new laws to control campaign finance. He felt that Congress should conduct any further hearings "with more fairness and decorum." In spite of his interest in the hearings, Fletcher's basic attitudes and daily activities were not modified by his reactions.

Martha Weeks followed the hearings with interest—to the extent of some seven hours a week—and decided that President Nixon must have had prior knowledge of the cover-up of administration involvement. Other than supporting new laws to control campaign finance, she did not then consider any larger issues posed by the revelations.

Like Martha Weeks and Fletcher Barbera, the Kaubs followed the hearings enough to keep informed, but they felt no sense of emotional involvement in the outcome. Marie Kaub reported that she was much more concerned about the delay in the proposal for a new bridge across Upper Newport Bay, for she felt that Ramona Heights desperately needed a new access route. The Ervin investigation seemed remote from the needs of her family.

A CHANGE IN THEIR DAILY LIVES

A number of the Ramona Heights voters reacted so strongly to the constitutional crisis implicit in the Senate Watergate investigations as to modify, in varying degree, the pattern of their daily lives. In addition to seeking information, they were pushed over some "threshold of political activism" to engage in at least minimal political activity.

Piotr Pavel was not working regularly during the early summer of 1973, when the first weeks of the Ervin Committee hearings filled the television screen. He watched the hearings at least twenty hours per week, Myrna reported that she watched the hearings whenever she could, and both read and listened to all analyses they could find. As the prototypical liberal intellectuals of the microsample, the Pavels would be expected to react strongly to the Watergate disclosures.

Piotr: I am numb with disgust. Our founding fathers must be whirling in their graves like dervishes. . . . Nixon should resign and be tried as a criminal. We should establish a parliamentary system of government, as in Britain and France. . . . Watergate hearings being held and televised prove we are a great nation. Benedict Arnold is an angel compared with Tricky Dick.

Myrna Pavel responded in the same vein, but not quite so vehemently. Instead of calling for President Nixon's resignation, she proposed that he supply all papers or tapes requested by the Ervin Committee and then appear before it, to receive the same treatment as his helpers. "In a democracy," she wrote, "HE is no better nor worse than any other voter." When asked her opinion of the men who rose to positions of power in the White House, she answered:

Myrna: They are to be "admired" for their being able to use an opportunity; however, in this "gamble" do they win or lose? I prefer to think of them as the Orange County Bund and feared them as such. (Was I paranoid?)

The Watergate hearings changed the pattern of the Pavels' daily lives. They spent more hours following the hearings than even their usual compulsion to be informed would have dictated. For the first time since their campaign activities in behalf of Adlai Stevenson, they were motivated to influence the opinions of others, outside their normal circle of acquaintances. Piotr reported that they were expressing their disappointment and disgust in public, attempting to "convince people it is all Nixon's fault." Myrna added that they "speak to anyone who will listen, but too many feel 'poor Nixon' is being persecuted, or couldn't care less."

It seems fair to characterize the Pavels' reaction as a sense of betrayal of their trust in the American system and, at the same time, a confirmation of their worst suspicions of Richard Nixon. This powerful combination of emotions led them to the media for further knowledge; but the media impact was hardly narcotizing. They again became grass-roots activists, attempting to persuade their Orange County neighbors, including strangers, of Richard Nixon's iniquity. And, by the end of the summer, they counted a success with one of their "targets." A neighbor who was only a slight acquaintance, a wealthy professional man who had been a regular contributor of substantial campaign funds to the Republican party, severed all ties to the party in late October. They felt his change of heart was as much determined by events, however, as by their efforts at persuasion.

The most dramatic action in response to Watergate was taken by the Elliotts. Deborah had long devoted so much energy to the needs of the family that she hardly paid attention to public affairs, but the Watergate investigations fascinated and amazed her. At Deborah's suggestion, the goal of the family's summer vacation trip became Washington, and their goal in Washington became the Ervin Committee hearing room. Quentin described the experience.

Quentin: We camped in our van (Deborah, the two boys, a friend of theirs, and I) next to Union Station, arose at 4:30, stood in line for the hearing from 5:25 to 9:30 and stood at the back of the hearing room while Ehrlichman kept dodging. The hearing was quite revealing for me; not in the way I anticipated, though. What struck me most was the frequent talking-behind-the-hand asides of the senators and legal advisers who were not "on camera." It was casual, schoolboyish, and, I felt, in bad form.

Having driven across the continent to attend, Quentin was certain to be persuaded of the importance of the hearings. He was also convinced that President Nixon had prior knowledge of the cover-up. He felt the president should resign; failing that, he believed Congress should begin impeachment proceedings, rather than continuing with the Ervin investigation. He wrote in late August, 1973:

Quentin: The obvious need to impeach Dick Nixon is so great that protracted public hearings have only served to delay the real instrument of justice: due process.

For Quentin, Watergate was both a betrayal of his hopes for America and a confirmation of his worst suspicions, of Richard Nixon in particular and the national moral climate in general. He wrote:

Quentin: [Watergate has] much wider implications about acceptable personal ethics in our country today: the core of it being "If you think you can get away with it, DO IT!" . . . I pray for the soul of our president. Only God knows where Watergate will lead us.

Watergate marked an awakening for Deborah Elliott. In both 1970 and 1972, she constantly apologized for her lack of interest in, and knowledge about, American politics. Her interest was captured by her concern for integrity. She wrote in October, 1973:

Deborah: The present executive branch, I mean all of the people involved in the Watergate scandal, were not dedicated people to me, and had only self-interest. And I tend to judge Nixon by the company he hired. Reasonable men, it seems to me, would work together for the best interest of all, and Nixon doesn't seem part of this. To me, his real estate holdings prove he is a crook using my tax money. With Agnew, Cox, Richardson, etc., resigning, I have become interested in Politics now more than ever. I am 41 and haven't been the least bit interested up to now, it must be my age too, and more understanding of human nature.

In spite of the demands of her large home and two small daughters, Deborah watched the Ervin Committee hearings for ten hours or more a week in the early summer. Born in the United States, but educated in Canada, she had never studied American history. She wrote that the hearings were "a political science course for me." By November, 1973, Deborah favored the president's resignation; failing that, she felt Congress should consider impeachment. Quentin was writing to congressmen to demand impeachment.

Tina Roybal also emphasized the educational aspects of the hearings:

Tina: At first, appalled and contemptuous of those in power for their actions, which tore at my naïve ideals of representative government. Lately, a feeling that because of our system we can be more honest about such exposés without them endangering our system, but instead strengthening it.

She felt that the investigation would be more profitably turned over to the judiciary, and she predicted that "elected officials are going to operate with more trepidation (for a while, anyway)." But her most important reaction, the modification of her daily life, was related to her job as a teacher.

Tina: I feel a stronger conviction to uphold our constitutional rights and hope to convey this to my students in a nonpartisan manner.

Arthur Roybal, who, unlike his wife, voted to reelect President Nixon, reacted more mildly. He felt that the president was implicated in both the break-in and the cover-up, and he wrote in August, 1973, that the Nixon tapes should be released under ground rules established by the Supreme Court. He also emphasized the educational value of the hearings.

Arthur: The public's awareness as result of TV coverage will have greater impact than any laws could possibly do or have.

As for himself, however, Arthur's life remained the same. He reported that he discussed Watergate with friends, but "just like football, baseball or golf results, etc. (No 'Crusader Rabbit' approach.)"

Jan Markus was in the hospital at the time of the first round of Ervin

Committee hearings, for treatment of a recurrent malignancy. Eldene kept him informed of the developments, but the strain of visiting him in the hospital and providing convalescent care when he returned home meant that Eldene had little time for any political activity, aside from following developments in the media. Eldene was convinced of the president's complicity; she felt that Nixon should volunteer to appear before the Ervin Committee, and "if found guilty he should resign." She added, "*if* and when the tapes are turned in, they will have been tampered with and spliced." She labeled the Nixon staff "a bunch of Nazis," and suggested that "we need women to clean house." She wrote:

Eldene: The country is still a great place to live in. I'm proud of it. But the legal criminals should have their day in Court and pay the price for dividing the country. I.T.T. Wheat Deal. Vesco. Taxpayers' money on personal home improvements. This Administration has shown and is showing contempt for law and order and the Constitution. We supported him, but I sure am sorry.

The economy is the worst that I could remember in my life.

I would like to see law and order and decent morals.

Wish Martha Mitchell would hurry and write her book!!

Eldene had well-formulated suspicions of the character and associations of Richard Nixon as early as 1970, and she voted for McGovern in 1972, while her husband remained loyal to Nixon. Watergate confirmed her suspicions.

NEW PERCEPTIONS

Finally, there are two members of the microsample for whom Watergate created a personal crisis. The revelations led two fervent Nixon supporters, John Weeks and Maureen Barbera, to question matters they had previously accepted as settled. They were the betrayed; Watergate forced new perceptions upon them.

Their reactions to these new perceptions contrasted sharply. While Maureen was driven over the threshold of political activism and wrote a letter expressing her feelings to the editor of the *Los Angeles Times,* the Ervin hearings left John Weeks mentally paralyzed: although he was convinced of President Nixon's implication in the Watergate activities, he could not decide what should be done about it.

Maureen described her general reaction as being "horrified—I feel we have been 'duped.' " Like the Pavels, she became fascinated and spent at least four hours a day watching the hearings, in spite of caring for a large house and three small children. She decided that President Nixon had prior knowledge of the cover-up; she wished he would cooperate with the investigation; and she hoped that new legislation to control campaign spending and finance would emerge. Maureen wrote to me, as she wrote in greater detail to the *Times:*

Maureen: I feel that this is perhaps all pervading. The moral tone of the country should change. Being part of the late 50s generation, this has hit us like nothing else would. But what do you do to change it? I can handle my own family—but the nation? I feel helpless there.

For Maureen, the phrase "late 50s generation" summed up much anguish. A member of the so-called silent generation in college, she adhered to the standards of dress, manners, and convictions about the structure of society that were challenged in the 1960s. She was never sympathetic to that challenge, and she remained convinced of the superiority of her own values, which somehow seemed vindicated by the landslide reelection of President Nixon and the defeat of the adherents of the counterculture who supported George McGovern. Watergate revealed that the winning campaign organization did not adhere to the rules of fairness or even to the law. More important, it indicated a widespread ability, on the part of the class and generation with which Maureen identified, to conduct its affairs on the basis of an ethic of sheer expediency. This called into question her own expressions of moral outrage at the attitudes and actions of the youth of the 1960s. A floodgate of new perceptions was opened up. Among other emotions, Maureen shared the blunt reaction of Eldene Markus. Wrote Eldene, "Clean shaven, short haired, clean-cut looking lawyers as lawbreakers. Not fit to hold office!"

More of her deepest convictions than Maureen might care to acknowledge are symbolized by the portrait of Fletcher's great-grandfather that hangs over their fireplace. His stern Yankee visage, the lively look in his eye, and the artifacts of his ship chandlery in the background bespeaking the promise of honest value for an honest dollar, together suggest a solidity and virtue which the demonstrators of the 1960s threatened. Yet the men whom Maureen assumed, consciously or not, to be the inheritors of those virtues, and the models for her own children, turned out to be moral dwarfs. After the resignation of Attorney General Richardson—a New England Republican of transparent virtue —Maureen felt that President Nixon's handling of the Watergate crisis had grown irrational, and he should resign. Failing that, Congress should, in an orderly manner, consider impeachment. Fletcher agreed with her, although he was reluctant to see Gerald Ford, then Vice

President designate, or Carl Albert, Speaker of the House, become president.

The impact of Watergate upon John Weeks was less cosmic, being related to his partisan identification, rather than to his perception of himself and of the legitimacy of the social structure. Rather than confronting the immorality of his party, he was struck by its incompetence. He was engrossed by the Ervin hearings, spending some ten hours a week (while working full time) following the Watergate developments. He adjusted to the revelations in part through the "so's your old man" technique, pointing out that corruption must be at least as widespread in the Democratic party as in the Republican, and noting that the committee controlled by Democrats did not seek skeletons in their own closet.

John: Unfortunately, because of sheer stupidity, an administration which could have been great, being remembered for ending wars, decreasing world tensions, etc., will now go down in history remembered for Watergate.

In the most complete comment of any of the respondents, he elaborated on his feelings at the beginning of the summer of 1973.

John: There are several things which bother me about Watergate, i.e.:

1. Apparent use of government domestic and foreign security agencies in campaign activities or campaign-related activities.

2. The dishonesty of course, but also the stupidity of such actions when Nixon's election was virtually assured. People that stupid running our country is worrisome. [Weeks said in 1970 that "not enough idiots" could be assembled in one place at one time to start an atomic war.]

3. The actions of the Committee (Democratic dominated) to go far afield of their stated investigation in an attempt to discredit the Republican party in general.

4. The failure of the Committee to investigate Democratic campaign practices.

5. The Committee actions assure that not one of the witnesses, regardless of guilt, will ever be brought to trial. The circus atmosphere on international T.V. produces the common and undisputable defense, "They can't get a fair trial because of the publicity and being tried by the news media"—witness the predominance of Watergate cartoons involving every Watergate principal.

John wanted to punish individuals for their transgressions, pinpointing the blame, to keep scandal from tarring his entire party. He was convinced that President Nixon had some prior knowledge of both the original break-in and the subsequent cover-up. He hoped that Congress would enact new legislation to control campaign finance and spending. But he was undecided what other actions Congress should take. Reporting his indecision, John wrote:

> I'll wait until *all* the data are in. . . . Watergate is the predominant conversational subject—the general reaction I hear is "They *all* do it." Perhaps not fair but mirrors general opinion.

John thus found ample support for his feeling that the Democrats can boast no greater integrity than the Republicans. Adopting that conviction did not ease his pain very much. For John admired Richard Nixon and his administration extravagantly, disdaining Hubert Humphrey and George McGovern in turn. The trust he placed in Nixon—the delegation of both knowledge and decision to the president—was betrayed. A period of minor spiritual desolation was the result. By early November, his doubts were resolved. He said it was obvious that Nixon was "as guilty as sin," but it would be hard to prove in impeachment proceedings. He favored the president's resignation.

AND WHAT OF THE FUTURE?

Despite the differing vigor of their reactions and disagreement over what should be done as a result, the microsample held unanimous opinions about certain aspects of Watergate. Except for Arnold Garcia, who had no opinion, the microsample came to believe that President Nixon was implicated in the activities investigated by the Ervin Committee. Their search for integrity in high places was frustrated at the White House.

Asked their reactions after the first round of Ervin Committee hearings, even those who praised the hearings for their educational value or for demonstrating the greatness of America felt that the hearings had gone on long enough. They volunteered the opinion that the time had come for the judicial process to determine guilt and punish it. With this hope and expectation, they were shocked by the firing of Special Prosecutor Archibald Cox and the resignation of Attorney General Elliot Richardson, which seemed an attempt by the president to obstruct justice. A few insisted on the president's right to fire Cox; all but the McGees expressed admiration for Richardson's action. Even the Rineharts, staunchest Nixon partisans of the microsample, praised Richardson as a man of integrity.

In spite of the impact of the televised Ervin hearings, only two voters —Piotr Pavel and Quentin Elliott—were persuaded, at the time those hearings were recessed for the summer, that President Nixon should be impeached. Myrna Pavel wanted him to resign. The events of the fall —Vice President Agnew's resignation, the firing of Cox and the resignation of Richardson, the two nonexistent tapes of the nine promised to Judge Sirica—changed a number of minds. When I contacted the microsample during the second week of November, 1973, eleven voters favored the resignation of the president, his impeachment by Congress, or both. Piotr and Quentin had been joined by their wives, as well as by Maureen Barbera, the McGees, Markuses, and Weekses. The Porfilios did not favor resignation, but Ralph Porfilio predicted that the president would, in fact, resign. The McGees said that a Nixon resignation could only "make matters worse," and they doubted that impeachment proceedings would reveal the full truth about power in Washington, but they hoped Congress would make the effort.

When asked what should be done about weaknesses in the American system revealed by the Watergate scandals, the members of the microsample universally supported legislation that would enact stringent controls on campaign spending and finance. But this was passive support, like they gave in 1970 to welfare reform. The concern of Eldene Markus, Quentin Elliott, and Maureen Barbera was directed toward a more general target—the moral climate of America. The grass-roots activism of the Pavels was intended to persuade others of Nixon's culpability. The chance that the microsample would join in demanding specific campaign reform legislation was slight, unless they responded to leadership initiatives by reform groups or party factions led by persons in whom they could have confidence.

Voters do not react to public events with dispassionate objectivity. Established attitudes and values, as well as psychological needs, influence the content and vigor of their response. This obvious truth was demonstrated by the voters of Ramona Heights, when confronted by Watergate. Their reactions in 1973 were consistent with what I had learned about them in 1970 and 1972. The common denominator in the attitudes of those who turned against President Nixon in the fall of 1973 was their concern for integrity in public life. Those who continued to support him were either deeply cynical about politicians, like Garcia, fairly apathetic, like the Johnsons, or so strongly attached to the Republican party, like the Rineharts, that they could not fully credit their own perceptions.

CHAPTER TEN

Suburban Voters in a Coalition of Hope

It is only a calm realization that our main myths are dead or dying that can make us, as a nation, live on. We are shaped by those beliefs, but we are something more than they ever were, we can outlive them. We remained more than our self-flattering tenets—our individualism, self-regulation, discipline, achievement, "markets," Causes. It is comforting—needed comfort—to reflect that this is so, that we can survive our own creed's dissolution; for Nixon, by embodying that creed, by trying to bring it back to life, has at last reduced it to absurdity.

—*Garry Wills*[1]

"Richard Nixon is as guilty as sin."

—*John Wesley Weeks, 1973*

THIS BOOK has been about twenty-three voters in Ramona Heights, California, their life histories, aspirations, beliefs, and their political behavior, which is mostly limited to voting. The unstated premise has been that voting is important; elections make a difference. Despite their imperfections, which abound in an age of over-

[1]Garry Wills, *Nixon Agonistes: The Crisis of the Self-Made Man* (New York: New American Library, 1971), p. 546.

crowding and mass media, elections are the only means by which the American people, acting together, influence the direction of the nation.

Every election does not have the same impact. For an election to make a difference, the voters must be offered meaningful alternatives, which they perceive as being significant. The victorious party must then be able to make changes in the direction mandated by the people. This combination of circumstances rarely occurs.

When the Constitution was written, there had been no experience of democracy in a large nation. The founding fathers wanted to involve the people in determining the course of the nation, but not too directly. The House of Representatives was elected, senators were appointed by state legislatures, the president was designated by the Electoral College, and the judiciary was appointed by the president with the consent of the Senate. Supporting the new Constitution before the Pennsylvania ratifying convention, James Wilson spoke of the new structure with easy confidence. "When you examine all its parts," he said, "they will invariably be found to preserve that essential mark of free governments—a chain of connection with the people."

The Constitution provided for elections, but it also created a separation of powers (more accurately, a separation of personnel sharing powers) which created separate and jealous branches of government that had to cooperate in some harmony if significant new policies were to be adopted and executed. With so many points in the system where it is possible to obstruct change, the structure is well designed to protect the status quo.

Political parties have made the Constitution workable, providing that needed "chain of connection" with the people. Not foreseen by the founding fathers, a two-party system was in full operation by the time Thomas Jefferson was elected president. When executive and legislative branches were staffed by members of the same party who acknowledged similar commitments to the people, change became possible.

But fundamental change was never inevitable, or even likely. In the last few years, a reexamination of American history has shown that really significant political change has come to America only sporadically, when economic and social change built up pressures which created the conditions for a critical election.[2] In the period between critical elections,

[2]The concept was formulated by V. O. Key, Jr., in a seminal article, "A Theory of Critical Elections," 17 *Journal of Politics* (1955), pp. 3–18. A comprehensive recent elaboration is Walter Dean Burnham, *Critical Elections and the Mainsprings of American Politics* (New York: Norton, 1970).

which lasts thirty or forty years, one of the two major parties is supported by a constellation of groups in the electorate that usually constitutes the majority. It is the dominant party, and the opposition's behavior is determined by its reactions to fluctuations in the fortunes of the majority party.[3] The interests that are dominant in society also dominate the political system and reap its benefits. The electorate perceives little difference between the two parties, which sound quite alike, for both are serving the dominant powers.

With the political system protecting and extending the benefits enjoyed by the dominant interests, which win repeated contests over the allocation of scarce resources, other elements in society increasingly recognize political injustice. When disadvantaged groups seek redress for grievances through the political system, the response is sluggish, until economic recession or some similar event triggers the conflict that produces a critical election. The result is a realignment of the two parties.

When a realignment is imminent, a coalition demanding important change forms within the electorate and forces itself upon the attention of the established party leaders. Then a coalition opposing change is formed, and the two forces clash in one or more critical elections. Such clashes occurred in 1800, 1828, 1852–56, 1896, and 1932–36. In four of the five cases, the coalition favoring change was victorious, and reforms in the name of the people were carried out by Presidents Jefferson, Jackson, Lincoln, and Franklin D. Roosevelt. In 1896, the coalition opposing change triumphed with the "full dinner pail" of William McKinley. In all five cases, a new majority party was established and the policy output of the political process was belatedly adapted to social and economic change. With the defeat of Populism and William Jennings Bryan in 1896, reform sentiment found an outlet in the Progressive faction of the dominant Republican party.

If this historical pattern is to continue, the critical election of our own era is overdue. According to Walter Dean Burnham, the nomination of Barry Goldwater in 1964 and George Wallace's American Independent party candidacy of 1968 provided early warnings of an impending critical realignment. Kevin Phillips, adviser on voting patterns to John Mitchell, Nixon's 1968 campaign manager, developed a cyclical theory of political change in America and described *The Emerging Republican Majority*.[4] In 1972, the Nixon campaign capitalized on the disaffection

[3] As Samuel Lubell put it, the minority party plays the role of moon to the majority party's sun. See his *The Future of American Politics* (New York: Harper, 1952), chap. 10.

[4] Kevin B. Phillips, *The Emerging Republican Majority* (Garden City, N.Y.: Doubleday, Anchor Press, 1970). I have compared the works of Burnham, Phillips, and Richard M. Scammon and Ben J. Wattenberg's *The Real Majority* (New York: Coward, 1970),

of traditionally Democratic voting groups, particularly in the South, to win a historic landslide. President Nixon headed the coalition that wanted to slow or revise the social changes begun in the 1960s, which many voters, including those of Ramona Heights, perceived George McGovern as championing. But the Republican party received no mandate, as a Democratic majority was returned to Congress. The critical election did not come to pass.

Critical elections are recognized only in retrospect. Candidates always insist that the fate of the nation hinges upon their own victory, but voters are seldom persuaded. When the Ramona Heights voters were asked if they felt the 1972 election were more important than the usual presidential election, they replied that they did not find it so. It is hard to recognize critical elections when they are happening, because the permanent party realignment comes about in response to the actions of the victorious candidates in office. Franklin D. Roosevelt's 1932 election represented a vote against Herbert Hoover and the depression; Roosevelt's most concrete campaign promise was to reduce government spending. Only in 1936 did the electorate endorse the measures of the New Deal.

The preconditions for a critical election were present in 1968 and 1972. The social explosions of the 1960s, triggered by resistance to the involvement in Vietnam, resulted from the failure of both Democratic and Republican administrations to respond effectively to the building pressures for domestic change. The responses that were made, through such programs as President Johnson's War on Poverty, while more symbolic than real, created conflicts within the aging New Deal coalition that were more important than common opposition to the Republicans. Wedded to the ethic of achievement, the rank-and-file of organized labor, the "white ethnics," and Middle America were ready to revolt against the presumed granting of governmental largess to groups —blacks, and the residents of inner cities—who had done nothing to "earn" such rewards, other than disrupt society.

Failure of the Marketplace Metaphor

Why had the system reacted so slowly to the pressures for change? Why, when changes came, were they inadequate, wrapped in a rhetoric which stimulated opposition but could not hide the failure to effectively

formulating an extended version of the present argument, in "Plotting the Electorate's Course in Dangerous Waters," 2 *Political Science Reviewer* (1972), pp. 39–65.

deal with the needs of America's disadvantaged?

A complete analysis of contemporary American government, and its historical roots, is beyond the scope of this volume. Such analyses have been performed by others,[5] and need only be summarized here. The achievement value, held so dearly by the Ramona Heights voters, is related to the theories of John Locke, who preferred minimal government, and the economic theories of Adam Smith, who called for the separation of the political and economic spheres. The desire of classic liberalism for a free marketplace—of talents, of goods, and of ideas—influenced the framers of the Constitution, and it has influenced the practitioners of American politics. Past critical elections placed men in office who sought to restore the individual's equality of opportunity by limiting the power of private interests. In the case of Jefferson, Jackson, and Lincoln, these changes were carried out without deliberately increasing the authority or personnel of the national government.[6] By the time of Franklin D. Roosevelt, society had grown so complex that the power of private organizations could only be monitored and controlled by establishing governmental organizations, with a corresponding growth in the scope of government, if not in its authority.

The New Deal replaced Hoover's rugged individualism with a system which saw the group, or organized interest, as the basic unit of the political structure, but retained Locke's suspicion of unified governmental power. Instead of directly controlling big business (which might have been accomplished by taking seriously the earlier antitrust laws) the ability of labor to organize and bargain collectively was guaranteed. A new private interest was created to counterbalance the existing one that had grown too powerful. Specific needs in the society were answered by establishing specialized governmental bureaus. Some of them provided little more than governmental sanction for the activities of private interest groups, as had been the case in agriculture since long before FDR. The scope of government grew, but not its competence, for the maze of competing and overlapping government agencies served to

[5]See Wills, *Nixon Agonistes;* Theodore J. Lowi, *The End of Liberalism* (New York: Norton, 1969); and Grant McConnell, *Private Power and American Democracy* (New York: Knopf, 1967). The brief analysis offered here, based on these and other sources, parallels the longer one in my *The People; Maybe,* 2nd ed. (North Scituate, Mass.: Wadsworth, Duxbury Press, 1974), Chap. 11.

[6]Jefferson and Jackson were agrarians who defended states' rights, when it suited their purposes. Lincoln freed the slaves only with the aid of civil war and a large army. But the Homestead Act opened federal lands on the frontier to the common man: Jefferson's small freeholder was resurrected.

prevent exactly what classic liberalism sought to prevent: the ability of government to exercise unified and central authority in response to the interests of the people as a people. "Interest-group liberalism" became the new pattern of government, as competing government agencies served competing clients.[7] The metaphor of the marketplace scored another intellectual triumph.

The result was to add a new list of groups to those which already benefited from government policy. The normal procedures of American government served to protect and expand those benefits. Conflicts of purpose were built in. Long after government supported the civil rights movement, the authority of building trade unions to deal with employers was guaranteed by government, although union members were determined to exclude blacks. Federally supported mortgage guarantees accelerated the building of suburban tracts which drew the white middle class away from the central city, contributing to its collapse; federally financed urban renewal projects then attempted to rejuvenate the central cities, but they were designed to serve business interests, rather than the needs of the slum dwellers being replaced. Interest-group liberalism was no less exploitative than laissez-faire capitalism. New groups were admitted to share in the bounty of industrial productivity, without reducing the allotment of established groups. The realization that there is a limit to the natural resources of the United States, and of the planet, could not be accommodated within the boundaries of interest-group liberalism, which depends on an ever-increasing national product to provide general prosperity, without that reduction in the comforts of the wealthy that would result from a redistribution of income. Not even social security payments are redistributive; they are financed through taxes paid by workers and employers.

The importance of governmental policies to private interests was emphasized by the Watergate investigations of campaign finance. Leaders of industry reported a systematic, and illegal, "shakedown." They felt they had to contribute, to insure the continuation of government policies which, in the name of a free market, shield certain enterprises from the forces of the marketplace. Think of the milk producers' price increases, or the burgeoning profits of the oil industry.

The perception of politics as the winning of "unfair" advantages by persistent groups should include the revelation that no invisible hand

---

[7]Lowi argues that "interest-group liberalism" became the dominant ideology, obscuring unresolved questions about the proper nature of governmental power (*The End of Liberalism*, Part 1).

operates in the political process to assure general benefits through com-petition. Can we then expect that the voters of Ramona Heights will abandon the marketplace metaphor as an explanation of reality, recog-nize that "equality of opportunity" is an impossible goal, and demand that an electoral majority, rather than the influence of narrowly based pressure groups, determine the national future? Garry Wills claimed that Richard Nixon has been our inevitable president, as he embodied the virtue of individual achievement which has been made irrelevant by postindustrial society, but which many Americans still cling to. Wills argued that, in attempting to restore the creed, Nixon demonstrated its absurdity.

Ideologies are powerful. Even if the Watergate revelations underscore the absurdity of the underlying theory, it seems unlikely that the mem-bers of the microsample will abandon their belief in equal opportunity as the great goal of government. Quentin Elliott saw the results of the corporate version of the competitive ethic and decided that it was not the life for him. He retains a firm belief in the benefits of competition, both economic and athletic. He would only insist on the duty of govern-ment to prevent the corporate rape of public resources, just as he accepts the imposition by the referee of minimal order on a hockey game.

The genius of American politics has been to agree on policies, making agreement on principle unnecessary.[8] Ramona Heights voters of diverse persuasions on other matters agreed, after Watergate, on the need for stringent regulation of campaign finance and spending. The main result of such laws, like that of the antitrust laws, could well be to reassure the public without affecting the fundamental distribution of political power. The most radical means for restoring public confidence would be to finance campaigns from the public treasury, entirely eliminating private groups as a source of campaign funds. The adherence of Americans to the competitive ethic may prevent such proposals from being seriously considered; they have, in any case, overtones of erecting unconstitu-tional limitations on the freedom of political expression.[9]

In discussing the 1972 campaign, Harry Johnson volunteered the opinion that campaign expenditures should be strictly limited "to such

[8]Daniel J. Boorstin argues, in his *The Genius of American Politics* (Chicago: University of Chicago Press, 1953), that America's sole exportable commodity is technology; we have no real political theory, because all theoretical issues were seen as resolved by the Declara-tion of Independence and the Constitution.

[9]For a capable argument against the public financing of election campaigns, see Ralph K. Winter, Jr., *Campaign Financing and Political Freedom* (Washington, D.C.: American Enterprise Institute for Public Policy Research, 1973).

a small amount that they wouldn't have to look for contributions from General Motors." Harry pulled back from the brink of endorsing public campaign finance, but he wanted to require the television networks to donate free time. Except for Eldene Markus, who was intrigued with the possibility of public finance, he was the only respondent to suggest limitations on campaign spending before the Watergate scandals erupted. By November, nearly a third of the microsample volunteered an interest in public campaign financing.

The historic pattern of significant change following critical elections has depended on the viability of the political parties as organizations able to support the vision of a popular leader. This implies a president and Congress of the same party. Parties in the past have had a base of faithful adherents so that a popular leader could build a majority without needing to convert a massive segment of the population. At present, however, the parties are losing their hold upon the loyalty of voters. This process is more advanced in California than in the rest of the nation, for the Progressive era left a tradition of nonpartisan local elections and subdued partisanship on the state level. The pride in their independence of the microsample members is typical of California attitudes.

But Ramona Heights is little different from suburbs in other states. In contrast to the older cities, most suburbs manage political conflicts by deemphasizing partisanship, and suburbanites take pride in their removal from the influence of urban political machines.[10] Have the ties of party been so weakened that parties will no longer be able to fulfill their crucial roles after a critical election? If the Ramona Heights experience of 1972 may be generalized, it is easy to imagine a future in which the electorate swings wildly from one election to the next, seeking a candidate of integrity while disdaining his party label, on the basis of personality clues communicated by television. This would produce a series of meaningless landslides (with 1972 being the first), because the winner would not be able to command a partisan organization able to achieve his purposes.

What role can be predicted for voters like those of Ramona Heights in future elections?

---

[10]For the nonpartisan nature of suburban politics, see F. M. Wirt et al., *On the City's Rim: Politics and Policy in Suburbia* (Lexington, Mass.: Heath, 1972), Chaps. 10 and 11. For a finding that suburbanites are less likely than city dwellers to perceive policy differences between the parties, see pp. 107–108 of the same volume.

A VISION OF THE FUTURE

Walter Dean Burnham offers a chilling vision of the American political future: fascism. His argument begins with finding that the traditional lower-middle-upper division of social classes has been replaced, in postindustrial America, by new categories, based on the mastery of technology. They are the technologically competent, the technologically obsolescent, and the technologically superfluous.[11]

The technologically competent class includes much of, but is not limited to, the old upper class. Its members manage large organizations, oversee the further development of technology, conduct research, plan advertising campaigns, command the use of computers, and invest the nation's savings. This class is divided within itself by conflicting attitudes about its duty toward the other elements of society. Those newly arrived in these higher circles by virtue of their own efforts tend to feel that every individual must achieve wealth—or even subsistence—strictly on his own: "I made it; why can't they?" Those who have lived with their wealth for enough generations to feel secure in it support governmental programs to improve the welfare of society's least fortunate members. Instead of achievement, they emphasize the value of equality.

The technologically obsolescent are those who have achieved comfort in the present system but are ill prepared for further change. They include most union members, small tradesmen threatened by national chain stores, and the elites of small inland towns and cities which are dying because of the population movement to metropolitan areas on the East and West coasts. They are engineers unable to keep up with the pace of developments in their own fields. They are the Middle Americans. They are also the numerical majority.

The technologically superfluous have no skills that can be employed by the system, for the kind of labor that requires pure strength has been taken over by machines. They live in such places as eroded farms, Indian reservations, and the ghettos of large cities. Their lack of salable skills results from their lack of education, or from a lifetime in agricultural labor before being uprooted from the soil, not from a failure of personal

[11]Burnham, *Critical Elections*, pp. 135–193. Burnham takes his social class labels from David Apter's essay, "Ideology and Discontent" in D. Apter, ed., *Ideology and Discontent* (Glencoe, Ill.: Free Press, 1964). Burnham does not make the distinction, which I regard as crucial, between the newly arrived members of the technologically competent class and the politically active offspring of established families.

ambition. Middle Americans accuse them of laziness.

According to Burnham, American politics has been transformed by this change in the class structure. The New Deal coalition was cemented by the changes which brought the middle group to its modern level of consumption, but that comfort is now eroded by inflation, rising taxes, and an energy crisis. Recently the Democratic party has paid dramatic attention to the woes of the technologically obsolescent, the true outcasts of modern society. Elements of the technologically competent have formed a coalition with them. The nature of that alliance was clear in the 1972 Democratic National Convention, but the same impulse exists within the liberal wing of the Republican party, where the heirs of established wealth like Nelson Rockefeller (and John Lindsay, until he was forced out of the party) also argue that the lowest social strata deserve payments from society—enough to assure subsistence—although they are unable to contribute to its technological work.

Middle America tends to see this inability to contribute as an unwillingness to work. Middle America also realizes that the technologically competent need not pay a proportional share of the cost of their own charitable impulses. Integration comes to their own neighborhoods on the rim of the black ghettos; it does not disturb the country estates. Pupils are bused to achieve the integration of the public schools; busing does not touch the private schools, where the wealthy have enrolled their children. Most important, the cost of government welfare programs is financed by the income tax, which falls heavily upon the middle group. They cannot utilize the capital gains provisions, depletion allowances, and other tax loopholes that are available to the wealthy. Yet, at their cocktail parties, the wealthy complain of "hard-hat" bigotry.

In Burnham's view, the motive power of recent American politics has been resentment. The middle group resents the coalition between the upper and lower elements of society; above all, it resents the ability of individuals—black unwed mothers, for example—to obtain rewards for which they do no work. George Wallace understood this resentment, and capitalized on it, in his 1968 third-party candidacy, and in his foreshortened 1972 campaign to "return the Democratic party to the people." Richard Nixon appealed to that same resentment in both elections, in part because both Hubert Humphrey and George McGovern were seen by the middle group as agents of the upper-lower alliance.

Burnham wrote that the best prediction for the American future is a period of fascism, when the resentment of the majority will be implemented by political leaders through the repression of political and cultural dissent and the curtailment of welfare programs.

A prediction of fascism for America must stand or fall on the accuracy of the presumptions it makes about the political convictions and desires of the majority—in Burnham's scheme, Middle America, the technologically obsolescent class. To the extent that he identifies the values of this middle group with suburbia, Burnham offers a low opinion of their motives. He views the suburbs as tight little islands, way stations on the middle-class escape route, where homeowners shut themselves off from any sympathy for the needs of the central cities.[12] He implies that appeals to racism and envy by political leaders will strike a responsive chord in suburbia, second in strength only to the reaction of white ethnics in the cities.

The twenty-three voters of Ramona Heights are located within the upper levels of the technologically obsolescent class. They must suggest some modifications in the common stereotype of suburbia, although they do not, in any statistical sense, represent Middle America. They have been described as "affluent technocrats," persons who perform useful work for modern society and have been rewarded by it with substantial comfort, although none has risen to the positions of power that characterize members of the technologically competent class. They are similar to other affluent technocrats who live in other suburbs and, indeed, in cities.[13]

The voters of Ramona Heights adhere to a political ethos which is rooted so deeply in the American experience that it is unlikely to be dislodged by a single political event. Their adherence to the marketplace metaphor is both an asset and a liability. The asset is that open political warfare between social classes is unlikely. There is in the American tradition no justification for a conviction that permanent advantages should be enjoyed by persons simply because of their birth or status, who make no contribution to the work of society. Welfare mothers are resented; the other side of the coin is that the "beautiful people" who star in gossip columns about the jet set would be laughed at if they pretended to political leadership. Maureen Barbera's experience perhaps exemplifies a rediscovery of this attitude. Her disdain for the groups

---

[12]Burnham, *Critical Elections*, p. 172. Burnham does not recognize that Middle America is asked to pay a disproportionate share of the costs of the charitable impulses of the technologically competent.

[13]The common conclusion of studies comparing urban and suburban political behavior is that the significant variable is social class, not place of residence. See Wirt et al., *On the City's Rim*, pp. 51–57. Also see William M. Dobriner, *Class in Suburbia* (Englewood Cliffs, N.J.: Prentice-Hall, 1963), and Herbert J. Gans, *The Levittowners* (New York: Random House, Vintage Books, 1967), p. 266.

which disrupted American society in the 1960s was based on an assumption of the moral superiority of her own class and generation. That assumption was belied by the Watergate investigation, and she was forced to recognize the legitimacy of a diverse cultural pluralism in American society. If the group of young men operating out of the White House could not rightly claim moral superiority, there was no legitimate reason to justify their power.

The liabilities of attachment to the marketplace myth are related to this asset. Disdaining a politics of class, the feeling that the state should remain neutral leads to the perception that politics, and the wielding of power, is essentially a despicable enterprise. This conviction can breed a deep cynicism about politics and politicians and encourage a retreat entirely into private life. Such is certainly the case of Arnold Garcia, and it is at least partially true of the Kaubs and the Johnsons. The same conviction makes it likely that political activity, stimulated by the candidate of perceived integrity, will be launched in an idealistic atmosphere, only to be frustrated by political realities. The Pavels worked with enthusiasm for Adlai Stevenson; looking back on the experience, they feel that Stevenson was "too good" for the game he was in. The perception of political parties as brokers between the demands of specific groups—groups seeking "unfair" competitive advantage—further loosens the ties of the political party upon their imaginations, when they themselves do not identify with one of the competing groups. Yet it is only the party that can be the vehicle of significant political change.

Does the marketplace metaphor then lay a dead hand of mythology on American politics, preventing the system from coping adequately with social and economic realities? Without abandoning the myth of the marketplace, the public can perceive that the power of specific interests destroys the freedom of that assumed market, thus limiting the equal opportunity of both organizations and individuals.

Such is the case with the vaunted "military-industrial complex." When the cold war mentality held sway, military requests were ritually approved by the armed services committees and passed by both House and Senate. Individual congressmen were concerned with getting an adequate share of defense installations and contracts for their own districts. The engineers of Ramona Heights, who themselves are employed or have been employed by defense industries, agree in questioning the purposes and claims of need made by the armed services. John Weeks regarded the antiballistic missile as a public works project.

The most obvious issues of this kind, however, center upon protecting the ecological balance of nature. California, trumpeting its pride at becoming the most populous state, had been devoted since the gold rush to uncontrolled growth based on the rapacious exploitation of natural resources. In the last few years, this boosterism has been dramatically reversed, as Californians have realized the dangers of repeating eastern developmental mistakes on the West Coast. They have taken action to preserve (or, nostalgically, to recapture) the natural beauties that attracted so many residents to the state. The movement has scored impressive victories. Plans for yet another skyscraper were abandoned in San Francisco. Utility companies agreed to build nuclear power plants away from the coast. Development-oriented county supervisors have been defeated for reelection. Even Governor Ronald Reagan senses the intensity of feeling on the issue.

The most impressive accomplishment of the ecology movement was the passage of Proposition 20 in the November, 1972, election. This initiative measure placed a moratorium on further private development within a thousand yards of the high-tide line along a thousand miles of California coastline, until comprehensive land use plans can be developed by a coastal zone conservation commission and six regional subcommissions. The initiative was opposed by big business and big labor, land developers, and mortgage lenders; in the campaign preceding the vote, they outspent the conservationist supporters of the measure by about twenty to one. The measure passed with a 55 percent "yes" vote. All but four voters of the Ramona Heights microsample were among that majority.

A concern for the depletion of natural resources spreads easily among the members of an affluent middle class. Unlike the technologically superfluous residents of the central city, they have achieved a good life in their suburban tracts, and the continued outpouring of industrial production can add only incrementally to their personal comfort. Such events as the pollution of the Santa Barbara beaches by an oil spill caused by off-shore drilling, as well as air and water pollution in general, arouse their ire and direct their political decisions. But not one of the families of Ramona Heights has sold its second car in order to cut down the consumption of gasoline.

THE TERRITORIAL IMPERATIVE

Ecological issues hardly provide common political ground for the affluent suburbanites and impoverished ghetto dwellers of the same metropolitan area. The argument of overconsumption can have no attraction for one who receives but a minute share of the bounty of the

American system. Metropolitan areas are a single unit in an economic sense, and the central city still provides a focus for the commercial and cultural activity that gives suburbs their reason for existence, although this function is declining with the suburbanization of industry. Metropolitan areas are politically fragmented, as the separately incorporated suburbs defend their territory from the city's claims on their tax resources and their human talent. Racial divisions increase. The flight of white middle-class residents creates black cities encircled by white suburbs.[14]

The decay of her great cities is America's most pressing problem. Can the future hold anything other than conflict? Is there no common ground for cooperative action, as the suburbanites gird to defend their territory against all threats, both real and imagined? The attitudes of the Ramona Heights microsample toward policies commonly proposed to ameliorate the urban crisis—the city income tax, metropolitan area government, the construction of publicly subsidized housing in suburbia, school busing to achieve racial integration—offer few grounds for hopeful answers.

Most of them had not heard of the concept of a payroll tax levied on all who work in a city, regardless of where they live. Upon discussion, however, they agreed that simple justice supports the notion that those who work in a city, placing a burden on its transportation and waste disposal systems by day, but who commute to bedroom suburbs, should be expected to contribute to the city's maintenance costs. Agreement with this principle came easily, for Orange County does not have a single metropolis ringed by suburbs. Los Angeles is the major city of the region, but it is not the center of a spider's web of commuter railroads, highways, and bus lines. Industry and residential areas are intermingled in a sprawl that covers Southern California. Thus, when the microsample agreed, passively, to the principle of an income tax levied by cities on persons who work there but live elsewhere, they saw no danger that they would be asked to pay it.

The question of metropolitan area government was posed in terms of formulating a single government for all of Orange County which would supersede the separately incorporated municipalities. Most of the respondents had never heard of such a proposal. Fletcher Barbera said that

[14]The pattern is not universal. Middle-class blacks—the teachers and policemen who serve the city's residents—are beginning to live in the suburbs. But the development of black suburban enclaves so far resembles only "patches of coal on a snowfield." Wirt et al., *On the City's Rim*, p. 40.

he would blame me if anybody ever seriously proposed it; best to designate dangerous ideas according to their source! Fletcher argued—as did most of the microsample—that the municipality of modest size is an important source of the suburbanite's sense of identity, and that his life is enriched by the chance to meet personally the candidates for local political office. However, Arnold Garcia felt that metro government for all of Orange County could well be more efficient, by eliminating the expensive duplication of municipal services and assuring their uniform quality. He cited the varying competence of the fire districts in Los Angeles County as an example. Harry Johnson also felt the proposal merited consideration. But other members of the microsample said that their neighbors would not like the idea of consolidating the municipal tax bases of the county, so that more of the property taxes paid in Ramona Heights could be spent in alleviating the problems of Santa Ana. Myrna Pavel said, "Ramona Heights isn't that altruistic!"

The resistance of the microsample to the construction of publicly subsidized housing in Ramona Heights, as has been shown, stems in part from their knowledge of high-rise public housing developments in big cities, which have in some cases become new super-slums. In the fall of 1973, President Nixon proposed using public housing funds to provide rent subsidy payments for those unable to afford decent living space. The poor would then be able to seek housing on the open market, and there would be no need for their neighbors to know that their rent payments were subsidized. This proposal shares features of President Nixon's 1969 proposal for a Family Assistance Plan, which the microsample supported. There is every reason to expect that they would support the rent subsidy, for it would meet their objection to the construction of identifiable public housing in suburban neighborhoods.

Public housing, as designed in the early 1950s, was one solution that often made the problem worse. Can school busing to achieve racial integration be another? In the Orange County context, busing could come to the schools of Ramona Heights only if all the school districts of the county were lumped together to determine the appropriate racial balance. (Several members of the microsample, including Arthur Roybal, cite the Los Angeles school district as an elephantine, bureaucratic nightmare.) Minority children would have to be bused more than fifteen miles, from the black ghetto and Chicano *barrios* of Santa Ana. Would a resulting equalization of educational opportunity offset the cost of the transportation in dollars and the cost to the children involved of inconvenience and separation from their neighborhood friends? The voters of Ramona Heights—including Quentin Elliott and the Roybals, who are educators—do not think so, and they voted for the antibusing initiative on the 1972 California ballot. They were joined by such passionate liberals as the Pavels.

The consideration of Ramona Heights' reactions to four "solutions" to urban problems holds little hope that suburbs and central cities will together recognize the social problems of metropolitan areas as being their common responsibilities. However, these are not the only possible solutions. The Markuses, Elliotts, and Barberas will not resist other solutions simply because a tax increase may be involved. While nobody can match the enthusiasm of the Markuses for paying taxes, it is not likely that the Weekses, Johnsons, Roybals, and Pavels would join an Anti-Tax Vigilance Committee.

In November of 1973, Californians were offered a chance to establish a constitutional limit on state governmental expenditures by limiting state taxes to a specific, and declining, percentage of the total of personal incomes in the state. The initiative constitutional amendment was presented in a special election called by Governor Ronald Reagan after the legislature rejected the measure. Reagan claimed that the proposition afforded an opportunity to reverse the historic pattern of governmental growth and the pandering by legislatures to the demands of special interests. Legislative opponents charged that the governor's presidential aspirations were tied to passage of the measure.

The people of California rejected the lengthy and confusing proposition by a vote of nearly 58 percent. Many feared that a reduction in state taxes would only bring increases in the local property tax. State employees and elements of the Democratic party fought the measure heroically. Although Orange County approved the measure by a vote of 59 percent, and the Ramona Heights precinct approved it by 62 percent, thirteen of the twenty-three members of the microsample voted against it, approximately the same proportion as rejected it statewide. As Harry Johnson put it, "Taxes are inevitable, and this wasn't the way to go about trying to limit them."

America's urban problems are not likely to be solved on the basis of local or even state tax revenues; federal funds must be involved, along with federal energy. A federal program to combat urban poverty couched in terms of equalizing opportunity and restoring initiative, in the manner of the Family Assistance Plan, could win the acquiescence of Ramona Heights voters.

One window into America's political future may be opened by the children of the Ramona Heights voters. Is it possible for a new generation to abandon the myth of the marketplace, while their parents remain wed to it? The actions and declarations of the activist college student minority in the 1960s suggested that the children of affluence—those who have never known want—in taking their affluence for granted, may be better able to share it. There are two encouraging examples in Ramona Heights. Arnold Garcia proclaims his disgust, which may mask deep-seated pride, that his oldest son, now completing dental school, does not plan to make a free enterprise fortune. Instead, he will serve in a *barrio* clinic for a relatively modest salary, treating the teeth of Mexican-Americans who cannot afford to pay free enterprise rates. Similarly, the Pavels' younger son is now completing medical school and entering his residency. He plans to specialize in pediatrics, and he too plans to serve in a clinic for poor children, rather than establishing a fashionable practice in a chrome-plated office.

As noted before, the parents of Ramona Heights remain in communication with their children, and they are instructed by their children's values as much as they attempt to instruct the children in their own. This suggests that those who hope for political change as the result of a dramatic conflict between the upcoming generation of the children of affluence and their parents are wrong. Instead, the influence of new voters is but another factor to be weighed in the balance.

Because of the decomposition of the parties, which is so well advanced in Ramona Heights, it may be that a critical election on the model of 1896 or 1932–36 is impossible. The higher educational level of the voters, coupled with their intimate perceptions of the candidates made possible by television, may have destroyed the political party as the "action intermediary" of American politics.[15] It is hard to imagine Quentin Elliott, for example, abandoning his pride of independence to march in the torchlight parade of either party. He is quite likely, however, to march in the parade for a particular candidate: a Charles Percy or a George McGovern or an Elliot Richardson. Quentin will ignore the party label if the candidate displays the proper prerequisite of integrity. Quentin's moralistic approach to politics bypasses the parties as the vehicles of compromise and accommodation.

Although Quentin supplies the most striking example of this trait, it is a general one in the microsample: the search is for personal qualities in the candidates, secondarily for congenial positions on issues, and not at all for that camaraderie which was a hallmark of nineteenth-century

---

[15]This argument is made very capably by Everett Carll Ladd, Jr., and Seymour Martin Lipset in *Academics, Politics, and the 1972 Election* (Washington, D.C.: American Enterprise Institute for Public Policy Research, 1973), Chap. 2.

parties and is found by the McGees in working to save America and by Alice Rinehart among the Republican ladies. The question then is, To what kind of leadership are the members of the microsample most likely to respond? Does their cool reaction toward proposals intended to ameliorate urban-suburban political conflict foreshadow a demand for repressive governmental measures? Or are they potential supporters of a more hopeful coalition?

A Suburban Ethos, and the Political Future

The relationship between citizens and their democratic leaders varies with the circumstances. When the nation is caught up in a great cause, articulated by a Woodrow Wilson or a Franklin D. Roosevelt, the leader is elevated to a nearly supernatural status by much of the population. At other times, a Harry Truman or a Calvin Coolidge will win respect, if not admiration, for entirely human qualities. Surely, at all times, the people place a degree of trust in their elected leader. A president holds office as a result of majority choice, and no better method of choosing has been devised. Even the well-dressed capitalists who went "down to the Trans Lux to hiss Roosevelt" in the famous New Yorker cartoon must have realized that the president proposed new policies in response to needs widely felt among the electorate.

Richard Nixon's reactions to the Watergate disclosures, which only seemed to implicate him more deeply, shattered that trust for many Americans. Among the voters of Ramona Heights, the series of crises, scandals, and resignations which grew out of Watergate came closer to challenging the legitimacy of American government than all the agonies of the previous decade—ghetto riots, campus confrontations, and antiwar demonstrations. Throughout that time of turmoil, these suburbanites expressed varying degrees of sympathy for protesting groups. They felt that the decisions of government were made by duly constituted authority and should be obeyed for that reason, if no other; the grievances would be handled in due course. A president can make mistakes, but he is still the president.

Their admiration for the presidential office always included some ambivalence of feeling about its incumbent. Politicians, they felt, normally rise to the top by making bargains and pandering to interests that are far from savory. They expected, however, that the occupant of the

White House would be relatively immune from self-enriching corruption, and they hoped he would surround himself with men of honor, rather than morally insensitive technicians. For more than half the microsample, Watergate was a betrayal of their trust.

How will the voters of Ramona Heights, and of the nation, face the future in the aftermath of Watergate? The interpretation of any new event is influenced by past experiences and the idea systems utilized in interpreting them. The Ramona Heights transcripts have revealed an ethos that is shared by all the respondents, in spite of their differing life experiences and convictions regarding specific policies. Since the elements of this creed have deep roots in American history, the beliefs of Ramona Heights must be similar to those of much of Middle America. As delineated in Chapter Six, that creed has three elements:

1. We are a successful society, governed through inspired institutions.
2. Most citizens are free to achieve.
3. Political action yields limited results; the contest between groups inhibits any search for the common good.

The contradiction involved in holding these ideas concurrently reflects the American ambivalence toward the phenomenon of political power: a realization that politics involves conflict, coupled with a yearning for political leaders who might, in serving the best interests of all, make those conflicts insignificant.

The response to Watergate of various voters draws upon these three attitudes unequally. Insisting on the first suggests a separation of the incumbents and their deeds from the offices they hold. Trusting in the inspired nature of the Constitution, such voters may be led to seek a reduction in the extraconstitutional personnel and pretensions to authority in the executive office of the president. The activities of Congress and the courts in exposing the facts of Watergate are seen as a vindication of the separation of powers, showing the American political system as worthy of support and participation. By contrast, when the third attitude is drawn upon in interpreting Watergate, and the activities exposed by the investigations are seen as normal political practices, the result is a heightened cynicism. Among the Ramona Heights voters, this attitude was best expressed by Arnold Garcia.

Arnold: They're all crooks; Agnew just got caught. . . . Nixon shouldn't resign, he should stay in and fight. They're all crooks. The Republicans got caught, the other guys just haven't gotten caught yet.

Pressed to its logical conclusion, such an attitude suggests at least a retreat into privatism, if not a surrender to despair. But despair was not the reaction of Ramona Heights. The constitutional crisis did not radically alter their daily lives, although time spent in following the unfolding events did modify the pattern of life in several households, and the scandals created a personal crisis for Maureen Barbera and John Weeks. The ability to separate a judgment on Richard Nixon and his associates from the offices they held was less difficult than it might have been, because the respondents did not perceive either Nixon or his 1972 opponent, George McGovern, as paragons of integrity. Since their expectations were not high, the Watergate revelations did not constitute the shock or stimulate the outrage that would have resulted from such discoveries about a more universally admired president.

If the Ramona Heights voters are at all representative of voters in general, the challenge to the legitimacy of American political institutions implicit in the Watergate disclosures will not lead to a widespread revulsion against democratic practices. Such events as the dismissal of Special Prosecutor Archibald Cox and the resignation of Attorney General Elliot Richardson, followed by the surrender of the long-disputed tapes and a revelation that some were missing, affronted a sense of decency based upon a common understanding of the essence, if not the details, of democratic practices. The president's refusal to reveal the evidence was based on technicalities of the Constitution, rather than any need or privilege of the people to know. Many voters felt that their rights—and the due process of law—should take precedence over certain constitutional details, and that the Constitution never contemplated establishing the president as being above the law.

The mere absence of revulsion directed against institutional practices offers no clue to the nature of positive leadership or the content of enlightened policies that the voters are likely to seek and accept. Significant political change will win the enthusiastic support of voters like those of Ramona Heights only if the third component of their ethos—the belief that political action yields only limited results—is modified. The most likely impetus for such a modification is through the accentuation of one or both of the other elements of that ethos.

The belief that ours is a successful society, governed by inspired institutions, is a historical judgment. It elevates the founding fathers to heroic stature and insists that their design has served well in the past and should be adequate for the future. This conviction may be related to the failure of the microsample to find political guideposts in Utopian thought. It is certainly a reaffirmation of the allegiance of allegiant citizens. And it may be even more: an expression of a kind of patriotism that rises above vulgar nationalism to express kinship with others who share the same history and accept the same covenant, formulated in the

Declaration of Independence and the Constitution.[16]

The failure of radical politics in the 1960s was in part a failure to respect this perception of historical continuity. Student activists did not recognize Middle Americans as being, for better or worse, their fellow Americans. The labeling of their country as "Amerikka" was not a tactic calculated to broaden the appeal of the movement. The voters of Ramona Heights were appalled by the antics of the antiwar movement, even after they had come to oppose the war. A comparison of public attitudes toward the Korean and Vietnamese wars revealed that the pattern through which public opposition developed was very similar, even in the lapse of time. The Vietnamese war stimulated a vocal opposition, while the Korean war did not; public opinion unfavorable to the war in Vietnam developed independently of the antiwar movement.[17] The experience of Ramona Heights, then, was probably fairly typical. The perception of both wars as being meaningless wastes of resources was suggested when they dragged on inconclusively and was confirmed when one's own friends or relatives became involved in the conflict.

An appeal for meaningful political change which involves these voters must be couched in terms of the national values and traditions they accept. Political leaders must be dedicated to the restoration of presumed past grandeurs. These voters will not follow those who tell them they have accepted a misinterpretation of history or claim that the promises of America were always fraudulent. Using Burnham's categories in the same vein, it will not do for the technologically competent to tell the technologically obsolescent that they are prevented by bigotry from attending to the needs of the technologically superfluous.

The institutional corollary of the renewal of political virtue is the restoration of the governmental balance of powers. One clear message of Watergate is that members of the executive office of the president, loyal to him alone, their appointments not subject to confirmation by Congress, asserted and exercised secret power which only the scandals brought into public view. Secret power is not subject to the control of

[16]The most noble tradition of American patriotism, as expressed by Abraham Lincoln, is based upon adherence to these covenants. This is in contrast to patriotism based on tenancy of the ancestral land, or citizenship in the city, developed by the ancient Greeks. See John H. Schaar, "The Case for Patriotism," *American Review 17* (May, 1973), p.71 ff. Schaar's essay is also the source of the judgment that radical political leaders in the 1960s failed to approach others as fellow Americans.

[17]John E. Mueller, *War, Presidents, and Public Opinion* (New York: Wiley, 1973), Part 1.

public opinion, and thus it unbalances the system.

The Ramona Heights voters are likely supporters of political efforts couched in terms of restoring the balance of government. But what kind of policies will they endorse which attempt to resolve the problems of American society? Their responsiveness in this area is related to the second component of their ethos, the belief that "most citizens are free to achieve." As a belief, it is both descriptive and normative. Policies aimed at making it possible for everyone to prove himself on an equal footing in the marketplace of talents and skills are likely to win support. For varied reasons, the members of the microsample approved of President Nixon's Family Assistance Plan. Proposals for achieving greater equality must also recognize these voters' concurrent attachment to the value of achievement.

These voters resist many of the common proposals for ameliorating tension within metropolitan areas. They oppose massive long-distance busing to achieve racial integration in the schools, they resist the construction of public housing projects in their neighborhood, and they lack enthusiasm for metropolitan area government. But there are signs of support for other programs intended to achieve equality of opportunity. Such a staunch conservative as Fletcher Barbera recognizes the inequity of public school finance that depends heavily on the local tax base. Several parents feel that the neighborhood gives their children an artificial view of life by providing only playmates of their own social class. Many of these voters would endorse proposals for a rent subsidy (or perhaps an interest subsidy in the case of purchase) which would permit the social makeup of Ramona Heights to become gradually more heterogeneous.

In short, these voters are not strangers to decent impulses, nor to human sympathy. Such a statement only seems remarkable when placed in such contexts as the assertion by a political leader like Frederick Dutton that the "suburban way of life" is a new, negative force in American politics and the assumption of a political scientist like Walter Dean Burnham that repressive fascism will be supported by suburbanites as a matter of course. In view of the ultraconservative reputation of Orange County, it would seem that, if signs of hope can be found there, signs of hope can be found anywhere.

The same myth of the marketplace which nourished the ethic of achievement provides justification for a governmental system which is minimal in its scope and authority. But the dedication to minimal government is an aspect of rhetorical conservatism which need not determine policy attitudes. A majority of the microsample joined the majority of California's electorate in rejecting Governor Ronald Reagan's constitutional amendment limiting the taxing powers of state government. Californians, and probably Americans in general, will not rush to support an apparently Draconian attempt to limit the decisions of future generations about the scope and authority of government.

A number of current issues undermine the authority of the marketplace myth without displacing it. They are the issues of ecology. The Ramona Heights microsample overwhelmingly favored placing a moratorium on the further development of the coastline. This was a recognition that the rights of property ownership are not absolute; property must be utilized in a manner congruent with the public interest; and the public interest is not automatically determined by the forces of the marketplace. A similar recognition may grow from the energy crisis.

For all these reasons, the Ramona Heights microsample can hardly be used to support dire predictions about America's future. These are voters with mixed perceptions and mixed motives. Although some grow too easily impatient with life styles different from their own, they cannot be convicted of racial bigotry. They believe in human equality, in the abstract; they think this is best realized as equal opportunity, in practice. Like most Americans, they normally view politics as a spectator sport. They do not follow a single party; their allegiance shifts primarily in response to the perceived qualities of the candidate and only secondarily on the basis of agreement with the candidate's positions. Far from being the potential followers of a demagogue, they seek integrity, above all else, in a candidate. (They can be fooled; three admitted having been fooled by Spiro Agnew.) Some—Maureen Barbera, the Elliotts, and the Pavels—are available for enlistment into political activity that involves more than voting. If they should join the activists, the McGees and Alice Rinehart, it will be in support of candidates with a much more liberal style, who combine the image of integrity with a program to conserve natural resources, and seek new ways to bind up America's social wounds.

Can cautious optimism for the nation be based on an acquaintance with only twenty-three voters? Perhaps not. However, decision-making by government, and by campaign managers, which has been based on the best statistical knowledge of the social sciences, reducing human complexity to a system of punches on an IBM card, has so far created more political dilemmas than it has resolved. It may be that political leaders—and the people themselves—must risk a leap of faith.

Index